Is That You, Coolidge?

A Memoir

Mark Nichols Sims

Is That You, Coolidge?
Copyright © 2017 by Mark Nichols Sims

All rights reserved. No part of this book may be reproduced in any form or by any means without the prior written consent of the Author, excepting brief quotes used in reviews.

ISBN-13:
978-1-937908-69-0

Printed in the United States
Printed by
Rocky Heights Print and Binding, LLC.

Printing Number
10 9 8 7 6 5 4 3 2 1

Foreword
By Alabama Governor Bob Riley

"...he stood only 5' 4", but he was a giant..." While there are many truths in Mark Sims' book, <u>Is That You, Coolidge?</u>, this quote struck me as the most insightful, for Mark could not have described his father and my friend more perfectly.

From the moment a young Coolidge Sims stepped onto Utah Beach in Normandy, until an aged and wise man went to his heavenly home, this memoir is a portrait of man trying to adapt to a rapidly-changing world while his trusted foundations shifted beneath him.

Through daily conversations with his father during the last few months of life, Mark Sims achieves a goal most of us are not even aware we have: to know, to truly know, our parents. From a child's point of view, they are simply our mother or father— one-dimensional, uncomplicated caretakers of our world. Yet, Mark delves deeper to understand who his father actually was. In flashbacks that move effortlessly between moments spent with his father in an assisted living facility, to past memories that created his life, Mark poignantly relays his discovery of answers to questions silently posed long ago in his mind.

A master storyteller, Mark allows his readers to experience a turbulent time in American history from two distinct perspectives: a father, struggling to find the balance between change and tradition, between fundamental belief and an open mind; and a son who developed his own view of the world and clashed sharply with the father he so admired and respected. Through vivid imagery, raw honesty, and emotional dialogue, Mark places the reader in that time, in that town, and in that moment. He takes us from the joyful recollections locked away in Coolidge's aging mind, to heart-wrenching moments of his golden years, when his children were forced to decide how best to care for their father.

I would know. I grew up right next door to the Sims family. While I already towered over him by my sixteenth birthday, I still looked up to him with admiration and respect. Coolidge always embodied fierce conviction, but kept a quick wit and a twinkle in his eye like a mischievous little boy. Even now I cannot recall ever seeing Coolidge Sims losing his temper or being rude to another person. He had a perpetual joy and a love of life that was infectious. It was impossible to be in his presence and succumb to the transgressions of selfishness, ingratitude or cynicism. Coolidge understood the gift of each day and found gladness in each one.

I believe his peace and optimism came from a truly pure heart— one that put others above self. Many years ago, Coolidge literally saved my father-in-law's family business at a time when it could have easily collapsed. Although he would have surely benefitted from his chief competitor's loss, Coolidge never let it happen. That was the Coolidge I knew.

Coolidge and Marylyn raised their children with a spirit of moral absolutism— love of God, love of family, love of neighbors, and love of country. Theirs was a life built on the Solid Rock, not the shifting sands of the times. It's one that Patsy and I chose many years ago as an inspiration in raising our own children.

Perhaps Is That You, Coolidge? should serve as a timeless primer for parents; a moving illustration of the worthwhile struggle to raise children with an uncompromising set of values— but always tempered with unconditional love.

Bob Riley

Contents

Foreword	3	Alabama Governor Bob Riley
Contents	5	
About the Author	9	
Dedication	13	
Prologue	17	The English Channel 1944 – Utah Beach – Hedgerows
Chapter One	27	Return home - Marylyn - Sixty-Six Years Later - Surprise Summit - Decision Time – The Oaks
Chapter Two	45	Room 138 - Remember When– High Life – Measuring Love - Medicine Man
Chapter Three	61	Open Windows - Delta Dawn – The Rest of the Story - Papa's Pantaloons - Big Brother - Places in the Heart
Chapter Four	79	Choo-Choo - First Date – Small Town Friends - Woodchoppers Ball
Photo Gallery 1	91	

Chapter Five	97	Suspicions - Dance of the Razor - Money Matters - T'was the Month after Christmas - Powerful Lessons - Table Talk
Chapter Six	115	Cell Phone Rendezvous – Monday, Monday – Shuttle Service -Treasures - Hey Peetey
Chapter Seven	135	My Big Idea - Honor and Respect - Cheeseburgers - Complications - Turnaround - Good Morning? - Greasy Hair and Silly Prayer - Bathroom Humor
Chapter Eight	151	Coffee Talk - Drug Dealers – Pharmacy Fun – Michael Time – Sunrise, Sunset - Stressful Days - Crossing the Line – Mrs. Teel and Daddy's Girl - Dr. Mike – Sandworms and Bicycles - Life Lessons - Making the Call
Chapter Nine	177	Summer Songs - New Hope – Stacey and Company – Faux Pas -Friends and Neighbors – Nicknames – Entertainer Extraordinaire - Pranksters - Old '97 - Legacy Visit
Chapter Ten	201	Sadie – Nick and Nubbin' – Marylyn Memories – Little Prisspot - Good Times - Adrenaline Mom

Chapter Eleven	215	Family Secrets - May 25 - Lonely Days - Rebound – Miss Ayler - Teenagers Again - Thought Pegs
Photo Gallery 2	237	
Chapter Twelve	245	Yogurt Run - Just Like Family – Deep Divide – Courage and Grit - Mixed Messages - Big O - Scary Days - Collision Course
Chapter Thirteen	269	Divine Appointment - Ah Ha! Moment – Return to 138 - The Father in the Room – Panic Button - July Recess - Last Kiss
Chapter Fourteen	287	Unpredictable - Charlotte the Third - Final Resolutions - Taking Turns - We Three - God Encounter – Shutting Down - Oh Happy Day!
Chapter Fifteen	301	Grandkids Remember - Family Table
Epilogue	309	Eulogy - Q and A – Coolidge-isms
Acknowledgements	321	
Remembrance	323	

About the Author

Mark Nichols Sims and his wife Peggy live in Helena, Alabama, on the outskirts of Birmingham. Mark graduated from Samford University where he met Peggy. He also received a M.A. in Biblical Languages from the Assemblies of God Theological Seminary. For nearly forty years they have served the Kingwood Church family where they serve on the pastoral staff. Mark is also the founder and director of the Birmingham Metro Master's Commission program and has served on the Master's Commission International Network board of directors since its inception. An accomplished speaker and writer, Mark is most comfortable as a "Disciple Maker." Training young men and women in Christian discipleship and ministry is his life-blood.

Mark and Peggy Sims raised their two beautiful daughters in Kingwood Church where they and their spouses serve in leadership. Lindsay and her husband Joel have three children: Sophia, Grant, and Juliette. Betsy and Nathan have two children: Charlotte and Dalton. Being parents and grandparents are Mark and Peggy's greatest earthly joy.

"Why I wrote, Is That You, Coolidge?"

My father never considered himself to be exceptional, but his influence was widely seen in everyone he touched. As his son, he affected my life greatly—but alas, it took me years to discover how powerful that effect really was.

I am a prototypical *baby boomer,* born during the prosperous post-war years of the American Century, and came of age during the tumultuous cultural changes of the Civil Rights struggle, the sexual revolution, the Jesus Movement and the Vietnam War. I always considered myself a great, independent thinker, but in retrospect I see that I was hardly a thinker at all.

Ultimately, I want my children and my children's children to be affected by Coolidge Sims. The most powerful way to accomplish that is to write down the stories and experiences that have woven the fabric of our lives. If we do not preserve them, they will surely vanish within one or two generations.

We all stand on the shoulders of others, and our experiences are a reflection of those who have gone before us. My life has been enriched by the songs and narratives that I learned as a child. I want those same stories, plus new ones in ever increasing measure, to continually resonate in my soul, in the souls of my kin, and in the hearts of anyone who takes the time to listen to them.

> *"My son, keep your father's command*
> *and do not forsake your mother's teaching.*
> *Bind them always on your heart;*
> *fasten them around your neck.*
> *When you walk, they will guide you;*
> *when you sleep, they will watch over you;*
> *when you awake, they will speak to you."*
> *Proverbs 6:20-22*

I am a storyteller at heart. Is That You, Coolidge? is the story of my visits with him during the last five months of his life. I gleaned more insight the short span of twenty-four weeks than I ever dreamed possible. The days were hectic, but contained the most poignant moments of my life.

Coolidge was not a perfect man. Nevertheless he was an inspiration, an example, an instructor, a father, and a hero to us who knew him best. Hopefully, even those who never knew him can now get a glimpse of the remarkable father that this stubborn *baby-boomer* finally discovered.

Mark Nichols Sims   August 2017

Mark and Coolidge 2010

*She brought laughter and music to
all who knew her. <u>Is That You, Coolidge?</u> is dedicated to the
memory of Miss Sadie Thompson.
1925-2017*

Is That You, Coolidge?

A Memoir

Mark Nichols Sims

Prologue

The English Channel 1944

A deafening series of four booms split the air without warning, shaking the transport ship as well as the nerves of the men who waited anxiously on deck. In perfectly choreographed form, they jerked their heads downward at the noise of the blasts, unsure if it was friendly or enemy fire. Coolidge snapped his head back and to the right where he spotted the source—the enormous battleship, *USS Nevada*, hurling massive shells toward the mainland, rattling their bones to the core.

He was one of the hundreds of young GI's crammed together on the open deck of the *USS Bayfield*, a modest-sized troop transport that had ferried soldiers across the English Channel since the very first wave of the D-Day invasion on June 6. Coolidge, a twenty-one-year-old American son stood on his tiptoes to catch a glimpse of the Normandy beach nicknamed "Utah," noting the thick plumes of black smoke rising into the sky from the fierce fighting inland, far beyond the beach.

The pounding of the *USS Nevada's* proud guns continued for several minutes, muddying the commands being shouted by the officers. Coolidge whispered a prayer, knowing that he would soon join the thousands of American GI's who had already landed at Normandy as a part of the largest amphibious invasion in history. His hair stood up on the back of his neck hearing the deep, distant rumble of shells pounding enemy targets just beyond the coast. He could smell the diesel fuel; taste the salt-water spray splashing against his face; and feel the weight of the heavy steel helmet on his head.

The invasion thus far had been a colossal undertaking, with mixed results. Some GI's cheered nervously; others vomited overboard; every one of them, including young Coolidge Sims, trembled in his boots.

    He took a long, deep breath hoping to chase away the waves of nausea that had plagued him throughout the two-hour trip across the choppy channel. Pressed against the starboard side rails of the transport ship he caught a clear view of one of the small, flat-bottomed landing craft known as a "Higgins Boat." Through the ocean spray's heavy mist he could see several of them approaching the *USS Bayfield*, each one seeking to load and deliver a new wave of fresh warriors onto the Normandy coast.

    Coolidge felt someone pulling him backward as a tall, older officer escorted a unit of Negro soldiers, a segregated unit of mechanics, truck drivers, and cooks, to the ships edge. It was the first people of color he had seen since leaving his native Alabama six months earlier. The tall captain shouted the order for the unit to load into the small landing craft temporarily moored on the *USS Bayfield's* starboard side. Right on cue, the sailor crew heaved a huge rope ladder blanket across the edge of the deck and down the side of the ship, resting about five feet above the Higgins landing craft.

    On command, a nervous wave of black soldiers loaded down with rifles, gas masks, leather boots, baggy pants stuffed with cigarettes, toilet articles, helmets, life jackets, and more climbed over the rim and worked their way chaotically down the rope web. All the while the small landing craft below them bobbed up and down and sideways in the rough sea, making the five-foot leap from the bottom of the ladder into the Higgins craft treacherous at best. Timing was paramount. A shallow leap could land a soldier into the space between the boats and into the cold English Channel to be crushed by the landing craft banging continually against the gray metal sides of the *USS Bayfield*. The tall, impatient officer yanked his hat off and yelled out instructions. The peeved lieutenant in the boat below echoed the orders, cursing the black soldiers for wasting precious time. Five or six at a time, they made the final leap into the boat, some feet first, others ending in a belly flop, scurrying toward the front of the boat before the next man landed on top of him.

Coolidge spotted a young colored soldier who had hesitated several times, wholly incapable of bringing himself to cross over the edge and onto the ropes. Soldiers around him pushed, shouted, and ragged him unmercifully for his paralyzing fear of climbing down the ropes where one misstep risked a plunge into the salt water below.

"I ain't no swimmer!" he protested wildly to no avail. "I be drownin' down in 'nair!"

The tall officer, infuriated with the young black private, rushed toward him, cursing madly. Eyes wide open, his gaze darting between the officer and the boat, the black soldier let out a high-pitched warning to the men below,

"Look out boys, here come Willie Dee!" His skinny, six-foot frame sailed over the deck like an albatross. "Hep me Lawd Jeesus!" he screamed as he launched. Butt first, never touching the ropes, Willie Dee landed squarely on top of the men below. Cheers and rousing laughter erupted from the men who watched his terrified flight from the deck above. Below, the poor fellows who felt the full weight of Willie Dee and his forty pound backpack collapsed like bowling pins, clutching their sprained necks, spewing all sorts of profanities.

Willie Dee's stunt made Coolidge laugh out loud, but did little to curb his apprehension about what lay ahead. The climb down the ropes and into the boat would not be a problem. He could handle that. A country boy, he had climbed trees, walls, fences, and ropes all of his life. It was the landing on the beach ahead that gave him pause. Sure, the initial landings on June 6 had cleared out the concrete pillboxes and beach fortifications and driven the Nazi defenders several miles inland. Still, the pockets of resistance, snipers, and occasional strafing by a BF-109 Messerschmitt fighter plane had posed a dreadful risk to subsequent waves of Allied troops.

The full-throttled engines of the Higgins boat thundered as it departed the *USS Bayfield* and sped toward the French coast while another one moved into its place. Coolidge knew this one was *his* boat—he and thirty-five other men were its cargo. Orders were given and they wasted no time getting into position. The loud engines continued to roar as the men descended the ropes post haste.

Unannounced, a round of shelling from the *USS Nevada* jolted the nervous troops yet again, accelerating the tension as they descended the ropes. Coolidge gritted his teeth, steadfastly focused on the task of climbing down, and then made a decent jump onto the craft. Adjusting his backpack, he moved toward the towering landing gate at the front, as the other GI's took their place in the crowded landing craft.

Utah Beach

The Higgins craft sent plumes of water into the stiff channel wind and all over the place. The company sergeant ordered the men to adjust their field packs and make sure their rifles stayed as dry as possible. In a matter of moments, the fully loaded landing craft began moving at breakneck speed headed toward Utah Beach. Coolidge saw nothing but the gray metal of the large landing gate before him, speaking nothing to anyone except God. Within a few seconds, the craft was as close as it could get to the shore. The gate of the vessel fell forward and the men began to scramble off into the waist-deep, bone-chilling cold water.

Other than the booming of the *USS Nevada's* guns and distant shelling, he heard no obvious signs of conflict. Fortunately, there was only sporadic German resistance if any at all. Coolidge followed the two men in front of him down the ramp toward the water, one peeled toward the left and the other to the right, leaving a clear path straight ahead for him. As instructed Coolidge hoisted his rifle with both hands high into the air, and stepped off of the ramp into what he expected to be shallow water.

Weighed down by ammunition and supplies, his five-foot four-inch frame plunged suddenly into about five and a half feet of salt water until his boots slammed into the bottom of the English Channel. He frantically churned his legs, struggling to gain a secure foothold. Instinctively, a tall GI behind him grabbed him by the collar and pulled him up out of the low spot just in time for a welcome gulp of air. Never dipping his rifle into the water, Coolidge finally gained traction and moved onto the beach; eyes wide open, heart pounding, and thankful that he had not died an embarrassing death at Normandy—in a random, stupid sand hole.

Utah Beach was littered with the residue of war— burned-out vehicles, sunken landing craft, barbed wire, and the sickening smell of all things dead. The bodies of the most recent casualties had already been removed, but the tide continued to vomit body parts and cadavers from the belly of the channel whenever it chose.

As the unit moved off the beach Coolidge and a buddy, Johnny Wise, took the time to duck into a burned out German machine gun bunker that had guarded Hitler's "Fortress Europe." Allied grenades and flame-throwers had ended the reign of death that this pillbox had rained down on the heroes of Utah Beach on D-day. The stench inside the bunker was unbearable. It was the kind of smell that could be felt. It clung to his hair, his clothes and penetrated his skin; soaked into his pores and permeated the mind. It's the kind of smell that burns itself into the memory, never to be erased. Coolidge held his breath tightly during their foray into the burned-out bunker. In the corner, he caught a permanent glimpse of the twisted, mangled, charred, and barely recognizable as human carcasses of two enemy gunners. They were probably two German guys no older than he and Johnny.

"Oh my God, why hasn't somebody removed these poor souls?" Johnny asked in a barely audible whisper, choking and coughing all the while.

"Heck if I know," Coolidge responded, darting out of the doorway for a gulp of air. "But I'm not about to do it."

Hedgerows

The 180th General Hospital unit re-formed and moved carefully a half-mile away from the beach, into the muddy plots and fields that for hundreds of years the simple French farmers of Normandy had bordered with hedgerows instead of wooden or wire fences. *Hedgerow* describes the thick vegetation, hedges, vines, and small trees growing in an earthen embankment three to five feet tall, and just as thick. From the sky, they appeared as interlocking boxes stretching for miles. From the ground, seeing beyond the next hedgerow was impossible, so an enemy sniper or machine gun nest hiding in a hedgerow was a natural death trap for soldiers walking on a side road or exposed in an open field.

His unit officers designated a muddy field between hedgerows as a safe place to establish camp for the night. Like worker ants, the GI's began setting up two-man pup tents and preparing campfires. A late afternoon drizzle made the task miserable for Coolidge and Johnny as they tried to come up with a plan to get sleep without getting soaked. Coolidge used his small entrenching tool to dig a drainage trench around their tent, while Johnny smoked a cigarette, carrying on a conversation with a tall new unit colleague, Tommy Grantham.

Crack, tzing! "Sniper fire!!" Johnny yelled, collapsing to the ground, hands covering his exposed head, a half-smoked cigarette still wedged between his fingers. Tommy took a nosedive behind the pup tent; Coolidge clutched his helmet against his head rolling sideways in a heap. A cold lump of mud pressed tightly against his cheek. The three men remained glued to the turf but listened intently as an infantry guard unit about forty yards away charged into action, shouting commands and moving in the direction of the unseen sniper.

"You okay, Johnny?" Coolidge shouted, his face jammed between the mud and his own chest. Instantly a succession of images raced through his mind— Sunday dinner in Alabama, drinking a Coca-Cola with his girlfriend Marylyn at Jordan's Drug Store—and then the two charred bodies in the Nazi bunker. He could smell it. The smell of death from the bunker was still on his body, and on his mind. Would he be next?

"Yeah, where's it coming from?" Johnny responded.

"Heck if I know," Coolidge hollered. Sporadic gunfire was heard past the hedgerow behind them. Coolidge hunkered down even more. Another burst of fire for about ten seconds was followed by a peculiar silence. "I hope that means the good guys won," Coolidge quipped. Everyone remained immobile until an *all-clear* shout was heard on the perimeter. Johnny was the first to sit up. Then Coolidge slowly pushed himself up out of the mud with his soaking wet left arm—soggy from the drainage trench he had just dug. Standing up, he watched Johnny take a deep drag on what was left of his cigarette. Johnny blew the smoke in Coolidge's direction.

"I'm not lying," Johnny lamented. "That scared the snot out of me."

"You're not kiddin'! When I saw you hit the dirt, I thought you'd been shot!" Coolidge said, scraping the black mud off his right cheek. Tommy just sat cross-legged, looking down at the ground.

"You alright buddy?" Coolidge asked Tommy.

"Yeah. I'm alive. But I think I peed my pants."

They got a good laugh at Tommy Grantham's expense, but it took several minutes for the entire unit to return to an uneasy normal. Coolidge found himself nervously scanning the hedgerows for another hidden intruder. He was really worried. Then suddenly out of nowhere came a fast-talking military photographer.

"Hey, men! Come over here; let me get your picture before it's too dark!"

"For what?" Coolidge quizzed him, "The Saturday Evening Post?"

"Not quite. *Stars and Stripes.* It's my army job," he responded with a thick Brooklyn accent. "I bet you'se guys think that Kraut was shooting at *me*, right?" The three chuckled tentatively, bunching up together for the quick photograph.

"Will we ever see the picture?" Coolidge bantered as the photographer hurried off.

"Sure, if you'se lucky to live long enough."

Indeed, they survived the war and saw the picture. Coolidge Sims is the one on the right—the short one. He was my father.

I thought I knew him well but later discovered that there was much about him that I had misunderstood, missed, or ignored. It wasn't until he was given only months to live that I raced to learn all I could about him. Was he really who I imagined him to be? Who was this man I called Dad? I only wish I had not waited so long to ask the question,

"Is that you, Coolidge?"

"When I was a boy of fourteen, my father was so ignorant I could hardly stand to have the old man around. But when I got to be twenty-one, I was astonished at how much he had learned in seven years."
Mark Twain

Chapter One

May 1946

    Hitler's war in Europe had been over for a year now. Calvin Coolidge Sims, or Coolidge as everyone called him, stared out the window of the troop train as it slowly pulled into the Atlanta railroad terminal. The 22-hour train ride from New Jersey had been especially long and boring, the last one this soldier would ever take bankrolled entirely by Uncle Sam. His right shoulder rested against the coach window. Hypnotized by the lazy clicking of the train, his tired eyes stared blindly at an empty track beside him, appearing and disappearing tie by tie from his vision.

    He had been away from home now for over three years. The train finally glided to a halt and the porter announced their official arrival into Atlanta. The second the doors opened Coolidge bounded out of the coach like a house cat trapped overnight in a tight closet. Lugging his sole possession across his back, an olive green duffel bag stuffed to the gills, he hurriedly made his way toward the terminal building.

    There weren't waving and cheering masses present to greet the soldiers in Atlanta, just as there hadn't been welcoming throngs when their troop ship arrived in New York Harbor a week ago. The adoring crowds and beautiful girls had exhausted all their post-war enthusiasm in '45 when the first shiploads of battle hardened guys, the ones who had been gone the longest, had returned home. It had been a well-deserved welcome for heroes, perfect for the newsreels and cameras.

    But by May of 1946, most Americans were content with moving on with their lives without much thought of the previous four years of war. They had better things to do than welcome every troop ship that arrived from

Europe, and there were lots of them. Over 16 million Americans had served their country overseas in World War II, and were now making their way home.

Coolidge recalled the nice, but the obligatory military band playing a patriotic tune when they had disembarked in New York, along with a few beautiful WAC's and WAVES smiling and waving as the boys walked down the gangplank back onto American soil. For a year now Coolidge had seen the photos in the Stars and Stripes newspaper highlighting the exuberant crowds that greeted the GI's as the first troop ships arrived home. But that was almost a year ago. He wasn't really expecting it to still be happening, but he was a bit disappointed nevertheless. After all, the young man was no less proud to have served his country, than the heroes who had returned with colorful fanfare nine months earlier.

Glancing to his left and right he saw a few tearful, happy reunions going on between GIs and the families who had come to meet them at the station. He noticed but didn't stop long enough to take it all in. Coolidge was trying to come up with a plan to get *all the way* home. His short legs pushed his small frame across the green and white-checkered tile floors of the train station at a breakneck pace. His duffel bag was wider than he was, but he carried it confidently. The heavy bag knew who was boss.

Still sporting staff sergeants' stripes on his jacket, and the familiar elongated garrison cap, stylishly cocked to the side like proud rooster's comb, he looked forward to being a civilian again. For the first time since 1943, he was a civilian now. He had to find his own way to travel the last 100 miles to his home in the tiny east Alabama town of Ashland. He *did* have money in his pocket. He had drawn a hundred dollars upon his honorable discharge from the U.S. Army at Fort Monmouth, New Jersey, but preferred to hold on to the money as long as he could.

Moving at a brisk pace through the huge terminal lobby he questioned whether or not he should buy a bus ticket to Anniston, and then hitchhike the last 40 miles, or save the money and hitchhike all the way home from Atlanta? He had hitchhiked plenty of times, so it wouldn't be difficult, especially as a friendly homeward bound soldier in army fatigues. But it was already three o'clock on Sunday afternoon, and either option might leave him with an uncomfortable overnight stay in the middle of nowhere. Coolidge ducked into the men's room for a quick minute when he saw it—just on the left, next to the "white only" water fountain—a telephone booth. He made the decision then and there to give Papa and Mama a quick call and let them know he was almost home.

His family had no idea yet that he had even left Europe. The army tended not to afford anyone the consideration of planning ahead. Coolidge was keen on the idea of surprising the family by just showing up, walking in the door, and shouting, *"Hey Mama, I'm home."* Hearing his mother's shriek and then becoming unglued with joy would mean more to him than if President Truman himself had met him personally when the troop ship arrived.

But the anticipation of seeing his family again got the best of him. *"Forget the drama; just go home!"* Coolidge said aloud to himself. Dropping the duffel bag just outside the phone booth he located a nickel in his pocket to begin the call. He dialed zero.

"Operator here. What number please?" It was probably the first time he had heard a female voice on the telephone in at least two years. As disinterested as she sounded, it sure was nice to hear something other than a gruff GI speaking on an army field phone. Her familiar Southern accent caused him to smell home even more.

"Yes Ma'am," Coolidge responded, feeling a flutter in his stomach. "I want to make a long distance call to the Cecil Sims residence in Ashland, Alabama, please."

"And what number would that be?" she asked in a gentle tone.

"Oh, we don't have numbers in Ashland," Coolidge countered. "It's just three short rings and two long ones. When you get the Ashland operator, she'll know." Barely a few seconds later he heard,

"Ashland phone operator, hello." A wide grin exploded across Coolidge's face. It was Miss Ola Thorpe. He had known her all of his life. She had been the phone operator in Ashland since telephones first appeared in the small rural town. Her abrupt, crusty telephone voice betrayed her. She was actually a kind, caring, spinster who made it her job to know everything, but not in a malevolent sort of way. Miss Ola was a simple old gal who knew everyone in town by name and was loved by all. Short in stature, with a wrinkling upper lip and thin nose, she wore her dark hair pulled back tightly into a small, neat bun on the back of her head.

"Yes, I have a long distance call for the Cecil Sims residence in Ashland, Alabama," the Atlanta operator announced. "Will you please...?" Miss Ola abruptly interrupted,

"Well, Cecil and Melvina are not at home. They're down at Thurmon and Nettie Brewer's this afternoon visiting."

Instinctively Coolidge gushed out, "Miss Ola, will you ring them down there for me?"

"Is that you, Coolidge?" Miss Ola drawled. A wide grin reappeared on Coolidge's face.

"I'm sorry, but you cannot have a conversation before this connection is made," the Atlanta lady warned.

"Oh yes we can," Miss Ola snapped back. "He's one of our soldier boys that's been gone from here for three years. Coolidge, I'll ring down at Thurmon and Nettie's and get a hold of them for you." The Atlanta professional kept silent. She had been overruled. Miss Ola rang two longs and two shorts and one more long ring at the Brewer residence.

"Hello."

"Nettie," Miss Ola blurted out. "Get Cecil and Melvina on the line. It's Coolidge!" Within seconds Melvina Sims was on the line,

"Is that you, Coolidge?"

"Just a moment," the Atlanta operator interjected. "The charges for ..." Melvina gave her zero time to finish.

" We'll pay all the charges."

"Thank you, it's been a pleasure," the operator said, reading her final line in the touching family drama.

"Mama, I'm at the train station in Atlanta. I'm getting a bus ticket for Anniston first thing tomorrow morning, and I'll hitchhike on home from there."

"Oh no you won't," his mother ordered. "You stay right where you are. Your Papa and I are coming straight to get you." Coolidge could hear his father in the background shouting that they could be there in a couple or three hours.

"Okay, Mama. I'll be waiting for you," he said. "Oh, and Mama, I don't know if she's home, but could you call Marylyn and see if she might want to ride over here with Y'all?"

"Alright, I will. Bye-Bye Coolidge." Before Melvina Sims even had a chance to hang up the receiver Miss Ola, still on the line, broke in,

"Melvina, y'all go on home and get ready. I'll call Marylyn and let her know to expect your call. I know she's in town this weekend. She will be so thrilled that Coolidge is back!"

Marylyn

Coolidge had known Marylyn Nichols since his family first moved to Ashland. They were in the second grade. Marylyn had gone home after the very first day of school in 1931 chattering to her mother about the new boy in class. Her big brown eyes flashed with delight as she recounted the day's events while her mother peeled rutabagas at the kitchen sink. Marylyn was especially animated that day, the pink bow sitting atop her thick, brown, pageboy haircut bounced around happily as she prattled on,

"His name is Coolidge. When Teacher asked us what we had for breakfast this morning he said, *'Syrup and biscuit, wanna see?'* Then he opened up his mouth wide, and stuck out his tongue!" Marylyn put both hands over her mouth and giggled wildly, her mother stopping long enough to share Marylyn's excitement as well. Coolidge and Marylyn had been sweethearts ever since. Yes, they had dated a few other people over the years, but everyone always knew that they belonged together.

Marylyn got the courtesy call from Miss Ola, and then the official one from the Sims. She got ready in record time, dizzy with delight about Coolidge returning from three long years in the army.

The only one more thrilled than Marylyn about Coolidge's return was probably Estelle Nichols, Marylyn's mother. She had loved Coolidge ever since seven-year-old Marylyn made such a fuss about him in the kitchen. He had spent a lot of time at their house over the years, endearing the entire Nichols family to himself. During the war, Marylyn's grandmother, who lived in the home with them, boxed up some fresh muscadine grapes in a cardboard shoebox and attempted to mail them to Coolidge during the Battle of the Bulge. Grandmother Nichols had no concept of where France was but thought a little fresh fruit would surely lift his spirits.

Marylyn was elated to ride to Atlanta with Coolidge's parents, although she did not want herself to be the main event. This was about their son returning safely from the war, not about her. Coolidge's parents were very fond of Marylyn as well, but they had not really spent much time together, at least not without Coolidge present.

Melvina Sims was not a strong conversationalist, and Cecil was the king of dry wit. For introvert Marylyn, the happy drive home with Coolidge would be heaven, but what about the two and a half hours in the car driving *to*

Atlanta? What would she say? How awkward would it get?

Marylyn remembered well the night when she and Coolidge, both high school seniors, were on a Saturday night date in Cecil's car. The deal was that Coolidge could use the family car as long as they were willing to interrupt their date to drive Cecil home when he closed his dry goods store at nine o'clock in the evening. As promised, Coolidge and Marylyn kept their end of the deal. When they got Cecil to his house, he had a difficult time getting the passenger door to open. Marylyn, seated in the front seat between the two men, dutifully reached across Mr. Sims' lap and opened the door for him. As Cecil got out of the car he mumbled,

"Strange to me you know more about my car than I do." Marylyn was aghast. She cried for two days. Although Coolidge laughed and told her that it was just his father's way of being funny, she didn't believe him. It had bothered her ever since. What did he think of her? Still, it never crossed her mind to decline the invitation to join them for the trip to Atlanta. The rest of the story is history, and a wonderful story it is.

Sixty-Six Years Later

My cell phone rang at around 8:30 that Monday night. I noticed the call was from Ashland, but I wasn't familiar with the number.

"Hello, this is Mark," I answered.

"Mark, this is Don Fulbright. I'm sorry to bother you. Do you have a minute?"

"Sure, Don. Is everything alright?"

"Well, it's your Dad again. Jo and I are really worried about Coolidge. We went by to check on him tonight and he's just not doing well at all. He's been walking around all day in his housecoat and pajamas, and I don't know that he's eaten anything at all. He seemed so frustrated."

"I had no idea, Don."

"He said he couldn't figure out if he'd paid all the bills or not, and couldn't seem to balance the checkbook. Jo offered to take a look at it for him since she's good with bookkeeping." Don's voice lowered to a near whisper. "Mark, it was a mess. It made no sense. He's so confused, and actually asked us not to tell his kids how messed up his bills are."

"I just talked to him Friday night, Don. He was happy and talkative and sounded great, other than complaining about the neuralgia in his left leg that was keeping him from sleeping well." I had a sinking feeling in my gut.

"Yeah. To just talk with him on the phone, he sounds like everything's fine," Don continued. "He sounds great for a guy about to turn 89 years old, but seeing him in person really tells a different story."

"I guess he hides it from us pretty well," I added.

"Yes, he does." There was a curious, silent pause. "I'm sure you'll pass the information on to your brother and sister," Don said warmly. "If there's anything we can do, you have our number now—just call."

"We thank you and Jo so much for caring. You're such good friends to Dad. We'll keep you in the loop when we figure out where the loop is," I assured him. "Good night, Don."

His call left me feeling somewhat like a bad son, embarrassed that I was clueless about my father's deteriorating health. Don and Jo were being the best of friends by calling me. I beat myself up for not recognizing it earlier. It shouldn't have surprised me, though. In the past, my father and I had all too often communicated on different wavelengths.

Despite some tough hurdles during my teen years, Dad and I *had finally* begun to grow closer, especially after I married and started a family. We talked regularly and I felt that I knew my father adequately. All of a sudden I now realized how much I still wanted to know. My iconic father would not be here forever—a realization came to me as suddenly and unexpectedly as the phone call from Don Fulbright.

My mom, Marylyn, had died thirteen years earlier, leaving Dad alone in the same house they had shared together for forty-two years. Amazingly, they had been happily married for almost fifty-three. Up until a few months ago, Dad had coped rather well with the role of widower. He had remained active in church and civic activities, played golf, worked part-time in the hospital pharmacy, and watched lots of sports and news on television. Coolidge Sims' social calendar stayed jam-packed, and his quiver of friends was full.

The Sims children, all three of us, lived close enough to be with him in less than three hours. Mike Sims, the eldest, lived in Columbus, Georgia; our younger sister, Donna Taylor lived in the Birmingham area, as did I. Dad regularly shared time with each of us and with his seven grandchildren whom he adored.

We saw Dad grieve when his younger sister Gail died of cancer and were very concerned about him when his only brother Bremon passed away in Florida. But when his older sister Gwynnelle died, he began to decline swiftly. He and his last remaining sibling had, for the last dozen years, been best friends. They lived on the same street, six houses apart, and virtually took care of one another. Her death was a tough blow.

Coolidge began spending more and more time alone and became increasingly feeble—falling several times at home and in public. Still, he kept his humor intact, finding some way to laugh his way through it.

> "It wasn't that bad a fall," he would explain. "I'm so short, I didn't have far to drop—the ground was pretty close."

In addition, his several driving accidents let us know that he was becoming a danger to himself and to everyone on the road.

Just a few months earlier he had agreed to travel to Columbus to celebrate the Thanksgiving holiday with Mike, his wife Kathy, and their family. They were expecting him by mid-afternoon, but he didn't show. As darkness approached, Mike and Kathy began to be very concerned. Mike called to ask if I had heard anything from him. I had not, but knew that he preferred to travel in daylight. He didn't answer his cell phone, but that wasn't unusual. He rarely carried it with him and often forgot to turn it on. Concern turned to worry.

At age 88, there were multiple reasons why he was delayed so long, but few of them were good reasons. Should the police be called? Should the family begin to look for him? Was he lost somewhere in Georgia, or in Alabama? Kathy and Mike dutifully swung into action, anticipating where Dad might have made a wrong turn, considering a feasible search and rescue plan, and praying for God to show them the next step to take.

To everyone's relief, he pulled into the driveway just as darkness set in. He had somehow become confused, disoriented, and had driven for a while in circles on *both* sides of the Chattahoochee River before he finally got his bearings. Dad had driven the very same route dozens of times before, but since Gwynnelle's death, Dad's mental focus had been off. Regardless of the logical reasons, Mike and Kathy knew then that something had changed with Dad.

After the alarming call from Don and Jo, I went to Peggy, my wife of thirty-three years, and told her the situation. Peggy urged me to contact my siblings at once, and to plan a trip to Ashland the very next morning. Dad had won Peggy's heart since the very first time I brought her home from college to meet the family. His charm and wit always delighted her, and Peggy's genuine affection toward him was unmistakable.

Our two daughters, Lindsay and Betsy, adored their Papaw. Already grown and married, they still remained closely attached to him. Lindsay mailed him pictures of his two great-grandchildren often, and looked for reasons to give him a call now and then. Betsy had spent lots of time keeping him company, especially after Marylyn died. She was the master of getting Papaw to tell stories of his childhood, making her an expert on all things "Coolidge."

Surprise Summit

Mike, Donna, and I agreed to meet at Dad's house the next morning for a surprise visit. He was glad to see us but knew something was up when all three of us arrived unannounced. Despite his best effort to appear normal, he was noticeably off his game—unshaven, unbathed, and still in pajamas at nearly noon. He had apparently been that way for days, ostensibly sleep deprived. Enunciating words and completing sentences seemed an unusual challenge for him. Something wasn't right.

After a tad of small talk, we gathered in the den for a meeting. Mike, a family practice physician, began the conversation,

"Dad, some of your friends have let us know that you're having a hard time right now. We are your children; we love you, and we want to help you."

"Look," Dad began, "You all have families to take care of, and I don't want to be a burden to you." Sitting by himself on the couch, he pulled his right knee up and held it with both hands, nervously pitching forward and backward while he spoke. He raised his eyebrows and glanced up at Mike who was standing next to him. "As long as I'm able to take care of myself, I'm going to."

"That's just it, Dad," I cut in. "You are at an age now where you can't do what you used to do. It's okay. We can take some of this off of you." Dad kept up his gentle rocking motion, his eyes watering slightly. I continued voicing our offer,

"Donna is more than happy to organize your bills for you, and help you keep up with your checkbook. I'm already talking with some people who we can hire to come cook for you, get your groceries, clean your house, and run your errands for you. Since Mike is a doctor, he's going to monitor your medicine, talk with your doctors, and help you make the medical decisions you need to make." Dad's lips formed an *"o"* and exhaled, sounding less like a whistle and more like a *wheesh*. He lowered his right foot onto the floor and sat with his hands folded in his lap. Donna sprang from the rocking chair to the couch, sat down next to him, and took his hand lovingly into hers and made a pledge to him.

"Daddy, you took great care of us all of our lives, and now we're going to take care of *you*. It's not a burden, Daddy, it's a joy." He looked squarely into her eyes,

"Y'all would do that for *me*?"

"Of course, Dad!" Mike answered in a near whisper.

"I'm sure with just a little help, I could pull things back together," Dad assured. "Now, one thing, uh, I don't think we need to spend too much money on outside help..." I had to interrupt him,

"Dad, you've been saving money for years, saying it was for when you got old and needed it. Well, guess what? It's time! You're old. You turn 89 years old in two weeks and it's time." Coolidge responded with a playful grin on his face,

"I'm not old! I'm just experienced!" We all needed a good laugh before Mike brought up the item that could be the most contentious. Taking a deep breath Mike waded into the deep water.

"Now Dad, one more thing that's really important. I'm a physician and I have lots of patients that are your age. It is my professional opinion, and my opinion as your son who loves you very much, that you don't need to be driving anymore. You have too many physical and medical problems to be on the road. Your judgment isn't as clear as it used to be, nor are your reflexes. It's not safe." Mike paused for a few seconds. "We're going to ask you to give up your car keys."

The air suddenly got thick in the room. A peculiar, uncomfortable silence filled the same space where there had just been laughter. Dad broke the awkward silence,

"Well, I don't think a son is supposed to tell his father what to do. I thought it went the other way around. I pay my insurance. I don't think that's your decision to make." Without a moment's hesitation, Mike volleyed back,

"Dad, if you die in a car wreck we know you'll be in Heaven. But what about that innocent person you may crash into? They may not be ready for Heaven. I don't think you want something like that to be the legacy you leave behind."

Coolidge was stunned. God had helped my brother appeal to the one thing that could best move our Dad's heart—living a Christian life with no regrets. It was like the wisdom of Solomon had supervened. Without one vestige of resistance, Dad rose from the couch, walked to the side table, picked up his car keys and handed them to Mike.

"You're right, Son. I would never want that to happen." Dad never balked at our demand, and never changed his mind about it. He never even spoke about it again—not even once.

Decision Time

For a short while, the help came three days a week to cook, clean, and make sure he got his medicine. Often his good friends from church came by to check on him. Connie, a long-time employee of Ashland Pharmacy, did the same. She considered *Mr. Coolidge* like family, keeping a close eye on him for us.

Nevertheless, within a month the word we got from Connie and the others was—he's still on a steep, downward spiral. He remained confused about his medicine; refused offers to run his errands; failed to answer the door when his friends came to check on him;

and stayed in bed much of the day, except when the help came to clean and cook. It was so unlike him. It became clear that something had to change quickly.

Donna and I drove to Ashland to see him. He was awake when we arrived, but looked debilitated. "Dad," I said. "We talked to Mike this morning, and he has spoken with your doctors. We have made a decision together that we know is best for you. We're going to take you back to Birmingham with us today and check out an assisted living center for you—at least until you get better." Dad was not blindsided by what I said. His empty brown eyes gazed at me, defeated.

"We're not doing anything with your house or your stuff," Donna added. "We're just going to take you to my house for a few days until we can get you into a facility where we can be close to you, and see you every day, and make sure you get the help you need." Donna and I held our breath—having no idea how he would react to our firm diplomacy. Dad cleared his throat, coolly declaring,

"Well let's go. I'm just glad y'all are here to help me. I can't do it anymore." Tears squeezed softly from his eyes, resigning completely while still restraining himself from an avalanche of emotion. Donna rushed to hug him, her tears flowing freely. I pulled a tissue from the box next to him, and placed it in his hand. Dad wiped the moisture from his eyes, and then fumbled the ragged tissue between his fingers. Amidst the tears and hugs, Donna and I glanced at each other in amazement and relief. Within an hour we had packed some things and were all on our way back to Birmingham.

I was strangely silent during the car ride to Donna's house. I did the driving and let Donna occupy Dad in conversation. During the entire trip, I could only think of one thing—I was now engaged in a race against time. A thousand questions to finally ask my father flooded my mind. Am I too late? Has he already turned the corner on remembrance? Will the things I longed to reconcile remain hidden forever? Or is this God's wonderful wake-up call to a son who desires so deeply to understand the full measure of his hero? I decided to believe the latter.

The Oaks

It was a windy, bright spring morning when we arrived at our Dad's new home. My sister had somehow uncovered the perfect place for him-- a senior retirement community called, The Oaks. Turning left from the main road onto the grounds, we crossed a quaint bridge over a stream, and wound around until we could view the main building—the Lodge, reminiscent of an Adirondack lodge from the early twentieth century, only newer. Situated on top of a grassy hill and surrounded by acres and acres of woodlands, the sprawling one-level building had the distinct appearance of a country hotel topped with a square windowed cupola as its crown. Bungalow styled columns lined the long, covered walkway that led from the drive onto an open viewing porch and into the main foyer.

Amazingly, the entire campus was tucked in-between a busy golf course, and several housing subdivisions that covered suburban hills just south of Birmingham—all completely unseen from the facility itself. As Donna pulled into the parking space, I glanced over my left shoulder at Dad seated alone just behind the driver's seat. He didn't say a word, but looked pleased.

"So far, so good," I whispered to my sister as I opened the car trunk to retrieve his walker.

"He'll love it here, I just know it." Donna sounded confident, but showed me that her fingers were tightly crossed. She opened the car door for Dad while I locked in place the folded handles of the aluminum walker. "Okay Daddy, let's go inside and see if you like it," she said. We had already made the decision that this is where he would be, but we wanted him to feel it was ultimately *his* choice. In reality, there was no backup plan if he refused.

Flanking him on the right and left we made our way through the covered breezeway and toward the front door.

Tilting his head and glancing toward me he declared, "I see y'all have sentenced me to an old folks home, Mark."

"Why do you say that?" I responded, searching to see if this was his first hostile jab or a just a playful joke.

"Because I can see about a dozen old codgers on the porch checking out the new boy in town." We chuckled at the wisecrack, so typical of him. Dad was not resisting. Still, I could tell how difficult it was going to be for him to start over—new friends, new faces, in new places. He had always used humor to endear strangers to himself. It worked in his second-grade class eighty-one years ago; it would now have to work at The Oaks as well.

The facility was incredible. There was nothing about the place that resembled a nursing home. There was no stale hospital smell or sounds of old people crying out in lonely misery. Streams of warm sunlight coursed downward toward us as we first stepped into the towering foyer. I could tell Dad's spirits were lifted. There were windows everywhere, with wide halls, high ceilings, and beautifully carpeted floors.

Moving into the main hall we noticed a television viewing room on the left, complete with at least ten comfy leather recliners, and a wide-screen TV. On our right was an enormous living room area. A large hearth and mantle were central to the room with a sizeable sectional couch facing it. Paned glass windows adorned two walls, with seating areas and small tables throughout. At one end, was a piano; at the other, a library with shelves and shelves of books.

The intersection of the entrance and the main hallway was like a slow-motion pedestrian crosswalk spanning a busy wheelchair roundabout. We paused as a smartly dressed old gentleman sauntered across the busy junction on his electric scooter, giving Dad a nod and a quick wave. Dad waved back, visibly amused, but not every pedestrian was so charmed by the elderly driver. Facing us was a short, rotund old woman with swollen ankles, sighing heavily with annoyance. She scolded the flashy driver's slow-motion recklessness, heaping shovel loads of disapproval on him with one wicked gaze. To our left, two frumpy gals careened side-by-side around the corner, eyes focused on the great room doorway, racing slowly to get the best seat for Friday morning bingo about to commence.

A meeting with the administrators went well, although Dad said very little. He simply told us to make the decision. "I'm not hard to please," he quipped. "It's a very nice place, but it seems more like a busy mall than a rest home. I'm not sure these people do much resting."

"Oh, Mr. Sims, The Oaks is a bustling place in the mornings, but it gets a lot quieter by evening," the charge nurse assured him. "Shall I show you your new room, Mr. Sims?"

We sealed the deal, signed the last of the papers and agreed to move him in the next morning. I felt hopeful. We had done the best we could do, provided him a place where he could *live life,* not simply a comfortable place to mark time until he dies. He would surely miss his friends in Ashland, although he had already outlived many of them. Still, even the best of friends can only provide peripheral care. Loving care is for family. He needed his family now, and his family had never been more ready to be there for our Dad.

"You don't choose your family.
They are God's gift to you, as you are to them."
Desmond Tutu

Chapter Two

Room 138

He was sitting in his faux leather recliner when I appeared in room 138. His strong brown eyes were trained on the doorway anxiously anticipating my arrival with another box of his stuff. I had cleared my schedule to stay with him most of the day.

"Hey Bud," he blurted out as soon as he caught sight of me. An odd grin crept across his freshly shaven face. "I was wondering if you were ever going to get here." He had already called me twice before 7 o'clock this morning to inquire of when I would be coming.

"What do you mean?" I said playfully. "Dad, it's not even eight o'clock yet. How was your first night's sleep? Was the bed comfortable enough?" I set the cardboard box down with a thud on the floor beside him.

"Not too good, Son," he muttered. His head moved from side to side, letting out a frustrated sigh. "I didn't sleep worth a flip last night, and then two orderlies woke me up for a bath at five-thirty in the morning, for crying out loud!" He was still visibly irritated. "I told them I would take one myself later, but they said I was a *fall risk* and had to have help." Nervously clutching and rubbing his forearms he continued, "So I guess taking a bath around here is not going to be carried out according to *my* wishes." I felt so sorry for him. He had just discovered that his privacy was gone.

"Dad, they just don't want you to fall and break a bone, and that kind of thing happens so easily." I hoped he had not said something awful to the nurse's aids that could come back later to bite him in the butt. "I'm so sorry, Dad. But maybe we *can* do something about them showing up at the crack of dawn."

"I sure hope so," he snapped. His strange silence and reluctance to look up at me revealed his level of aggravation at the early morning events. I watched him stare at his wrinkled, knotty fingers, opening and closing his fists to relax the tension he was feeling. I matched his silence, picking up an activity schedule sheet to check out the social events of the day. Then, suddenly perking up, eyes wide open he asked: "Hey, Bud, you ready to eat some breakfast?"

"You've been up since 5:30 and haven't eaten breakfast yet?" I responded matching his sudden change in mood. Hopefully, his early morning ruminating was over; his usual cheerfulness restored.

"I've been waiting on *you*. But we'd better hurry, they're going to run out of food before we get there." I helped him stand to get to his walker. As was customary, he reached for his Auburn ball cap and fixed it in place, carefully tucking his snow-white hair inside the bill. Even though we were a very short distance from the dining hall never taking one step outside the building, he was going to wear a hat. I had seen it all of my life. For Coolidge Sims, a hat—any hat—was part of being thoroughly dressed.

We ambled into the beautiful dining room, taking our seats at a table dressed in linen tablecloths and napkins, with a vase of two fresh daisies in the center. The smell of bacon was in the air. We took our seats at a table with two other gray-haired gentlemen.

After a pleasant exchange of names and greetings, the friendly Oaks staff delivered our breakfast choices to the table. There was no shortage of conversation between Coolidge and our new acquaintances. I kept quiet most of the time, but I listened intently to their predictable conversation. For members of my father's generation the common denominators were always the same: Where did you serve during World War II; where did you live; and what did you do for a living? They followed the playbook perfectly.

Back in room 138, I began helping Dad get his room in order. Donna had already done a yeoman's work of organizing his clothes, and her husband Allen had made certain the cable TV was ready and available. My wife, Peggy soon joined us carrying bags of necessities she had purchased to help finish the task of settling in. I started arranging his personal toiletries in the bathroom, while she filled the linen shelves with brand new towels and washcloths.

"Dad," I called out as he tried to locate ESPN on his new flat screen TV, "Did you shave yourself this morning, or did the staff do it for you?"

"That's one thing I did for myself," he answered from the other room with a forced chuckle. "I had plenty of time to pretty my face between 5:30 and when you *finally* got here." Thankfully, his wit was intact. He had not lost his sense of using humor to lighten any situation.

He's a little stressed, I thought to myself, but not depressed. As long as we're close-by, I think he'll be okay.

Locating and attaching the recharger cord to his electric razor, I heard someone making their way into the room. I assumed it was the nurse with the medicine cart arriving to dole out his morning meds, but the sound was more like the shuffle of feet than a rolling cart. Peggy and I peeked around the corner just in time to see a thin, silver-haired woman in housecoat and slippers moving right in front of the television, taking a nosy gander around the room. She sported an aluminum walker with yellow fluorescent tennis balls covering the base of its four legs. Dad sat with his feet propped up in his easy chair, clutching the TV remote. Silently observing her actions, he cocked his head to the side and furrowed his brow.

"You got a nice room here," the wrinkled stranger announced, pulling out one of his dresser drawers to see what was inside, and then shutting it back with a slam. "I'm Agnes McKay. I live acrost the hall from ya'." I could hardly hold back a snicker. Dad appeared so perplexed.

"Alright," he finally answered. "Pleased to meet you. I'm Coolidge Sims, and, uh, I'm new here."

"Yeah, I know," she whined. "We all saw you move in. We've been watching. You're an Auburn man. I like Auburn, but I mostly like Alabammer. How long's your wife been dead?" Peggy sank back against the bathroom wall for support, trying not to erupt into laughter. It was like my father was being *punked* by an octogenarian!

"She's been gone about a dozen years or so," Dad answered in a matter-of-fact tone. He lowered the footrest on his recliner and slid forward, still looking up at Agnes.

"Jenny Price and Ted Nall got married outside in the flower garden just last August," she drawled. "It was a pretty wedding. Now they live in one of the garden side apartments. Come see me sometime, Mr. Coolidge. I live in 133 acrost the hall." Agnes McKay moseyed out of his room, into the main corridor and headed down the hall, sliding her tennis ball shod walker in front of her before each step. I walked out of the bathroom as if I had seen or heard nothing. Peggy followed with the empty shopping bags in hand.

"Who was that, Dad?" Peggy asked.

"Some old woman from across the hall," he muttered as he slumped back into his easy chair, visibly annoyed. "I don't remember her name, but she looks like she'd been rode hard and put up wet." Dad's eyes scanned around the room at some of the things we had not found a place for yet. "Mark, where's that nice picture of your mother that I wanted to bring?"

"Oh, It's in the box I brought with me this morning," Peggy answered. "The one on the floor."

"Peggy, I think I'll put that picture on that bedside table next to where I sleep," Dad suggested. "What do you think?"

"I definitely think you should." Peggy answered.

"Mark, does my door lock?" Dad inquired. "Or can anyone that wants to just walk up into the middle of my room?"

"It locks. Here, put your room key on this ring." I handed him a blue plastic spiral ring that The Oaks had provided. "You can keep it on your wrist when you're out, so you won't lose it." Dad took it from my hand, examining it closely.

"Well isn't that something?" he whispered.

Remember When

Peggy gave Dad a big hug before she headed back home. Dad and I unloaded the final container of stuff we had brought, giving us a unique opportunity to talk about things past. In the box were a few pictures and some small items that had special significance to him. I placed the black and white five-by-seven picture of my mom next to his bed as he had ordered.

Among a few framed pictures of family and friends, one item caught my eye. It was a small, black leather book no larger than four inches square, packed full of names, addresses, and phone numbers. Turning back some of the pages, I saw that most of them were obviously quite old—entries written in fountain pens and even addresses without zip codes.

"What in the world is this, Dad?" He stopped digging in his billfold long enough to look intently at what I was showing him.

"That's my little black book. I've been keeping important information in there for years. Give it here; let me show you." He adjusted his gold wire frame glasses, lifting his head high enough to peer through the bifocal lens at the bottom. He fumbled through the brittle pages jam-packed with entries written in black or blue ink, and some in fast fading pencil. I eyed his knotted, swollen finger joints as they worked together in a clumsy fashion to separate the pages that the passing of years had caused to stick together. These were the same hands, once nimble, that I had watched in the prescription room type medicine bottle labels at breakneck speed, and then accurately count out capsules and tablets, load them into pill bottles, and screw the cap on—all with the deft precision of a concert pianist.

"Here's Dr. Wickersham's address; you remember him? And, look-a-here, here's one for Chief Elliot."

"Chief Elliot!" I responded incredulously. "He's been dead since I was a little kid. Look, Dad, his phone number has only four digits. How long ago has that been?"

"I'm sure *you* of all people remember Chief Elliot, don't you, Mark?" With a slight tilt of my head to the right, I gave him a puzzled look.

"I remember who he was—the Police Chief," I stated confidently.

"You don't remember the day Chief caught you playing with my German war souvenirs?" he asked. Suddenly it all came back to me.

"Oh, *that* Chief Elliot! Heck, yeah, I remember—I couldn't have been more than five or six years old. I had put that heavy German army helmet on my head, strapped the bayonet around my waist, and was playing in the front yard."

"That wasn't all," he added. "You had that Nazi flag I brought back from the war, tied it to a pole and marched up and down the driveway!"

"That's right," I recalled, "Chief Elliot pulled into the driveway in his police car and started screaming at me. I was petrified. I had no idea what he was saying to me." Dad could hardly stop chuckling as he finished the story.

"The Chief came into the drugstore afterward and told me what he had done. He was so embarrassed. He said that you threw the flag down and ran crying back toward the house. Chief said that the huge, heavy helmet was bobbing up and down on your head while you ran. He realized that he had scared you, and tried to call you back and apologize—but you were gone."

"I *do* remember that! I was scared to death of him from that day on." We continued our laughing and remembering. "I think I have emotional problems as a result."

"What you *didn't* know," he informed me, "was that he lost a loved-one in World War II. Seeing you in that Nazi gear was just too emotional for him. He was getting on up in years and kind-of snapped."

"I didn't know what a Nazi was," I said in defense. "I just liked to play army, and your souvenirs were fun to play with."

"Oh, I know," he said, still laughing a bit. "Do you remember what I came home and told you?"

"Not really. I guess it was too traumatic a day for me."

"I came right home to check on you," he said. "I let you know that I wasn't mad at you. You were too young to know what Nazis were, and you were so imaginative when you played. I didn't have the heart to tell you that you couldn't play with my souvenirs anymore. I just told you that the next time you played with them, do it in the back yard, not the front."

High Life

We hadn't laughed that much together in a long time. It was great fun remembering. And Dad had more to summon up.

"One of my funniest memories of Chief Elliot was several years before the incident with you," he recalled. Looking up at the ceiling as if he was trying to download thoughts he had stored in the cloud, he related a tale I had never before heard, of a certain Saturday afternoon when the Police Chief came into the drugstore for help.

I actually wrote the story down for posterity. Here it is in its entirety:

Clink-clink-tink—the brass bell on the door of the Ashland Pharmacy announced a customer.

"Coolidge," Chief Elliot shouted before the door shut behind him. "I need your help. We have a situation outside." Fearing the worst, Coolidge stepped out of the prescription room and onto the main floor to meet the chief.

"What's wrong, Chief?" he inquired; noticing right away that the officer was more amused than he was desperate.

"Well, the young Heath boy has a bull that got loose and is now lying down right smack in the middle of highway 9. He can't get him to budge, and traffic is beginning to back up in the square."

"What do you want me to do?" Coolidge asked with a smile breaking across his face.

"I need you to mix me up a dose of High Life to get the stupid bull to move," the chief requested. "How about it?"

"Alright," Coolidge said. "Give me a couple of minutes, and I'll meet you out there."

I hated to interrupt Dad's story. He was caught up in it, but I needed some clarification—what is *High Life*? He was happy to fill me in.

"It's *carbon disulfide*, but everyone just called it *High Life*. I always figured it was called that because when it was squirted on any animal, the poor victim came to life. A few drops into a hollow tree would bring a rabbit or possum out instantly, and it smells like c'airn." His information satisfied me, so the story continues:

In short fashion, Coolidge mixed the compound and darted out of his drugstore on the courthouse square to meet Chief Elliot at the scene of the disturbance. A large crowd was gathering around the young man and his stubborn bull, and cars were stacking up in every direction. The chief shouted out instructions to the crowd,

"Everyone needs to back away. We're about to get this bull up and moving." Then Chief Elliot motioned for Coolidge to apply the chemical to the lazy bull. Young Abe Heath held the rope firmly, but at distance.

"Here goes," Coolidge announced, pouring half of the bottle of High Life into the bull's hindquarter. The crowd waited in silence, but nothing happened. Coolidge moved closer and emptied the bottle of chemical contents onto the bull again. Still, there was no response from the animal.

"Go get some more, Coolidge," Chief said. "He must have a tough hide." Coolidge had not taken more than two steps back toward the pharmacy when the old bull snorted violently, lunged forward and stood on his all fours. His head was swinging wildly from side to side, blowing and snorting; his ears were pricked and he was showing the whites of his eyes.

The animal ran like a locomotive down highway 9, Abe Heath holding on to the rope and running as fast as his legs would take him. In a few seconds, the angry bull took a quick right, trouncing through a hedgerow and headed west down Second Avenue. The last thing Coolidge saw was Abe being dragged through the leaves around the southeast corner of Sarah Runyan's house, with old Chief Elliot limping in hot pursuit.

Dad and I could hardly catch our breath, we were laughing so hard. When the nurse came in to administer his midday meds, Dad could not even stop laughing long enough to take them. The afternoon shift nurse joined in the hilarity, having no idea what we were laughing about. According to Dad, It remained a topic of conversation and amusement in the Ashland Pharmacy for years. I suppose that some local yarns deserve to be remembered.

Measuring Love

An array of professionals from The Oaks streamed into Room 138 to make sure everything was as it should be for the new resident. An occupational therapist, a nutritionist, a geriatric counselor, a safety expert, an air conditioning repairman, and a bouncy young social director all visited us in one afternoon, leaving behind pamphlets, menus, and calendars galore. Dad was invited to participate in a hot three o'clock checkers tournament in the great room, but he declined gracefully—blaming it on me being there to spend time with him. He *really* wanted to simply watch a little television, and let me finish the work to be done in the room.

Fox News, ESPN, and the Golf Channel were about the only thing on television that Dad was interested in. He got comfortable in his recliner and then made a request.

"Hey, Mark. Could you plug in that heating pad and bring it over here. That neuralgia I have in my leg is bothering me more and more."

"You've been dealing with that for a while, haven't you?" I queried.

"Yeah. It feels like my shingles coming back, but the doc said he wasn't sure what it was. It bothers me most of the time." I laid the heating pad on the upper part of his left thigh, almost at the groin. "Thank you, Bud. I think I'll watch a little news for a while." I knew what that meant. It was code for: "I'm going to take my afternoon nap."

After the midday meal and several interruptions, the big box I had hauled in early in the morning was finally emptied. The room was beginning to look a tiny bit like home. The side table beside the chair, the TV cabinet, and the nightstand all became display pedestals for Coolidge's memories. Even the windowsill served as a place to line up pictures of family and friends.

With Dad softly snoring in the easy chair, I took the empty box back to my truck. When I saw the beauty of the spring afternoon, I regretted not getting Dad outside into the sunshine. A walk about the premises gave me time to reflect on what was happening to my father. In a matter of only four days, he had pulled up roots and left his hometown of eighty-one years. That was no simple adjustment. Are we being fair, or do we have a better option?

I prayed earnestly for God to give me peace about where we were in our journey with Dad. The Lord gently reminded me of a heated exchange I had with Dad in 1972, when I was a fifteen-year-old fool. I remembered it well.

He was sitting on a kitchen stool, preparing to polish his shoes for Sunday church.

"Dad, the Valentine banquet is next Saturday night."

"A week from tonight. Great. You have a date?"

"Yes sir, I'm going with Sheila."

"Would you rather me or your mother take you?" I knew that Dad had no idea where I was about to go with the conversation. I hesitated, clutched the back of my neck, and swallowed hard before coming out with it.

"Dad, I have a plan."

"Alright, let me hear it," he responded, continuing to apply shoe polish to his size seven black wingtips. His jovial tone caused me to hesitate even more. I wondered if it was really worth even bringing it up. But rather than stand there like a fool, I came out with it.

"Uh, well, I'm only six weeks away from getting my driver's license, and you and Mom both say that I'm a really good driver. And since we live so close, uh, I want to, uh, drive Sheila to the banquet."

"Okay," he agreed. "You can drive. I'll sit in the back seat and leave the front seat to you two." Obviously, Dad didn't get it. I tried to explain again,

"I mean, uh, just me and Sheila." The shoe polishing stopped cold. He cut his eyes up at me from the stool as if I had lost my mind.

"You want to do what?"

"But Dad, it's just to Sheila's, to the church, and back. It's not that far."

"You don't have your drivers license, Son, until you turn sixteen. It's the law." His reaction didn't really surprise me.

"Now, I must unload the big guns," I whispered to myself. "Dad," I pleaded as my voice began to shake,

"Everyone else's parents let their kids drive alone, especially when they're so close to getting their license." He was silent for a few seconds as he looked down and flicked a sliver of black polish off his thumbnail.

"Son, I don't believe that for a minute." His eyes met mine again. "Most parents in this town are not so stupid as to let their fifteen-year-old drive without a license. What if something happens?"

I wasted no time with my rebuttal. "You told me yourself that you learned to drive *without* a learner's permit. Wasn't that against the law? So what's the difference?" I couldn't believe I was actually saying this stuff to my dad, but I felt that I had at least scored a hit.

"There wasn't such a thing as a learners permit when I was fifteen, smart aleck. In 1939 you just went to the courthouse and got a license when you turned sixteen." His voice rose slightly, "No I did not break the law then, and I will not do it now."

With my throat tightening, barely holding back embarrassing tears, I gave it my last shot,

"I just don't understand why other people's parents have no problem with stuff, but my parents always do. It's not fair." Dad stood up, set his half-polished shoes on the stool, looked me square in the eyes. I felt his breath on my nose and cheek. I was expecting the worst.

"Well, obviously other parents don't love their children as much as your parents love you." He stared me down silently for no more than three or four seconds and then quietly sat down to finish his shoes.

Strangely, a sudden flush of anger in me was instantly eclipsed by a greater sense of relief. Rules had not won the day. Love had. And his firm takedown of my fifteen-year-old hide was not one I ever wanted to repeat.

As I finished my afternoon walk around the premises, I couldn't help but notice how much the wind had picked-up since I had been outdoors thinking and praying. I spotted dark black clouds on the horizon, a certain indicator of a cold front coming through, and the chance another round of spring storms in Alabama—hopefully not severe.

Medicine Man

"Dad, are you ready to get some supper in the dining hall?" I asked softly. I hated to wake him up, but if he wanted me to share dinner with him, we would have to do it at the early seating. Rousing from his nap he opened his eyes wildly, straightened the glasses still sitting on his nose, and looked around—obviously unaware of where he was.

"What?" he answered, catching his balance with a quick jerk?

"It's supper time, and I want to eat with you before I have to go."

"What time is it?" he asked in a panic, as if he had overslept or missed an appointment.

"It's about 5:30, Dad."

"Five-thirty! Oh, no. Have I slept here in my clothes all night?" His initial confusion soon melted into bewilderment. "Oh, Lord...."

"No, Dad," I squatted down beside the chair and leaned with reassurance into his personal space. "You've just taken a nap. I'm here. We're at The Oaks, and we are about to go eat a nice supper together." He let out a huge sigh of relief.

"Oh," he paused, taking another deep breath. "Oh, good. I... I, thought I had missed something important." My father didn't like the feeling of being *out of control*. He was the dependable one; never late, and always up for a challenge. He was a teetotaler and had ethically dispensed narcotics since graduating from pharmacy school in 1949. Never had he personally used any controlled drug to numb or escape pain. He had the opportunity, but never succumbed to the temptation of substance abuse. I had never seen him out of control.

For the first time, I understood how difficult it was for him to face the mental, emotional, and physical roadblocks that aging brings. Frailty and neediness had not been a part of his life. My father was keenly aware that something was going wrong, but he had no idea of why or what to do about it.

Within five minutes, he was up, back to normal, and on his way with me to the dining room. This time we didn't use the walker so I held tightly to him. It was a bonus that we found seats at a table of six. Again the conversation hovered around 1944—where were you on D-day? Even the two ladies present shared their memories of that fateful day. I listened to every word; delighted that Dad was ending his first day at The Oaks with good social interaction.

Dad left dinner on such a high note that I didn't want to leave him. This was the perfect time to talk, to ask questions, to discover. As soon as we got back to his room, I floated a random question.

"Dad, in all those years working at your drug store in Ashland, did you ever wonder if you had missed your calling, or that you should have taken a different path?"

"Originally I wanted to be a dentist, but at the time there was no dental school in Alabama. I was on the waiting list for the University of Kentucky dental school, but I would have had to wait two or three years to get in. So, I decided on pharmacy and went straight to Auburn on the GI Bill. The retail drug store business has been good to our family. I actually enjoyed serving the public all those years. It's the stupid paperwork for the government that I grew to despise. No, Son, I have no regrets."

"I want to ask you something else, if you don't mind," I said. He nodded his assent.

"Bob Riley's wife Patsy reminded me the other day of how blessed I am to have you as my father. She said her family would never forget that wonderful thing you did for her daddy many years ago. What was she talking about?"

"I'm not sure," he answered. I knew that he was avoiding my question.

"Dad, I told Patsy that I had no idea what she was talking about." I looked deeply into my father's eyes. "So, she told me." Dad glanced toward the muted television screen. I asked boldly, "Why did I never hear about it before?"

"Because it wasn't any of your business," he answered. " Besides, you were young." There was a short, awkward pause. "What all did Patsy tell you?"

Patsy Riley's father was John Adams—the owner of Adams Drug Company—my dad's only retail competitor in Ashland. Everyone in town was aware of a strange oddity, that the two pharmacists in town were each named after famous presidents: *Calvin Coolidge* Sims and *John Adams*.

"Patsy told me that her parents, John and Verna Adams, were on a very long trip to Europe, and had left the drug store in the hands of a relief pharmacist. For some reason, the fill-in druggist couldn't fulfill his obligation and simply closed Adams Drugs until John could return. His customers were in a panic. The entire business was on the verge of collapse. She told me that out of the goodness of your heart, you kept both drug stores going, without allowing any of Adams' customers to transfer their prescriptions to your store. Is that what happened, Dad?"

"Basically, yes," he admitted. "It was no big deal. I'm sure he would have done the same for me." He tried to change the subject, but I pressed him.

"Your only competition would have virtually gone out of business, by no fault of yours, and yet you prevented that from happening. Dad, that's unheard of in this world."

Dad looked into my eyes and pointed his finger straight at me.

"Son, John had worked hard to build his business. He was a good man. No one should suffer the loss of his livelihood because of bad luck. I did what I could do to help my friend, and John Adams was my friend. It was the right thing to do. What else could I have done, Son?"

I was so grateful that Patsy Riley had mentioned the situation between my dad and Mr. Adams. If she had not shared that story with me, I might never have learned of my father's courtesy toward his friend and competitor.

Bob Riley was Governor of Alabama at the time Patsy told me. It meant a great deal to me that on a busy evening, the First Lady of Alabama would take the opportunity to reminisce with me. Bob and Coolidge were very good friends as well, each admiring the other's good character.

I drove to my house that night with the incredible satisfaction that Coolidge Sims was a much bigger man than I had realized. My father might have been no taller than five feet, four inches, but still, I was the son of a giant.

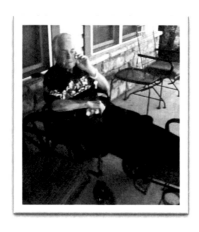

"Live so that when your children think of fairness, caring, and integrity, they think of you."
H. Jacks

Chapter Three

Open Windows

It was exactly 14.8 miles from my driveway to the front parking lot of The Oaks. I could make it in twenty minutes on a normal traffic day. A beautiful drive, north across the Cahaba River and over Shades Mountain, it provided time for me to prepare my mind, collect my thoughts, and pray about Dad. It came to be my favorite ritual of the day—speaking with one Father about the other.

Tuesday was my afternoon visit day. Donna had the morning visit covered. It was just after 3 o'clock when I parked my Nissan Frontier pickup two spaces down from the Lodge's main entryway, hugging closely a blue handicap-parking stripe on the left. The truck actually belonged to Dad. He had turned the keys over to me knowing that Peggy and I were a one-car family, and that I would be burning the road up daily between our home and The Oaks.

I was grateful for the extra set of wheels, but the small truck looked like a blitzkrieg survivor. The rear bumper and tailgate had been compressed into an inverted V when Dad backed it squarely into a telephone pole at Ayler Caldwell's house. The front left corner panel was crushed, having rolled into the wall of Shotgun Giddens' barbershop when Dad forgot to put it in park, and the entire passenger side sported a racing stripe, beautifully engraved by the parking meter in front of the dentist office. Decidedly, the sight of my vehicle caused fellow motorists to be extra-cautious if not downright wary of the metallic blue truck—mayhem on wheels.

My eyes connected with the blue and white handicap placard wedged between the console and my seat. As long as I was Coolidge's chauffeur I could use it if needed. Perhaps taking Dad to get some ice cream after dinner would be just the thing.

Fully expecting Dad to be dormant in his easy chair, I took my time getting into the room, greeting the nurses at the desk with a quick joke, and then stopping in to say hello to the dining room workforce. They were the friendliest of all. Instinctively I knew that my father would ultimately be the beneficiary of my kindness toward the staff. His door was wide open with television blaring when I finally peeled into the room.

"Hey there, Dad," I greeted him. He was sitting upright, bearing down closely at something in his lap. He returned my greeting with an equally bright response,

"Hello, Markle." Dad loved nicknames. When I was small I was *Cowboy*. Later I became *Bud* and lately, *Preacher*—a reference to my calling and chosen occupation. *Markle* had been created by accident when he once introduced my older brother and me as his sons, *Michael and Markle.* We got a good laugh about it then, and it stuck.

"What's that you're looking at?" I asked. Dad held up a yellow, faded photograph.

"It's a picture of your old man when he was a kid. Can you find me in the picture?" he dared.

"That's easy. There you are," I announced, pointing him out with ease. "You look the same as you do today, just less shriveled up."

"Hey, you better watch it," he retorted playfully. "You know Son, I remember when this picture was taken. That's Grandpaw Jenkins' house in the background, and it's my daddy's car we're standing in front of a 1928 A-model Ford."

The old photo had been taken around 1929 in the tiny community of Delta, Alabama when Coolidge was only six-years-old. The gathering of just over twenty well-attired family members had posed around Dad's aging grandparents for the traveling cameraman. It was most likely his grandmother's birthday—or "Little Grandmaw" as we called her. She lived into her late 90's. I even remember celebrating her birthday annually as a family event in the 1960's.

"Do you recognize all the people in the picture?" I inquired.

"I was trying to write their names down when you came in. I was hoping you would get here so you could help me. Look a'here, Mark— I'll call out their names and you write them down." Dad enjoyed trying to remember their names and faces. He was in a race against time to get it done.

"Where did you find it?" I asked. "I've never seen this pic before."

"I brought it with me in that box," he said pointing to a dilapidated cardboard box sitting on the foot of the bed. "It's full of old pictures that I got from Mama before she died. I actually haven't seen most of these pictures in a coon's age, but I figured I would finally have time here to go through and identify them while I still have a mind left to do it with."

"Great idea, Dad. You know I'd love to help with that." We had our work cut out for us, but I knew that it would be worth every minute. This would be an ideal forum—an open window—for Coolidge Sims to talk, and for me to learn.

Delta Dawn

Located at the base of Alabama's tallest mountain, the tiny community of Delta, population one hundred and fifty souls, was the birthplace of Calvin Coolidge Sims, and his father, and his grandfather before him. The area was flush with Scots-Irish settlers and a few Cherokees, and a hilly terrain that rarely supported farms of more than fifty acres. Corn was the only cash crop. Moonshine abounded.

Dad and I processed our way through the old photos. "Here's a picture of an old log building. Is that the place you were born?" I asked.

"No! That's my Grandaddy's corn crib! I wasn't born in a corncrib. You've got me mixed up with Baby Jesus." I laughed at his quip but pressed him for information.

"Dad, I have always bragged to my friends that you were born in Delta in a log cabin."

"I never told you that."

"Yes you did," I protested. "I promise, you did."

"No, my grandfather Sims' house—Grandaddy we called him— was two log buildings joined together by a covered breezeway, but I never lived there," he instructed me. "I probably told you about when I was a little boy and would *stay* with them overnight in that house."

"Wait a minute," I reminded him, "You used to recount for us how you could see through the slats in the floor, and you would watch the dogs fighting under the house. And you talked about how they papered the walls with newspapers and calendars like it was something incredible."

"Yes, that was all at Grandaddy Sims' house—it burned down in nineteen twenty-nine or thirty. I only have a few memories of that old house, but I have lots of memories of my Grandpaw Jenkins' house."

"That was where your *mother* grew up, right?" I asked for clarification.

"I would spend two or three weeks with them every summer, even after we had moved to Ashland, twenty miles away. When I was ten or so, I rode my bicycle all the way from Ashland to Grandpaw's house, all by myself."

"Twenty miles, on a bike, at age ten? Are you kidding?" I asked incredulously.

"I sure did. It took me most of the day. It was six miles to Lineville, five to Barfield, and nine more to Delta. Papa let me do it as long as I rode in daylight."

"And I'm sure you would have let me or Mike do that at age ten!" I expressed sarcastically.

"Of course not," Dad said, forcing a restrained laugh. "The highway's too dangerous now. Back then, I probably didn't meet a dozen cars on the dirt road the whole day." Then, with a tiny snicker, he raised his eyebrows and began his yarn,

"At Grandpaw's house, we always got up before daylight. On the morning that I was supposed to ride back home to Ashland, I wanted to get an early start, while it was still dark. Grandpaw Jenkins gave me a big firecracker and two matches and told me to shoot off the firecracker when I made it to the main road to Lineville, right where highway crossed Ketchamadogee Creek. I got there just as the dawn was breaking and lit that firecracker. I remember that loud crack as it ricocheted between the hills and echoed down Ketchamadogee Creek all the way to Grandpaw's place.

When Grandpaw heard it, he knew I'd made it safely to the main road. It is one of my favorite childhood memories. I can still see the white mist hovering over the creek in the valley in the first morning light. It has to be the most peaceful moment I've ever experienced." He sat relaxed and calm, his eyes staring into a safe place of warm memories.

"Nothing like ruining a peaceful moment with a deafening firecracker Dad," I muttered.

His eyebrows shot up suddenly, catching my eye for a stunned second, and then we both broke into a short series of laughs. Eventually, we moved back to the old photographs that began our conversation.

"And who is this?" I asked, showing him a picture of a young boy posing next to two young girls who both had hair like Rapunzel—neatly brushed and reaching all the way to their knees!

"That's my Mama—Mama Sims, your grandmother, and Aunt Eunice, and the young guy is Lenoice."

"Lenoice? I don't remember him," I returned.

"That's because he died when he was in his late twenties," he explained. "I think there's another picture of him when he's older." He fumbled through the box, scanning through three or four photos when all at once it came to him, "Wait, he's in the picture I showed you at first! Look, there he is, the big guy on the left, towering above everyone else."

"There's no way someone with our DNA is that tall, Dad," I declared. In the old photo, Lenoice stood head and shoulders above the rest. His size, in addition to his deep eyes, dark features and large jaw provided a roguish veneer to an otherwise common fellow.

"Oh, no, he was tall, but not *that* tall," Dad explained. "I think he's just standing on the running board of Papa's car." Dad settled himself in his chair, closed his eyes to more clearly recall the memories, and then took us both on a journey that reached back over eighty-five years.

"Lenoice never married. He was my uncle, but he was a lot younger than his brothers and sisters, and was somewhat spoiled—at least that was what everyone in the family said. He was always like a big kid to me."

"Was he lazy?" I asked.

"No," he answered firmly. "He was a hard worker. He helped Grandpaw run the farm and bring in a crop every year. He just seemed comfortable living at home and taking care of his parents." His eyes brightened; he leaned in my direction and lowered his voice as if he was about to tell me a delicious family secret. I leaned in too and met him halfway.

"Now I don't want you to think bad about Lenoice. He was a nice man, but he liked to drink a little bit too much. He made his own home brew, moonshine, and hid it in jars that he kept tucked away at the spring below the cornfield."

"Oh, yes. Prohibition. *All* liquor was illegal during the 1920's," I rejoined. "He had to hide his homebrew!"

"No," he corrected me. "Lenoice wasn't hiding it from the law. He was hiding it from Grandmaw Jenkins!

She didn't allow it in the house, and neither did Grandpaw."

Dad leaned back in his easy chair, looking up at the ceiling as he recalled, "Like I told you a minute ago, during the summer I used to go spend a few weeks with them to help them on the farm. I'm sure I didn't help a lot, but I felt like I did. I usually worked with Grandpaw, but sometimes I was with Lenoice.

Well, I was about ten or eleven-years-old and I had been helping Lenoice that afternoon and he wanted to take a trip to the spring to get a swig of his brew. He made me promise not to tell. Since I was there, I asked to take a little drink too, so he let me."

"He let you drink moonshine? At age ten?" I asked, surprised and amused at the same time.

"Yep. He sure 'nuff did. And that wasn't the end of it. I got *so* sick." Dad snickered, shaking his head from side to side. "I took a big gulp. It burned my goozle, and then…" Dad took a rapid gasp, "it took my breath away. I couldn't breathe."

"'*You alright, Coolidge?*' Lenoice said, slapping me on the back to help me catch my breath." Dad was animated like I haven't seen him in a long time. This was a new story for me; I had never heard it. My father was taking great delight in recounting it to me, in *real* time, just as he was recalling it.

"I told Lenoice that I was okay, but I wasn't. My hands were clammy; I got the cold sweats, but I was burning up; I became nauseated. It felt like there was a bowling ball in my gut. Lenoice was worried about me so he toted me back to the house, begging me not to reveal to Little Grandmaw what just happened. '*You must have just got too hot,*' he told me. '*Just tell Grandmaw you got too hot and need to lay down and rest.*'"

"Did you finally rat you uncle out, Dad?"

"No, I didn't." Dad paused and pursed his lips purely for dramatic effect, no doubt. "I went along with his plan, but a short time later I threw my guts up—and I guess Little Grandmaw smelled it.

In any case, she tore out of the house yelling like a banshee, marched down into the middle of the cornfield and beat the fire out of Lenoice with a broom." Dad cackled out loud as soon as he had finished the story, and then I followed. We laughed so hard we cried. When I finally got control enough to comment I asked,

"Could you see it? Could you see her smacking him with the broom?" Dad broke into another round of laughter, hardly able to launch the words from his mouth,

"No, but I heard it. She was screaming, and he was a'hollering!

Later Grandpaw said, *'Rhoda purt' near killed Lenoice over it.'*" That caused round three of laughter. For the rest of the evening, every time either of us pictured Little Grandmaw with the broom, one of us would say,

"Purt' near killed Lenoice," and it would start all over again.

The Rest of the Story

We laughed a lot that night, at Lenoice's expense. Still, I wanted to know what happened to him. "Dad, you said earlier that Lenoice died in his late twenties. What was it, cancer? An accident? Little Grandma?" Dad chuckled at the quip but turned serious quickly.

"On a foggy Saturday night, Lenoice and one of the McCullough boys drove about twenty miles away, to Oxford, for a night on the town. Prohibition had been repealed by then, and he had developed a wild streak, especially on the weekends. On their way home the fog had become so thick that they could hardly see the road." Dad described what happened that night in such detail that it plays like a tragic movie in my mind.

"Lenoice," Jim McCullough shouted, "Wake up. I can't see the road. The fog's so thick I can cut it with a knife."

"What d'ya want me to do?" Lenoice answered, rousing from his stupor. The revelry of the night had ensured that brain fog impeded the two young men as much as the cloudy vapor rising from the ground.

"Grab that flashlight behind your seat and shine it down on the edge of the road for me. I can't see squat." Lenoice scrambled around the A-model Ford Coupe until he found the flashlight. Directing its beam from the car to the edge of the road provided no real assistance to the driver. Still, the tired pair continued creeping down Highway 9 in the wee hours of the morning.

"Stand out on the running board and shine it straight down on the edge of the highway. Don't cha' let me run off the road," Jim directed. Lenoice lifted his large frame over the door onto the flat running board. With his left hand tightly holding the top of the doorframe, he leaned forward and to the right, shining the big flashlight down on the unpaved gravel road. On each side of the road were steep shoulders, dangerous enough for travelers who veered off the road even in good weather. The winding highway seemed to go on forever as they drove hesitantly along the right edge of the road.

"Where are we?" Jim inquired loudly. "How much further do we have to go? This is killing me."

"I think we're close to Bethel Church Road," Lenoice shouted, barely audible to Jim through the loud clatter of the old car.

"Then we're on a straightaway. I'm going to speed it up a little." Jim's confidence didn't sit well with Lenoice.

"The fog's getting thicker, Jim, I can hardly see the edge at all." They weren't approaching Bethel Church Road after all; they had made it all the way to Good Hope Road and about to miss the left bend ahead. Lenoice saw it, but only when it was right upon them, and too late.

Hearing Lenoice yell, Jim jerked the wheel sharply to the left. The coupe bounded off the steep shoulder at an angle sending both left wheels into the air and then toppled onto its side halfway down the embankment.

"Help me! God, Help me!" Lenoice's panicked scream pierced the night fog, even as Jim was thrown violently against the passenger side door. Lenoice lay no more than a foot away from his friend, trapped underneath the weight of the hissing car.

"I'm coming, Lenoice, hang on," Jim trumpeted, scrambling to climb straight up and out the driver's door window. By the time he got to the other side of the car, Lenoice's voice was weakening.

"I can't breathe! Get it off me! Get it off me!" Jim McCullough, standing on a muddy embankment tried over and over to lift the heavy car off Lenoice just long enough for him to take a breath—just one breath. Sliding in the mud over to Lenoice he tried again with all his might to lift the edge of the roof off of his friend's chest, but he couldn't budge it. Jim wept as he heard Lenoice, smothering to death, whisper finally,

"I don't want to die, Jim. I'm gonna die, Jim. I'm gonna die."

"Jim McCullough never got over that night," Dad recalled. "People always said that he was never right after that happened. We buried Lenoice at Good Hope-Delta Church. He's buried right next to Grandpaw and Grandmaw Jenkins. We had already moved to Ashland when it happened, but I remember it well. I was about fifteen when he died."

Papa's Pantaloons

Our conversation about his early days in Delta continued into dinner. A noticeable limp revealed itself during our walk to the dining room.

"Dad, what's going on with your left leg?" I probed. "Are you in a lot of pain?"

He didn't answer but kept pressing forward with his eyes locked on the doorway ahead. It was like he blocked me out for a moment, but I knew for certain he

70

heard me. I chose not to press him for an answer. The tiny drop of moisture on his top lip indicated pain—more than neuralgia, more than a superficial annoyance. Dad's was leaning from his hip toward his left side, and he was not prepared to talk about it.

We found our seats around a large table of eight. Following a polite exchange of nods and greetings, the white clad servers began to fill our requests. The Oaks had staffed the dining hall with good-hearted men and women whose outward friendliness had undoubtedly landed them the job. Young and old, blacks and whites, they filled more than the position of table servers—they were hosts, greeters, and part-time nursing advisors, keeping track of the eating habits of each resident. They were somehow educated to enforce good nutrition with a smile.

Dad's elevated pain eased as soon as he was able to sit. Before long he was back to his jovial self, making forays into almost every open conversation. In no hurry to finish the creamy tomato soup and ham sandwich, Dad became engaged in the table discussion of family times during the Depression. I laughed at every yarn. Like high-schoolers on a picnic, each talebearer one-upped the previous story, swearing each time that they were telling the gospel truth.

Bruce, the old gentleman who was most likely to raise the stakes higher than the others, entertained the table with a creepy story about what terrible things happened when his father had a little too much to drink on the weekends. There was an uncomfortable silence for a brief moment, and then Dad spoke up,

"Now I don't remember this personally because it happened before I was born, but my Mama swore it happened." Coolidge leaned forward resting on his folded arms, commanding total attention from everyone at the dinner table.

"Mama and Papa lived out in the country and came into town at least one Saturday a month for flour and sugar and medicine and banking, and for some socialization as well. Well, on one particular Saturday my Papa got fall-down drunk. It had happened several times before. Usually, Mama would get him home, let him sleep it off, wake up the next morning and go to church. Very little was said, and that's the way it was.

But this Saturday night was different. Papa had managed to act a fool and ended up putting on some women's pantaloons as a dare, just before he passed out. Mama took him home in the wagon, and let him wake up just as he was when he lost consciousness—pantaloons and all.

As soon as he awoke and realized what had happened, Papa was horrified." The entire table erupted with laughter and comments to one another. I even spotted a young Oaks staffer nearby trying to hide her wide grin, as if she had not been mesmerized by the anecdote. Dad continued,

"Papa went to the Baptist Church that morning and repented publically for his behavior, and later even tried to join a local chapter of the Women's Temperance Union! He never took another drink for the rest of his life."

Dad admitted to us that during the war he tried alcohol and even began to develop a taste for beer. Fortunately, he understood that he should quit before he became fond of it. He lived as a teetotaler all the remainder of his days. He made no allowances for his children as well. His axiom: "If you never take the first drink, you'll never have an alcohol problem."

He was a wise father.

Big Brother

Shortly after supper, I offered to take Dad out for some frozen yogurt. As tired as he appeared, he wouldn't miss a trip for ice cream for the world! They had twenty flavors and forty toppings to choose from at the *self-serve* frozen dessert place.

Dad's leg was paining him again so he took a seat, letting me fill his cup with the good stuff. He might have been in pain, but he knew exactly *what* he wanted, *how much* he wanted, and *which toppings* were his favorites—chocolate, vanilla, and strawberry yogurt and garnished with fresh sliced strawberries and dark chocolate chips.

We talked a little politics and exchanged small talk as we demolished most of our delectable treats. He seemed to be in a talkative mood. I put aside the lateness of the evening and pushed him for more.

"Dad, I really wish you had told us more stories about growing up in Delta."

"It wasn't all fun and games, you know," Dad responded. "We had to get up at the crack of dawn, milk the cow, churn, collect the eggs, ring chicken's necks, make lye soap, and all kinds of things. It was really hard work. Of course, I was pretty young when we lived there. Bremon had more chores that I did, but I was always following him around, asking him to let *me* do something.

I remember one time he was getting water outside at the well for Mama, and I was right under his feet. I peered into the well and asked him,

'Bremon, how deep is it?'

He suddenly got a wild hair and said,

'Coolidge, why don't you let me put you in this bucket and I'll lower you down in there so you can find out?' I was crazy enough to do exactly what he said. But once I got down in there, I got pretty scared, especially when he threatened to leave me there. I felt a little like Joseph in the Bible when his brothers put him in down in the pit. Of course, Bremon was just joking, but he did struggle to get me back up to the top. I was pretty worried there for a while. I remember him saying,

'Coolidge, don't you tell Mama we did this. She'll whup us both!'"

"Did you get all the way down to the water?" I asked.

"No, but I got down far enough!" he added.

"What's that one story you tell about Bremon and the rabid dog? Didn't you get bit by it?"

"No, but I came mighty close."

"Well, what happened, Dad?" He shoved another spoonful of pink and brown frozen yogurt into his mouth, taking his time to swallow the cold treat before he began:

"Papa left the house one summer morning, telling my brother Bremon to get our old hound dog out from under the house and put him in a pen before Papa came home for lunch. The dog had bitten our sister, Gwynnelle, and Papa feared that he was rabid. So Bremon came to me and said,

'Coolidge, I need you to go up under the house and aggravate Ole' Rebel enough to get him to chase you out from under there.'

'What?' I said. 'Papa said he might be a mad dog. What if he bites me?'

'Oh, he won't,' Bremon said confidently. 'Besides, if the dog's not penned up when Papa gets home, we're both gonna be in big trouble!'

'Nope, I ain't ending up in the pen with a mad dog. That's crazy!' I protested.

'Noooo,' Bremon assured me. 'You won't. As soon as you lead him into the pen, just jump over the back fence and get out. You're the fastest person I know, Coolidge. It'll be easy for you.' Of course, after Bremon stroked my ego so thoroughly, I agreed to his half-witted plan."

"How old were you, Dad?" I asked.

"Oh, about six or seven years old," he recalled. "That would have meant Bremon was about thirteen." Dad enjoyed telling this story so much! And even though I had heard it dozens of times before, I kept teasing him to continue.

"And you agreed? Good grief, Dad, did he offer you money or something?"

"Offer money? Bremon? Are you kidding? He was the king of tightwads. Bremon could pinch milk out of a nickel."

"So what happened?" I asked.

Dad took a big spoonful of yogurt with a fresh piece of strawberry. His eyes flashed in anticipation of re-living the story once again.

"Well, I heard the dog start to growl as soon as I crawled off the porch to take a peek under the house. There he was—foaming at the mouth and staring right at me. I whistled and shuffled my feet a little bit, and sure enough, I heard him coming—bap, bap, bap—his tail slapping the floor planks under the house. Ole' Rebel came charging out from under there a'slobbering, and a'snarling, and carrying on something fierce."

"I ran as fast as my little bare feet would take me peeling around the back corner of the house and toward Bremon who was standing like a statue at the gate of the old turkey pen. I could feel the mad dog gaining on me, so I turned it up a notch, racing through the muddy pen, scaling the fence, and then taking a diving leap head long to the ground! And after I had done all the work, Bremon had the gall to announce, 'Alright Coolidge, I GOT HIM!'"

Dad, as always, ended the amusing tale shaking his head in bewilderment, and with a whimsical smirk asked,

"Can you believe that?" Right on cue, we both laughed out-loud. Just watching Dad tell the story yet again was worth a million dollars."

"And Ole' Rebel never got to you, eh?"

"Oh, no, but that rabid dog turned right around, jumped up on the gate and bit Bremon smack dab on his hand! And so it ended up HE had to go through the round of twenty shots in his belly, just like Gwynnelle. Served him right!"

I still laugh every time I remember it, just as Bremon and Dad laughed about it every summer when we celebrated with the whole family. It was a Sims tradition to hear it at least once a year.

There were other oral traditions that the Sims family celebrated. The oddest might be the rhyme that delineated the birth order of Dad's aunts—"Hassie, Cassie, Clio, Claude, Teb, Ted, and Vida Maude." Hassie and Cassie were twins, as were Teb and Ted, whose real names were Essie and Lessie. And that was just the girls! My grandfather, Cecil, was among five boys in the family. They had nicknames, but no rhyme. I learned the rhyme as a child, as did all of my cousins. Today I can rattle it off with no problem. My wife even knows it by heart!

Places in the Heart

The drive back to The Oaks in Dad's Nissan truck brought me closer to Dad than I had ever been before. We had a great time together, laughing until we cried more than once. Still, there was something deeper that happened. He lit up every time he mentioned Mama, Papa, Little Grandmaw, Grandpaw, Breman, Gwynnelle, Lenoice—the ones he knew from the beginning of his life. They all remained with him, powerfully.

"Dad, you really miss them don't you?"

"Sure I do, Son. They are the ones who made me who I am. I grew up poor, but never realized it. We were rich in so many things. They put so much into me. Sadly, I didn't recognize it until my hair started to gray."

"Ok, I gotcha. Look at my hair, Dad. It's gray. That's why getting ice cream with you, and sitting with you out on the porch is so important to me. You have made me so rich."

"And you're trying to learn everything you can from me before I die," he concluded. "I know. I wish I had been able to do that. My Papa died suddenly before it was important to me." A long, peaceful pause ended our conversation.

April was fast coming to a close. The day's sunlight was lingering a few more minutes every evening. The lines of gentle clouds on the western horizon kindled a serene, golden glow that poured itself across the greening landscape. Sundown was just as it was supposed to be as I glided up to the covered walkway. Silence reigned until a faint squeak of the brakes broke the hush when I came to a stop.

"Dad, let me get your walker out, and I'll bring it around to you. Don't try to get out until I get over there." He was particularly self-reliant, usually insistent on opening his own doors and climbing out of vehicles unaided. He had struggled with leg pain all day, and I knew he was tired. I wasn't trying to baby him, I just didn't want to risk a fall. Dad never said a word in response.

I opened the truck door and prepared his walker. He slid out of the truck seat carefully, resting his right leg, his *good* leg, on the asphalt first, and then secured his right hand onto the gray, rubber grip on the walker. Reaching for my arm with his left hand he steadied himself before finally resting his other foot gingerly on the asphalt. I noticed a delicate tremble in his arm when he leaned on me with all his weight, and I heard a faint grunt and noticed his eyebrows wince the second his leg bore his weight. It saddened me that climbing out of his little truck was now such an ordeal. Dad took a deep breath, relaxed a moment, and spoke squarely into my eyes,

"Bud, I'll guess I'll try and stay around long enough for you to learn all you want to know."

*"Other things may change us, but we start
and we end with family."*
Anthony Brandt

Chapter Four

Choo Choo

My sister had placed a set of music CD's and a Bose CD player in Dad's room, just in case he wanted relief from watching TV—especially from the continual string of "Fox News alerts" punctuating his TV screen every few minutes. The media has certainly figured out how to keep a lonely, retired widower's attention for most of the day, moving from one alarming news alert to the next. My patriotic father would *never* want to be caught unaware that the republic was in jeopardy—although his blood pressure held a different opinion.

Making my way into the main lobby of The Oaks, I heard a familiar tune coming from the direction of his hallway—Glenn Miller's orchestra playing *Chattanooga Choo-Choo*. The closer I got I could tell it was playing from *his* room. From the hallway, I could hear him faintly humming along:

> You leave the Pennsylvania station
> 'bout a quarter to four
> Read a magazine and then you're in Baltimore
> Luncheon in the diner, nothing could be finer
> Then to have your ham and eggs in Carolina
> When you hear the whistle blowing eight to the bar
> Then you know that Tennessee is not very far
> Shovel all the coal in
> Gotta keep it rollin'
> Whoo Whoo Chattanooga there you are!

I paused and grinned before I entered, remembering how every time we traveled as a family and saw the word Chattanooga on any sign or advertisement,

Dad would break out into that song, first made famous in 1941—when my parents were just juniors in high school. Mom usually smiled and joined in on *"...then to have your ham and eggs in Carolina...."* That was my favorite line as well.

"Are you riding the Chattanooga Choo-Choo this morning, Dad?" I blurted out as I entered his room.

"Hi, Bud! You caught me singing again," he quipped with a quick glance in my direction.

"How was breakfast this morning?"

"I ate a *big* breakfast today, Mark. You should've come earlier. It was delicious." I noticed him fumbling around the room, obviously looking for something other than me. There was apprehension in his eyes.

"Dad, have you lost your billfold?" I quizzed.

"No." He paused, scanning the room, "I know I had your mother's picture here on my night stand, but for some reason, it's gone." Once before, in the middle of the night, he had accidentally, unknowingly, knocked it backward wedging it between the nightstand and the wall. Déjà vu. I took a quick look behind the furniture and there it was, just as I expected.

"Well look, Dad. It must have gotten accidentally knocked off the nightstand." There was no reason to remind him of what happened two weeks before. He would just get frustrated, embarrassed, and call himself stupid.

"I'll be Johnny," he responded, looking over my shoulder at the evidence. "That cleaning lady must have done it. She comes through here like a whirlwind and hardly even touches the place." I fished it out from behind the headboard, clawing at it several times before my short fingers could swipe it toward daylight. As I pulled it into view we both saw that the corner of the glass was cracked."

"Oops, looks like Mom got injured in that fall," I said to lighten the moment. One glance at Dad's countenance told me that he was feeling lonely today. He was more emotional than usual. He had likely dreamed about Mom and woke up missing her. He gently took the photograph out of my hands, looking adoringly at it.

"Well, I'll have to give you some money to go out and replace this frame, Son. This one's special."

"Of course, Dad. I'll take it home and bring it back tomorrow. By the way, I like that Glenn Miller music you're playing."

"It takes me back to when I was your age," Dad fancied.

"*My* age! Dad, I'm...."

"Oh, that's right, you're an old man now," he corrected himself.

"Alas. Fifty-six to be exact."

"Fifty-six!" he roared. "Where has the time gone! Big band music takes me back to when your mother and I grew up together in Ashland—when we were teenagers. And when I say 'grew up together,' I literally mean it. We've been sweethearts since the second grade." His voice trailed off into a whisper. "Some days I can hardly stand being without her."

First Date

"Dad, do you remember your first date with Mom?"

"Oh yeah, I sure do. It was in October of 1939. We were in the 10th grade, and it was the day after the first high school football game of the season—the very first football game I ever played in. We went together to a party at Dot Perry's house. Of course, I tried to put my best foot forward and impress her, but she already knew me pretty well. Everyone always said that Marylyn and I would be together."

"So she's the only girl you ever dated?"

"Not exactly. We did go out with other people, but not much. I dated a little when I was at Jacksonville State for less than a year, and she dated a few different guys all that time I was in the war, but we were always meant to be together.

In fact, your mother had a scrapbook that's packed away somewhere that has a little autograph book in it. It was given to Marylyn in 1932 as a Christmas present when she was only eight years old. She got everyone to autograph it—and I wrote something in it—twice! You ought to try to find it. My handwriting and spelling are terrible, but you can tell what was on my mind.

You'll see that on one page I wrote:
>Ducks in the mill pond,
>geece [sic] in the ocean;
>Boys' can't marry 'till the girl takes a notion.

And on another page:
>When you are married
>and live across the lake;
>please bring me a cocoanut [sic] cake.

I kept referring to marriage. It's obvious that there was no other girl for me. I planned on marrying her from the second grade on."

"Wow, Dad. That means you and Mom were actually *together* for sixty-seven years. Incredible. Thank-you Dad, for setting the bar high."

Small Town Friends

That afternoon I helped Dad sort through his mail. For some reason, it was one of those days when he got multiple "Thinking of You" cards from his friends in Ashland. Most included personal words and expressions of love beyond the printed words on the card. He assumed that the pastor at First Baptist had encouraged folks to send him a card—especially since most all the cards that day were from Baptists. Even so, he read them all with great appreciation in his heart. Most of the cards he read aloud to me as well.

"You know Son, you don't ever need to underestimate the value of friends. If you'll be a loyal friend, you'll always have loyal friends in your corner. I don't really know what people do who don't have a church family. It's so important to cultivate friendships in the church." Even in opening the day's mail, my father spouted so much wisdom. It came naturally to him. I could tell he was still in a talkative mood.

"Do you want a *Co-Cola,* Son?" he asked out of nowhere. "There's a couple of them in my little fridge if you want one." It tickled me every time I heard him say "*Co-Cola.*" Mom used to correct him each time, but without Mom around he had slipped back into what he grew up hearing from Mama and Papa Sims.

"No thanks, Dad. I'll get some coffee later," I said.

"Mark, this morning you were asking me about our courting days. Your mother and I did get in trouble together a couple of times. Once was during our senior year, when I talked her into sneaking onto a school bus with me one morning that was taking the juniors on an all-day field trip. Sadie dared me to do it, and Marylyn went along with it. It was the first time in her life that she had played hooky, and she couldn't enjoy the field trip because she was worried about what Mr. and Mrs. Nichols would say when we got home."

"Well, what did they say?"

"Your grandmother never told Mr. Nichols about it. I think *she* liked me more than Marylyn did." We both laughed. Grandma Nichols practically worshiped Dad. He could do no wrong.

"And I'll never forget a special summer outing with Marylyn to Cheaha Mountain. One Sunday afternoon, a group of us guys decided to drive up to Cheaha and have a watermelon picnic with our girlfriends. Of course, I took Marylyn, and my friends took their dates. Let's see, I believe it was Jack Nolen, Hugh Sparks, Ned and Speck Browning, and James Burroughs, and Leverett Pace—and all of us brought our dates. Well, James Burroughs, or

Goober" as we called him, was such a cut-up that he got all of us to agree on a story and pledge to stick to it, no matter what." Dad's excitement grew as he told me what happened.

"We had brought several "yellow-meated" watermelons to eat up on the mountain at the scenic picnic area. Yellow melons were not very common in those days, so when we began cutting them, one of the girls asked the obvious question, *'Hey, why are these watermelons yellow?'* Goober was more than eager to answer.

'All watermelons turn yellow when you cut them high up on a mountain,' Goober stated as fact. *'They're only red down on level ground. Since the elevation here is over 2000 feet, they always turn yellow.'*"

"Of course, the rest of us guys agreed with Goober, making comments like *'Of course,'* and *'Everybody knows that.'* We had them all convinced until Marylyn spoke up.

'Coolidge Sims, I KNOW you are trying to pull my leg! And I can tell you don't believe that phony tale either. Girls, it's not true.' Although I kept swearing up and down that it was the truth, Marylyn refused to believe it. She said my eyes gave it away."

"Oh Dad, I believe it!" I said wholeheartedly. "Growing up I knew that Mom could spot a fib a mile away. She always said she knew us *too well* to believe us if we tried to get away with a lie. Mike and Donna and I could *never* get away with it!" We spent several minutes reminiscing about her incredible *mother's intuition*.

"If she said, *'Look at me, Mark!'*— it was over and done—I was toast." He nodded in agreement.

"Dad, Cheaha has always been a good place for dating. You may not know, but I drove Peggy from Samford to Cheaha just to ask her to marry me. I slipped the ring on her finger sitting at Pulpit Rock!"

"Is that a fact?" he asked rhetorically. "I never knew that, Son!"

"Well, now you know," I threw in for good measure. Eager to keep talking, Dad worked his way around to a new topic.

"Yeah, those were great friends Marylyn and I grew up with in Ashland. I wouldn't trade growing up in a small town for anything. We were all close. We spent so much time together. Mark, do you remember a moment ago when I said that my first date with your mother was to a party at Dot Perry's house?

"I sure do."

"Well, Dot Perry was Ned Browning's girlfriend. Ned and Dot often double dated with Marylyn and me. We were close friends."

"On the day Pearl Harbor was bombed, we were on a double date with Ned and Dot. It was a Sunday afternoon, December 7, 1941, and we were sitting in Ned's car, drinking Co-Colas in front of Jordan's Drug store, listening to the radio. That's when the news came across about the Japanese attack on Pearl Harbor."

"That day was the last time we ever saw Ned Browning. He joined the Navy a few days after he heard the news that Sunday afternoon. Four years later he died in a submarine just off the coast of Japan, only a few weeks before the war ended. With close friendships also comes the possibility of great pain as well."

Woodchopper's Ball

"Dad, did you and Mom ever have a "favorite song" together?"

"Oh, mercy, we had so many favorites. The first one was probably *Stardust*. I remember hearing Bing Crosby sing it on the radio on the Hit Parade. He sang *White Christmas* too, one of our favorites. We liked Dinah Shore, Perry Como, and Frank Sinatra, and Tommy Dorsey. But we mostly liked dance tunes—big band tunes. We always enjoyed going dancing at Clairmont Springs on the weekends. During the summer Clairmont sponsored the 'Big Apple Dance,' and we wouldn't miss it for the world."

"Oh yeah, Sadie Thompson told me about that dance. She said she would drive her dad's big green Pontiac, packed out with friends with their dancing shoes on." I couldn't help but notice Dad's melancholy fading into levity as he reminisced.

"Sadie could *fly* in that big Pontiac!" he chuckled. "If Judge Thompson had realized how fast she drove down the Talladega highway, he'd never have let her drive again!"

"Did you have a car, Dad?"

"Not really. I borrowed Papa's big Mercury sometimes, but usually, he needed it in the evenings working late at his dry goods store. For a while, I got around in a vehicle that looked more like a dune buggy than a car! It was an old rusty Ford truck frame, with an old engine we mounted on it, a steering wheel, a gear shift, and a couple of metal chairs we strapped into it. Marylyn would ride with me around town, but not all the way to Clairmont. That was about fifteen miles away! She didn't want her hair to get messed up blowing in the wind!"

"Not to mention the safety issue," I added. "Metal chairs—strapped in? Really?"

"That *was* a little crazy, wasn't it?" he admitted. "But Marylyn only got hurt one time riding with me. It was actually in Papa's Mercury. The car was already full when I saw Marylyn and Sadie walking from town toward Marylyn's house. I wanted to give them a lift so I told them to jump on the running board and hold on.

It was about a mile and half to the Nichols' house. They held on fine on the highway, but when I turned into the bumpy, gravel road that let up to her house, Marylyn slipped off and fell up against a fence. It cut her leg pretty bad. She was really embarrassed and made us promise not to tell Mr. and Mrs. Nichols. She said if I told, it might keep Papa from letting me use his car again. I was always afraid that Mr. Nichols was going to talk to me about it, but he never did. Still, I always regretted not owning up to it. I was always overly protective of your mother—that's probably why."

"Well, I guess Mom considered having uninterrupted transportation was worth the pain."

"I don't know about that, but sometimes we would ride with Billy Saxon and his girl, Louise Guthrie. Billy's daddy owned a school bus and we'd double date in the bus."

"In a school bus? Two couples in a school bus? You've got to be kidding!" I had *never* heard that story before.

"Sure. It was transportation. If anyone ever saw a school bus out at night, they automatically knew that Billy Saxon was on a date." Dad laughed out loud. It was probably the first time he had thought of it in fifty years.

"So what was the Big Apple dance all about?" I quizzed. Motioning with his hands as if he was standing in the dance pavilion at Clairmont Springs, he responded:

"We all paid a couple of dollars to get in, and there were sandwiches and sweets and soft drinks for everyone on one side, and tables and chairs on the other side, and of course music for dancing," he explained vividly.

"A dance band too?" I inquired.

"Oh, no. We just played records on the phonograph. Those were some good times with your mother, Son."

"And if we couldn't go to Clairmont for a dance, we'd just go out to Pace's Lake, which was a big swimming hole in the middle of a pasture. We'd roast weenies and marshmallows and dance. Sadie would open up the doors of her big Pontiac, turn on the radio, and we would have a party right in the midst of the cow patties."

"You always did like to dance, Dad. I remember that well. You and Mom were in a square dance club when I was a kid."

"We sure were. We always liked to dance. But looking back, I remember Marylyn would usually get out of breath and get worn out at dances, even when we were teenagers. She would have to rest for a while. We didn't know it then, but she always had a heart condition that she got back when she was twelve or thirteen. I think she had rheumatic fever or something."

It all made sense to me. Mom had died of congestive heart failure in 1999, but she had obviously struggled with heart issues long before that. Nobody knew how serious her heart condition was until she was in her sixties.

Dad broke out into a grin as he remembered something else about the Big Apple dance.

"I believe Marylyn's favorite dance tune was *Woodchoppers Ball* by the Woody Herman Orchestra. She always requested it. It was their most famous hit. *Woodchopper's Ball* was a really upbeat, jazzy tune that made you want to 'jitterbug' all across the dance floor. There was a certain place in the song that the girl sort of danced a circle around the guy as they gazed into each other's eyes, all the while she pointed both index fingers, up and down to the rhythm of the music, into the air just like this." Dad pranced in a circle around me between the TV and his easy chair, index fingers bobbing up and down toward the ceiling. We were both laughing until Dad got out of breath and off balance, and had to catch himself on his recliner. I helped steady him for a couple of seconds before he plopped down into his easy chair, as we chuckled again. Then, slipping back into a pensive mood Dad uncovered his thoughts,

"I can still see Marylyn's beautiful, dark brown eyes gazing at me as we danced the *Woodchopper's Ball*. I'd give *anything* to dance it with her one more time."

Once, a member of my church congregation asked me a personal question that took me several days to discern the answer. It wasn't a Biblical question to research or a doctrinal stance to explain. Rather, it was a question that required deep introspection and examination; it demanded sober thought on more than one level of thinking.

The question was, '*What was your father's single greatest gift to you?*'

I came to the conclusion that Coolidge Sims' greatest gift to me was the gift of stability. I never questioned whether or not my father loved me. I always knew that he would take care of me and provide for me. I never feared that he would abandon my mother, or abandon me. He never came home drunk or caused havoc in the family.

He was the same man day in and day out. His faith in God never faltered, and his love for my mother never failed. He gave me stability. It is the gift for which I am the most thankful.

I traveled home as the sun was setting thinking about the relationship that my parents shared with each other for 67 years. On this Wednesday, my Dad had pulled back the curtain just a little further on what made their marriage union so special. I went to bed that night determined to give the same gift to my children and grandchildren.

"Lately all my friends are worried that they are turning into their fathers. I'm worried I'm not."
Dan Zevi

Baby Coolidge

Mama Sims with "Rapunzel hair", Eunice and Lenoice.

Coolidge, Gwynnelle and Bremon

Young Coolidge "fights" with Uncle Lenoice

Coolidge
2nd Grade

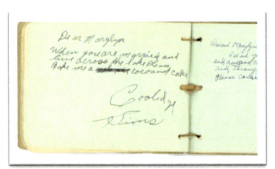

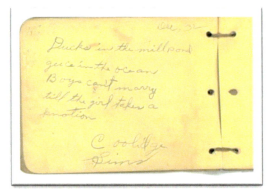

Marylyn
2nd Grade

Marylyn Nichols

Calvin Coolidge Sims
wearing "Three Bears" sweater

Ashland Panthers football team captain

Senior Play practice "Peck's Bad Boy"

Marylyn early 1940's

Coolidge Sims and Marylyn Nichols Clay County High School sweethearts

Charlotte Nichols
"Prisspot"

Marylyn and Coolidge
Senior Portraits

Freshman skit

Jax State basketball team Coolidge #6

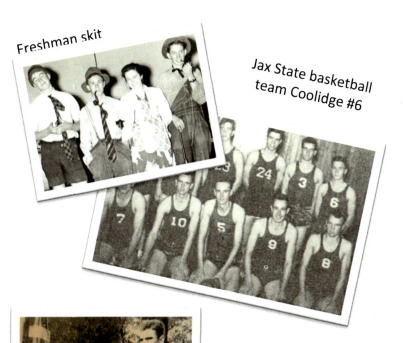

Coolidge on-leave before overseas deployment

Jax State's shortest and tallest students –
too tall, too short for the U.S. Marines
(newspaper clipping 1942)

Favorite portrait of Marylyn kept at Coolidge's bedside.

Beach 1947

Wedding Day 1946

Chapter Five

Donna called me at 11 pm. She and Allen were with Dad at the emergency room. He had experienced an anxiety attack, causing his heart to race dangerously. Back in 1985, he had suffered a major heart attack that rendered nearly half of his heart muscle non-functioning. Fortunately for the last twenty-five years, the good muscle in the heart had compensated beautifully.

"There's no reason for you to come down here tonight, Mark. They've gotten him calmed down and I'm taking him back to The Oaks shortly," she explained. "He said his leg was bothering him so bad that he could hardly breathe. Then the nurses called the paramedics—and here we are."

"They never called me," I insisted.

"No, I live the closest, so if I answer, they won't call you," she clarified.

"What's with his leg, Donna? He keeps complaining about it."

"They keep saying it's severe neuralgia from his recent bout with shingles. In older people, it can be horribly painful. They prescribed Tramadol to take for pain; not a narcotic, but stronger than ibuprofen."

"I was with him tonight until almost eight o'clock. We went out for some ice cream. He didn't say a word about it," I added.

"I think you wore him out," Donna said half-jokingly.

"He did seem tired when I brought him back. I'll bet he's embarrassed."

"Yes, very. He keeps apologizing over and over for being such a burden." Her voice quivered slightly before trailing off into a whisper, "It's so hard for him, Mark. He's never felt this helpless." Our dad's uncharacteristic frailty had broadsided her. This was hard for a "daddy's girl" to handle.

Suspicions

I tried to get to The Oaks before Dad went to breakfast, but traffic wouldn't cooperate. It had been drizzling rain since daybreak and the roads were messy. Upon arriving I checked with the head nurse to get an update. She hadn't seen or heard from Dad all morning. Perhaps he was still asleep after his rough night.

To my surprise, he was sitting on the edge of his bed when I eased into his room. His hair was tousled, oily and smashed down on the left side, sticking straight up in the back. He squished his wiry, salt and pepper eyebrows tightly together as he ran his hand slowly through his hair. Not yet seeing me, his worried eyes wandered around the room as if he was searching for something.

"Morning, Dad." He turned in my direction but was not startled by my presence, appearing agitated, or maybe just confused. "Have you been to breakfast yet?" I asked.

"No, I'm not hungry this morning," he snapped as his face hardened in disgust.

"What's happened, Dad?" I asked guardedly. "What's wrong?" My eyes darted around the room looking for clues.

"I guess I'm going crazy, Mark," he said gazing up at me with stormy eyes. "I can't find my money anywhere. I've looked, but can't find it." I spotted the open drawer on the nightstand, and his open billfold lying on the bed beside him.

"Did you have your money in your billfold, Dad?" He shrugged his shoulders and scrunched his face together, exasperated,

"I don't know—I thought so." He carefully slid himself off the bed and clutched his walker, still glancing wildly about the room. I searched his billfold again, just in case he was mistaken.

"How much money are you missing, Dad?"

"About sixty or seventy dollars. I don't know," he barked. His breathing had become labored since I entered the room, his frustration mounting.

At that tense moment, Phyllis, a friendly but brash dining room staffer came barreling into his room. She knew Dad well, serving him most every weekday breakfast and lunch. He normally joked around with her, delighting in the way she laughed at his every witty quip. Tall, overweight and a bit overbearing, she kept up with every dining room detail, remembering what each resident under her care ate the day before, and perhaps even the week before. She wore a wig every day, but never the same wig two days in a row. Phyllis relished questions and comments aimed at her hairstyle, usually ending the conversation with,

"That's right, I'm jus' stylin' and profilin', Baby," with the *y* in *baby* mostly missing, sounding more like *'babe'* with a tiny inflection at the end.

"Mr. Sims, we didn't see you at breakfast this morning. You gonna eat something, aren't you?" I jumped into the conversation before Dad could respond, afraid of what he might say.

"He's not too hungry this morning, Miss Phyllis. Maybe you could bring some raisin bran and juice to the room?"

"Alright, Baby. That sound like a plan for the little man!" Phyllis left as boisterously as she had arrived. Dad said nothing until Phyllis was long gone down the hall, but then turning toward me he alleged in a muted tone,

"I wouldn't be at all surprised if that colored girl was who my money." His lips curled in disgust, "She came in here this morning, moving around the room and making noise, trying to wake me up early. I don't like the way they just come in without my knowledge. I wouldn't doubt…"

"Dad," I interrupted, "I'm sure Phyllis is the last person who'd want to steal something from you." He didn't respond but ambled with his walker into the bathroom and closed the door. I continued to search for his missing cash, praying I would find it. Then it dawned on me,

"Hey Dad, don't you have a money clip you usually use for cash?" There was a brief pause, a toilet flush, and then he called out from the bathroom,

"Yep, check my pockets from the pants I wore yesterday." Sure enough, a quick check of the pants in the hamper produced the missing sixty-five bucks, tucked tightly into the clip.

"You're right, Dad. Here it is. Sixty-five dollars, safe and sound." Pleased, he expressed his relief,

"Oh good! That's great! Thank-you Son. It had me worried to death!" Dad's whole demeanor changed as soon as he emerged from the bathroom. When Phyllis showed up with the cereal and juice, Dad was as playful as ever.

"Mr. Sims, here's your breakfast, just like you axed for," she squawked.

"Well, looks like Big Mama has her fancy hair on today." His wisecrack was just what Phyllis was waiting to hear, laughing as if they had been friends all their lives. Phyllis shot back,

"Mr. Sims you so short, I'm shocked you can even see my weave way up here!" Together they hooted and cackled, exchanging good-natured barbs while she prepared his breakfast on the tray table. The morning had started off edgy but was looking better by the minute.

Dance of the Razor

Helping Dad with his shower had become a much easier task than I imagined it would be; not an inconvenience at all. Dad was usually his best in the mornings before the exertion of the day lit a painful bonfire deep inside his left thigh. He had relished his morning relationship with his electric shaver since he first used one in 1952. Now, at eighty-nine Dad's shaving precision with an electric shaver wasn't quite as accurate as it once was, but the high value he placed on a clean morning shave had not changed in sixty years.

I picked out his clothes and socks for the day, laid them across the bed, and joined him in the bathroom. He stood barefoot in front of the vanity mirror wearing his favorite cotton housecoat, forest green with tan piping. He was leaning firmly against the marbled beige vanity to steady himself, his gut pressed snugly onto the cold, curved laminate edge. I slid between the old timer and his walker, which virtually blocked the doorway, and peered at him in the mirror just as he touched the buzzing razor to his right cheek.

"Dad, do you need any help shaving?"

"Naw, I got it, Markle," he garbled, never meeting my eyes in the mirror. His jaw contorted oddly in the direction of his left shoulder blade. For a moment, I stood again like a four-year-old boy watching my father shave, mesmerized by the perfectly choreographed *dance of the razor*— a dance that partnered his shaving instrument with his worn, much-experienced face.

Flawlessly he guided the razor to perform four perfect pirouettes on his right cheek followed by a flowing vertical leap to the whiskers just below his temple, and then a deep plié' downward onto his neck, chin pointed upward and skin pulled tautly. A series of graceful spin moves floated across the silver stubble on his chin, his lower lip delicately timed to receive the twirling razor, grand jete', leaping, gliding across Dad's morphing facial stage, coming to rest just beneath the left cheek bone.

He paused briefly before performing the lyrical *dance of the razor* again—only this time in reverse. I watched him slap on a generous palm-full of Old Spice, and then it suddenly dawned on me—I enact the same dance every morning of my life with my Norelco, replicating the same movements in meticulous detail.

Staring into the wide bathroom mirror I recognized the incredible resemblance shared by the two men staring back at us—same brown eyes, same thin lips, same ears pinned closely to the head. And at fifty-six my hair was as snow white as my father's, graying early just as his had done. Why had I never seen this before?

Dressed and ready for the day, Dad rested for a few minutes in his easy chair talking all the while about presidential politics. The son of a lifelong Republican, Coolidge was named for the Republican vice-president in 1923. Calvin Coolidge actually assumed the presidency four months and one day after my father was born. Dad always made the best of his lifelong association with the famous American president, but truly relished the annual teasing that surrounded his birth date—April 1. When asked for his date of birth he usually responded with, "I'm an April Fool from 1923."

No one, I mean *no one*, engaged in more April fools jokes than Coolidge Sims. He called himself a charter member, an active participant, and lifelong loyalist to the *Order of the April Fools*, his convenient reason for never following his father into the Masonic Lodge. Dad viewed the Masons as oddly boring and time-consuming, preferring to focus his secret society obligation onto one really fun day every year. It worked for him.

Money Matters

"Dad, you really got worked up this morning about losing your money." I thought his crazy over-reaction needed another look. "Your heart doesn't handle that kind of stress very well."

"Mark, I grew up in the Depression, and we...."

I jumped in quickly, "I know that, Dad. That' not what I'm talking..."

He pushed ahead of me, "You *know* that I grew up in the Depression, but you *don't know* what it's like to grow up in a depression." I sat still. For once in my life, I decided not to push back against his patented *Great Depression lecture*. He obviously thought I hadn't gotten it yet, despite having heard it a thousand times over. This might be the last time I would ever hear it, so I listened with my heart.

"Papa was tired of being a part-time blacksmith, part-time farmer, and part-time school teacher in a one-room schoolhouse in Delta. Being a big talker and a well-connected kind of guy, he ran for county tax assessor in 1930—and he won. So that meant we had to move twenty miles away, to Ashland where the courthouse was located. By 1931 the Great Depression had reached Alabama, and Papa lost everything. So did almost everyone else.

The county had to pay him in *script*, a sometimes-worthless bank draft—depending on the health of the county's tax receipts. Those were tough times, but we had a garden, and a milk cow, and hogs, and chickens, so we didn't go hungry. But we only had electricity half the time, and had to make clothes and shoes last a whole year."

"I remember you telling us about that brown sweater you wore for years," I threw in to show my interest. He responded with a chuckle,

"Yeah. I got it for Christmas in the second grade. It had three little bears on the front of it, and it was way too big for me then. By the time I was in the fourth grade it fit, and then by the fifth grade, it was threadbare and really tight. The three little bears were pretty embarrassing by the fifth grade.

We'd go to Anniston once a year to buy shoes. Until then, Mama would cut out cardboard to line the inside of them once they got holes in the soles." Dad folded his gnarled hands and rested them on his stomach, looking me right in the eye. "Money was scarce, so we had to make a dollar stretch—something I'm *glad* you've never had to do."

I got it. What he was trying to do was make me appreciative, not guilty. He and my mother had worked hard so that my brother, sister, and I would *never* have to do without the way they had. He could have withheld from us like a selfish miser proving a point to teach his lesson.

But instead, he chose to make our lives comfortable, risking the creation of a whole new transgression—entitlement.

"Dad, I'll always remember the talk you had with me when we rode together to Birmingham the summer I left home and moved into the dorm at Samford. You said,

'Son, don't buy things you can't afford, and always pay your bills. It says a lot about a man when he pays his bills on time. If for some reason you get behind, talk to your creditors, pay what you can, and do without until you can get caught back up.' I'm sorry to say I haven't always been that prudent, but you taught me right."

"Do you remember Mrs. Mitchell that lived up at Shirey's Mill? Do you remember her coming in the drugstore when you were working there?" He stretched my memory muscle. "You were just a teenager."

"I think so. She was short, rotund, and wore her hair pulled back tightly into a little knot on the back of her head, always smiling."

"Yes, that was Mrs. Mitchell." He lowered his voice slightly, but the movement of his hands and body was as animated as that of a preacher. "Mark, she and her husband were rather poor (Dad pronounced it, *purr*), and I kept letting her charge more medicine, even before she cleared off her balance. And you know why? It was because she always kept her word. She would come in every Saturday like clockwork and say,

'Mr. Coolidge, I know I owe you twenty-six dollars and fifteen cents. I don't have it all today, but I've got nine dollars and seventy-five cents I can pay on it. I'll get it caught up as soon as I can. I sure do appreciate you working with me on this.'

I never refused anything to her on credit. She was as good as her word, unlike some people of means who would charge things and not pay on it for months, even years at a time, without so much as *'sorry I'm late,'* or an *'I'm going through a rough time right now.'*"

It was that entitlement thing. It really bothered Dad. Living through the Great Depression taught him to value honesty *and* thrift. Gratefulness was high on his list of preferred character traits.

"Dad, I laugh when I remember hearing Aunt Ginny and Aunt Gail call you and Bremon their *tight-fisted, penny-pinching brothers,* but I don't believe it. Mother always said you weren't even in the same league as Bremon. Bremon's kids have told me that too."

"Mama used to hear me trying to bum a nickel off of Bremon for an RC Cola," Dad responded, "and she would say, 'Coolidge, you know your brother is tighter than Dick's hatband.'" We both chuckled as we thought about it.

"I probably would have been really stingy, had it not been for your mother. She had no problem giving anything away. We shared the checkbook, so that meant that I never ended up with as much money as I thought I should have at the end of the month!"

"Dad, I've just got to ask you. How much did Mom really spend on Donna's wedding?"

"Oh, Lordy mercy," he said pursing his lips tightly beneath an impish smile. His bushy eyebrows lifted upward as he opened his eyes wide and declared,

"To tell you the truth, Bud, I have no earthly *idear.*" Occasionally Dad added an *r* to the end of any word ending in a vowel, just like Mama Sims used to do. When I was younger it embarrassed me to hear my college-educated father say things like *potater,* or *tomater,* or *diahrrear* in public. But now, that's just Dad, and I love it. He continued his humorous rant.

"If your baby sister and your mother ever went shopping together, it was a guarantee that some big bucks were going to be spent. All Donna had to say was, 'Momma, I might like these shoes for Christmas or my birthday next year,' and before they walked out of Wakefield's Department Store that pair of shoes was in the shopping bag, or on Donna's feet!"

"So did you ever find out how much her wedding cost you?" I asked again.

"I told your mother to handle the whole thing, just please don't plunge us into bankruptcy. Donna and Allen were married two years before I even checked the balance in the checkbook! When I was at the reception and saw the people lined up for boiled shrimp, I knew that I didn't *ever* want to know. I told Marylyn to put the receipts somewhere I could never find them—and she did."

Truthfully, no one in the world was happier to give than our Dad. He just sometimes needed our mom's direction in what was the most important, and she was a rather conservative gal herself.

After she died in 1999, Dad's "thrift compass" went slightly awry. Sometimes we would find the dishwasher loaded with disposable plastic cups, and noticed he was using and reusing paper plates—Dad saving money. All the while he was ordering the newest kitchen gadget from QVC or Home Shopping Network on late night cable TV. Packed into seldom-opened cabinets was a collection of unused Ginsu knives, slicer dicers, and salad shooters, the purchase of which my mother would have never allowed.

T'was the Month After Christmas

Parenting means preparing their children for life, and that isn't accomplished in one big lesson—rather it happens in increments. I can go back and remember one such lesson as vividly today as when it happened. My father didn't waste an important opportunity for me to learn a lesson in taking things for granted.

Christmas always arrives with a bang (gifts, sweets, cheer, and holiday prayers) and then quickly leaves us suffering from symptoms of straight-up withdrawal! And with children, it's even more pronounced. *"Every day should be like Christmas,"* a little tyke imagines, leading to his demands of even *more* presents and *more* sugar-- or else! Chaos inevitably erupts in the house and "kid naughty" summarily takes out "kid nice" in the first round. By New Year's Day, parents are fed-up, broke, and ready for a break from the spoiled sugar addicts.

"Out with the old and in with the new" is the New Year's motto. However, for youngsters, the "new" doesn't mean "new toys" and "new treats." Instead, January comes down like Thor's hammer on the ungrateful young urchins. School reconvenes and reality sets in.

It was in January, the month after Christmas, that I had the first of many "great awakenings" about how things *really* are. For weeks television ads had touted all the new toys available for Christmas. More than anything I wanted a *Playmobile*-- one of the top toys for little boys that year. It was a plastic car console with horn, moving windshield wipers, a gear shifting stick and working blinkers, all made to sit nicely on a table top for playing.

In my mind, it was the most incredible toy that had ever been invented. The Playmobile was the talk of the boys on the playground at school, and would certainly prove to bring hours of enjoyment to every kid who was fortunate enough to get one. And it WAS fun-- for maybe a couple of weeks.

But by the middle of January, it became one of the most boring toys in the universe. All one could do was sit there and steer the car to NOWHERE. There was no gas pedal to rev-up the motor, no radio that blared music, and no wheels to take a person anywhere. It just sat there! It was more boring to a little boy than listening to a sermon in big church! And if (and when) the batteries wore down, it became a totally useless hunk of plastic.

But as it is with most kids, my vivid imagination came to my rescue. What could be more exciting, I thought than a wreck? I could just pretend to run off the road and smash into a tree-- or better yet, I could swerve back and forth on the highway, sideswipe a car, and then collide into an embankment!

I rehearsed each crash scenario in my mind, upping the ante each time. Finally, my imagination led me to race down the side of a mountain, lose control, and then fly off the edge of a steep cliff and onto the rocky boulders at the ocean's edge-- just like like it was on the TV show, *Route 66*.

Obviously, my beautiful Playmobile could have never survive such a terrible fate. That's when I got the idea to do something *really* exciting. I raced to the storage room and pulled Dad's hammer out of the tool box. For about five minutes I hammered my new Playmobile into oblivion, carefully placing each blow exactly where the car would have smashed against the sharp boulders at the bottom. It was incredible fun—truly it was—until Dad showed up!

He had heard the commotion coming from my room and decided to check on his inventive son. I never heard him coming. With the hammer lifted high above my head I saw him enter my room, eyebrows raised and eyes bulging.

"Mark, what do you think you are doing? Are you crazy?"

"No Dad," I responded as I lowered the hammer gently to my side. "I had a wreck."

"A wreck, my hind leg! That was your Christmas present! Toys cost money! What were you thinking, Son?"

"It didn't cost anything. Santa brought it to me." I was hoping he would just say, "*Oh yeah Son, I forgot,*" but I was badly mistaken.

"Well, who do you think paid Santa for it!!!" Dad was not reasoning with me, he was shouting at me. But I had *never* heard that Santa charged for his kindness to kids. Actually, that night, Santa Claus lost some of his charm in my eyes. Reality set in, especially after the spanking. Dad was never cruel to me-- or *anyone*, for that matter-- but he sure had a way of getting me in touch with reality. Ouch!

After our discussion about the cost of Donna's wedding, I made reference to the lesson he taught me many years earlier and joked about the wreck of the old Playmobile. He remembered it as vividly as I did.

"Son, I had to teach you a lesson that night, or else you might go through life thinking everything should be handed to you on a silver tray. But your mother and I laughed about it later. You really had a good imagination."

Powerful Lesson

By the end of lunch, his left leg was giving him trouble again, and he began to complain about his lower back as well. The Tramadol helped, but it was still not knocking the pain out. The doctor doubled the dosage as needed, and he needed it. He took the usual afternoon nap in his recliner as soon as the two pain relievers kicked-in. I used the time to return a few phone calls, answer my email, and stretch my legs, wandering all around the grounds of The Oaks.

I made a brief phone call to my brother in Columbus recounting the latest about Dad's pain, his racing heart rate, and his general disposition. Mike let me know that he was coming for the weekend to give Donna and me a break. It was welcome news because I found it difficult to explain everything over the phone. Dad's condition was better seen than heard.

Dad awoke from his nap a bit confused but in less pain. After a few minutes he became fully aware of his surroundings and we continued our visit. Out of the blue, I said,

"You know, one of the greatest blessings you ever gave to us was how you taught us to be a giver to God." I had been thinking about it since our morning conversation. "I remember when I was in elementary school, about seven or eight years old, you began giving me a $2.25 per week allowance. That was big money to me, but it wasn't hard to spend."

"Not for you, Mark," Dad recounted. "Ten minutes in the *Five and Dime Store* and you were broke."

"True, true," I laughed to myself, "But do you remember where you placed the allowance cash every Monday morning, Dad?" He remembered precisely,

"On the mantle in the den."

"Yes, but you would only place the two one-dollar bills on the mantle; the last 25¢ you handed to me on Sunday morning so I could put it in the collection plate at church." Dad burst into laughing as soon as I said it.

"I sure did," he added jokingly. "I guess I sort of *forced* you to tithe."

"No, Dad," I responded. "You *taught* me to tithe."

Table Talk

Our dialogue worked its way all through the afternoon and until dinner. We took our sweet time together walking between room 138 and the dining room, Dad recalling the strains that economic collapse placed on the Sims family in the 1930's.

"You see, my Papa was elected in 1930 as a Republican, but with the depression and all, he lost the 1934 election to a Democrat by a landslide. Mama and Papa considered moving back to Delta, but Papa didn't want to uproot us again. He decided to open a dry goods store on the courthouse square in Ashland and try to make it work."

Halfway on our slow journey to the dining room, we crossed paths with Mr. Thomason, a lanky old fellow with a head full of white hair, not one of them out of place. He was the only male resident at The Oaks whose hair was perfect in every way, all the time—like a plastic Ken doll whose hair part is a molded indention into his head, but perfectly rounded on the top. In the front, a tidy, sharp ledge of hair protrudes over his forehead like a deep, chalky cave. Even sitting on the porch outside on a windy day, not a follicle is disturbed. It was as if he used lacquer instead of gel or hairspray. Dad said he had a *ninety-mile an hour hairdo.*

After a pleasant exchange of greetings, we three ambled into the dining hall and took a seat at a table of six, ladies on one side and men on the other. I asked Dad to finish his story about Papa Sims and the dry goods store before the dinner began. He spoke loud enough for the entire table to hear, so they all paid close attention to his story.

"Papa rented a vacant storefront on the square, for his new dry goods store. When I was a kid it was my job to get up early every morning and go to Papa's store and build a fire in the pot-bellied stove, and then sweep the floors before heading off to school. Papa had just enough money to start the business but had no money to pay our house rent so we had to find somewhere else to live.

Mama got the idea to offer to cook the meals for the boarders at the Woods Hotel for extra money to help out. They said they couldn't pay her anything, but would let our family live at the hotel free if she would serve as the unpaid cook. So we lived in a hotel for a couple of years, and I remember it as great fun."

From that moment on, our table was awash with stories about the life in the 1930's, each celebrating the hard times as the best times of all. Mr. Thomason was especially entertaining, offering a view of how times were for families in the city. I felt like a guest at a family reunion listening to the old timers recounting the experiences they all shared in common. Ours was the last table to finish dinner. By the end, even some of the dining staff had slipped-in close enough to hear Dad relate the final remembrance of the evening:

"Mama sent me to school nearly every morning with my lunch in a syrup bucket; it was usually a *cat head* biscuit stuffed with ham or sausage, and maybe a cookie or some cheese."

"Cat head?" Mr. Thomason interjected. "I don't recall what that was?"

"Yes, yes, I do." the frail, parchment-skinned lady directly across from me recalled, "It's a big old biscuit, wide and thick, sort of like a small burger." She spoke in a coarse and gravelly voice, rasping as if she had smoked most of her life. Her fancy rings floated around on her skinny, shrinking fingers. "The biscuit was about the size of a tomcat's head; good eating." Nods and agreements at the table pushed Dad to continue.

"Well, my buddy, Jack Nolen, came from a family that had more money than most. His mother, a cultured, proper Southern lady sent her children to school with bona fide lunchboxes full of good things. Often Jack's mother would pack him a pineapple and mayonnaise sandwich on white loaf bread. Every day M.L. Allen and I would race to get to Jack to see what he had for lunch, hoping to make a trade for something exotic. Jack was usually more than willing to trade his pineapple sandwich for my ham and biscuit. If I could get to Jack before M.L. got to him, I enjoyed some fine eating indeed!"

I left Dad at the table with his friends, slipping out to make it in time for Wednesday evening church. The nursing staff assured me they would keep an eye on him for the remainder of the evening. I reminded them he was interested in watching Fox News before bedtime.

I switched off the radio in the pickup on my way home. With only the muffled roar of the truck motor in my ears and the coolness of the air vent on my cheek, I reviewed the happenings of the day during a quick call to Donna.

"Overall a good day or bad day?" she asked me.
"It's hard to say, Sis. Days that are either good or bad don't really work anymore. Bad stuff happened today; good stuff did too. Right now, that's just the way it is."

"I'll be there by late morning tomorrow," Donna avowed, "and Mike will be coming on Friday for the weekend."

"Dad will really be glad to see Mike again," I inserted. "Should we tell Dad ahead of time that he's coming?"

"No, let's let him be surprised."

"Let's both show up there Saturday morning as well," I suggested. "I want to see Mike too, and get his perspective on how Dad's doing since he saw him last."

"Good idea," Donna said. "I'll call you tomorrow."

"Call it a clan, call it a network, call it a tribe, call it a family; whatever you call it, whoever you are, you need one."

Jane Howard

Chapter Six

Cell Phone Rendezvous

As soon as our Sunday evening church service ended, Peggy and I slipped out the door heading to The Oaks to check on Dad. Even before we exited the parking lot I dialed my older brother's cell phone number.

"Hello little brother," Mike answered, "I was just about to give you a call."

"We just got out of church, and Peggy and I are on our way. Are you still with Dad?"

"No, I'm already on the road," he said. "I need to get back to Columbus before it gets late. It's a three-hour drive, and I lose an hour crossing over into Georgia."

"Of course. I don't blame you. How did everything go today?" I asked. "I know he was thrilled that you were here this weekend."

"Well, I think Dad's doing pretty good. We did a lot of talking, and he says he likes it at The Oaks," Mike assured me.

"He was really pumped about you coming this weekend," I said. "I'm glad you could get away and come visit him."

"This morning he asked me how my practice was going in Columbus, and then he reminded me of my skill as a surgeon. I wasn't sure what he was talking about until he mentioned the word, *Frisbee*. Then I knew."

"Oh yes," I said with a smile. "I think I do. Let me turn my speakerphone on so you can tell Peggy the whole story. I want her to hear it."

"OK, well for almost as long as I can remember Dad had a big mole on the left side of his forehead, just on the edge of his hairline. And over the years it got larger and larger. One Thanksgiving, when I was in medical school at

UAB, Mark and Donna and I were playing a game we made up called *"Frisbee setback"* in the back yard. I threw the Frisbee as hard as I could and it hit Dad, ricocheting right off his head. I heard him say, *'Whoah! That hurt!'*

I ran over to him to make sure he was OK when I saw blood running down his face. I apologized profusely, and then I noticed that the big mole was gone! Amputated. Sliced off. Surgically removed with precision. And it healed up without a scar! Dad always said it was the cheapest, best-performed surgery he had ever seen. And I hadn't even graduated from medical school yet!" Peggy laughed, picturing the whole event unfolding in the back yard!

Before Mike got off the phone I asked him one more important thing, "What about his leg? Is it still bothering him?"

"He never complained about it," Mike explained, "But I can see he's favoring it a lot. When he walks he leans a little to the left. I asked him to tell me where it's hurting he can't really pinpoint it—sometimes it's his back, sometimes his hip, and sometimes his leg. I'll give Dr. Beale a call and consult with him about it tomorrow, but I'm pretty sure it's not residual pain from shingles."

"Ok. That sounds good. Let us know what he says. Hey, it was great seeing you yesterday. Drive carefully. Love you, bye." Because Mike is a physician with a grueling daily routine, his visits to Birmingham were often difficult to schedule. Still, he was the "go-to guy" on everything medical and the one Dad trusted most for advice.

Coolidge Sims had always lived in a town where a person's physician was a long-term friend and should be trusted completely with medical decisions. It never crossed his mind to sue or second-guess his doctor. If he didn't trust him, he wouldn't have chosen him. Mike could never be his personal physician, but Dad trusted his eldest son's opinion unequivocally.

We bounded into room 138 with all the optimism in the world, looking forward to hearing Dad recount the events of his weekend with Mike. Instead, we found two nurses in his room—one of them checking his blood pressure, and the other examining his right shoulder.

"What's going on," I quizzed. "Are you alright, Dad?" He never answered me but sat stiffly in his chair trying to answer all the questions the nurses were throwing his way.

"Your Daddy just had a fall. He said he got dizzy and lost his balance," explained the snappy nurse in the maroon scrubs. He wasn't in pain, so we felt certain that nothing was sprained or broken. Still, the entire ordeal was quite disturbing. The rules stated that if a resident at The Oaks fell more than three times in one month, they could be moved out of the assisted living lodge, and into the more expensive nursing home sector. To be a continual fall risk required too much supervision in the assisted living unit.

Peggy and I got Dad settled and comfortable before we headed home. Later I called my sister, and then my brother while Mike was still en route to Columbus. Mike said it might have something to do with his blood pressure, so we decided to get Dad a doctor's appointment to have him checked out—pronto.

We laughed in telling our brother that Dad always puts on a great show for Mike when he comes to visit, and then falls apart as soon as he leaves. And again, Dad had performed right on cue.

Monday, Monday

The following day my sister and I both came to The Oaks early hoping to get there before he got up and about. The risk of another fall weighed heavily on us. Unfortunately, Monday morning did not bring us glad tidings. Dad was still in the bed when we arrived. His back and leg had hurt him all night, and he was afraid to get out of the bed—feeling nauseated and dizzy. Unable to get a morning doctor's appointment, the nursing staff advised us to take him to the ER.

Our grueling visit to the emergency room resulted in Dad's hospitalization to find what was really going on. Was he having heart issues? Was it depression? Was it just a matter of regulating his blood pressure? Was it a pain management concern? We were in the dark and desperately needed clarity.

He saw a geriatric specialist who ordered an exhausting day of tests—X-ray, CAT scan, MRI, blood work, EKG, kitchen sink—you name it, they did it. It was taxing for all, but at least we felt like we were finally chasing answers.

On the following morning, May 1st, I got to the hospital early, not wanting to miss the doctor's visit. The lights were low and Dad was still snoozing when I arrived so I sat quietly beside his bed. I whispered a prayer for him while we waited. With only the gentle sound of the oxygen pump gurgling in the background, I watched him sleep, examining carefully the exact contour of his hairline and shape of his ears. For the first time, I noticed a crease that stretched diagonally across his earlobe. It was exactly like the one my wife once noticed on my earlobe.

I thought of the sound of his laugh; the quick gate of his walk; and the mole that used to be so prominent on the left side of his forehead just below the part in his hair.

Minutes later Dr. Perez, his gerontologist, bounded into the room. "Good morning, Mr. Sims," she bellowed. I rushed toward the door to greet her, explaining that he was still sleeping.

"The nurse said he had a restless night, and he hasn't awakened yet," I whispered.

"Oh, okay. I'm sorry. Let's step out in the hall for a minute," Dr. Perez suggested. I followed her into the corridor. The young, vibrant physician had impressed me the previous day with her compassionate, bedside manner, perfectly suited for working with the elderly. I noted how

Dad responded to her positive, upbeat demeanor. Rather than being Bubbles the Clown, she was personable and happy, coming across as the knowledgeable specialist that she was. I trusted her.

"Mr. Sims, I know you're not expecting to hear this, but your father has cancer." What? Alas. She said it—the "C" word. I was stunned because his heart had always been the issue. The good doctor continued her explanation, "The MRI indicates that we are dealing with a tumor pressing against the left side of his spine, just above his hip, which explains the pain he's been experiencing in his upper leg. It's a fairly large tumor, and I've got another team of cancer specialists looking at our best way to treat it."

"Is it curable, Doc?" I asked.

"No, not really. It's large and attached to his spine. But hopefully, we can treat it, shrink it, and prolong his life and his quality of life at the same time. At least that's what I'm thinking. Without treatment, I think we're looking at three to six months at the most; with treatment, maybe longer."

"I'm not sure what to say, Dr. Perez. I hoped this whole battery of tests would result in a simple medicine adjustment. A cancerous tumor was not on my radar at all." I paused to gather my thoughts. The doctor stood patiently beside me.

"I'll have to call my brother and sister," I mumbled.

"Of course you do," she assured me. "But I definitely still need to talk to your father personally."

"Okay. Let me wake him up." I spun around quickly to reach for the doorknob but felt her tug on my elbow.

"No, don't do that. He'll wake up dazed and won't remember a word I say. I'm used to working with his age group," she said honestly. "I'll be on the floor for a while, so I'll come back a little later, after he's up and has had his breakfast, ...and then I can sit down and explain it all to him if you don't mind." I was glad to agree and thanked her for her kindness and candor. Doctor Perez smiled and moved down the hall to continue making her rounds. I moved the opposite direction toward the window at the end of the hall, wrestling my phone out of my pocket and pressing the speed dial button for my wife, Peggy.

As always just hearing Peggy answer my call brought me comfort. I told her the news and we both cried for a moment. Afterward, I called Donna, who was already on her way to the hospital and then left a message for my brother who was most likely making his own rounds in a Columbus hospital. Preoccupied with my phone conversations, I didn't even notice that the hospital staff had delivered Dad's breakfast until I saw them exiting the room. "Is he awake?" I asked zipping down the hall toward them.

"He sure is," the white-clad food service worker answered. "He said he's really hungry."

"Oh, thank you, buddy." I paused a moment to plan my entrance, hoping somehow that my facial expressions would not give it away before the doctor returned. Both of my parents had been experts at reading our faces, no matter how hard we tried to hide something. Nevertheless, I hurdled into his room just as he was trying to remove the small clear oxygen tubing from his nose.

"Good morning, Dad!"

"Hey, Markel," he quipped. "I'm sort of tangled-up here. You showed up just in time." I got him situated and chatted with him as he enjoyed his breakfast. Dad always enjoyed a hearty breakfast. Many times I'd heard him say that a good breakfast was his favorite meal of the day. Cracker Barrel and Huddle House knew Coolidge Sims by name.

Donna sheepishly entered the room just as Dad was drinking a few sips of his morning coffee. He didn't mind drinking it black but always preferred it with a little tad of milk. I caught Donna's eye before Dad saw her. Her eyes said, "Does he know yet?"

"Well hello, Donna," I blurted out still eye-to-eye with her while managing a gentle *no, he does not know yet* head shake as she made her way into the room. The three of us enjoyed the time we had together that morning, although *two* of us had a sinking dread resting in the pit of our stomachs.

Doctor Perez soon reappeared, recounting the medical facts to Dad concisely and factually—promising good care but making no unrealistic assurances. I spent the entire time observing my father's every expression. Occasionally I would glance at my sister whose attention was focused like a laser on Dr. Perez. I knew she couldn't look at Dad for fear of breaking down.

Dad had no questions to ask, and we did not want to ask the doctor anything in front of him. We had plenty of questions, but they would have to wait until later. Dr. Perez agreed to call Mike and explain things to him. He would know exactly what to ask. For now, it was about managing Dad and his reaction to the bad news.

As soon as the door closed he looked squarely at Donna, "Well, I never thought it would be cancer that would get me. I always thought it would be my heart."

She gushed a response, "Dad, I am dumbfounded." Her voice melted into a whisper, "I don't know what to say." Her eyes moistened scanning in my direction. A lump tightened in my throat. Then Dad, with eyes bright and strong switched his gaze toward me,

"Mark, I couldn't believe she said it was cancer. *I didn't know whether to spit, wind my watch, or go blind.*"

For three seconds the world stopped. Then spontaneously, all three of us fragmented into timid laughter before finally letting go. Donna leaned across the bed and embraced Dad, gushing laughter while she cried, and then I joined them in the altogether bipolar-ish moment. In the blink of an eye, our father had lightened the most irreversibly bad report he had ever received—all to allay the unspeakable heavy burden that *he* felt we were bearing.

Having found out that Dad had cancer, our focus turned toward getting him the best treatment possible.

We already knew that we were in management mode rather than "cure" mode, but we weren't sure how it would look.

Over the next few days, we pulled together a plan, thanks to wonderful advice from Dr. Perez and her team of doctors. Dad would undergo 14 to 20 radiation treatments on the large tumor to shrink it, and provide relief from pain for several months, and maybe even a year. It was not a cure, but would at least allow him the best possible quality of life. Dad understood the treatment was only palliative in nature, but nevertheless, gave it the green light. Never had the value of time meant so much to me. I could not waste a minute of it.

Shuttle Service

The air was warm and the sky threatened rain as I rolled him in a wheelchair toward the truck parked at the entrance of The Oaks. It was way too warm and humid for the long sleeve shirt I was wearing, I thought to myself.

"Dad, you wanna take off your jacket before you get in the truck? It's really warm today. You might get too hot."

"No, Bud, I'm a little chilly this morning. I'll be fine." I helped him stand up and step away from the wheelchair but noticed how much he still wanted to do for himself. Locating the grip at the top of the truck cab he swung himself into the passenger seat with very little help from me. His arthritis-gnarled hands hadn't lost much of its ability to grip. I collapsed the wheelchair and loaded it into the narrow cab space behind our seats. When I climbed in I saw that he had buckled his seat belt, put on his sunglasses, and was facing forward, his right hand still firmly grasping the grip just above the door.

"Looks like you're ready to go, Dad," I quipped.

"Yeah boy," he responded with cheerful resolve. "Let's get this show on the road." It was his first radiation treatment ordered just a day after leaving the hospital.

"Are you ready for this?" I asked. "Any second guessing?"

"No, I'm looking forward to it. I'm looking forward to some relief." It wasn't his first time to deal with pain. Twenty-seven years earlier he had suffered a massive heart attack, and two years later brain surgery just behind his right ear to repair an excruciatingly painful condition known as *Tic Douloureux* or Trigeminal Neuralgia.

"Well Dad, if you can survive a heart attack and brain surgery, you can handle this," I encouraged.

"You know, Mark, as bad as the heart attack was I have never felt pain like Tic Douloureux," he said firmly. "When that pain started, and I never knew when it would hit me, it made me look forward to dying."

"Oh, I remember it well, Dad. There was one night when you had taken all of the family out to eat at Lloyds Restaurant and the pain hit you. You stood out in front of the restaurant and gripped the aluminum light post so tightly you put a dent in it."

"I remember that," he recalled. "That was the night I told your mother that I had to do something about it or God was going to have to take me on to heaven."

"Peggy and I came to visit you after that brain surgery," I added. "When we saw you shaking and barely able to walk, I thought they had messed you up forever."

"It took me almost a month to re-learn how to walk and brush my teeth and feed myself," he reminded me.

"So, it was that much worse than the heart attack?" I asked again.

"Oh yeah. But the heart attack wasn't a bed of roses. It happened on December 19, 1985. Your mother had gone to Anniston for a day of Christmas shopping with Donna. It was a Thursday, and I was off that afternoon, hoping to get some work done around the house. I was in the backyard trying to get the old push mower to start. I'll bet I pulled that crank cord fifty times when all of the sudden I felt a ton of pressure hit my chest, like two locomotives meeting head-on inside of me. I knew what it was. You know my Papa had the same thing happen at about the same age, and it killed him."

"How did you get from the backyard to the phone?" I inquired.

"I don't really remember. I could hardly breathe, and recall stumbling through the back door into the den and grabbing the phone. I called your Uncle Led because I figured he was home. When he answered I could barely whisper, *'Led, help me, it's my heart.'* I remember him saying on the phone, *'Is that you, Coolidge?'*"

"As soon as I could make my way out the carport door Led was there. He drove as fast as he could across town to the ER. All I remember saying was, *'Hurry Led, hurry.'*"

"Dad, Uncle Led saved your life," I said.

"He sure did, and I've thanked him a hundred times for it," he declared.

"Donna has told me that when she and Mom got back from Anniston that afternoon they saw your car, and noticed doors standing wide open, but couldn't find you. Mom knew something was wrong. About then the phone rang, and it was Donna Bickerstaff from the Ashland Pharmacy on the line.

"Donna, Coolidge has had a heart attack. It's bad, so y'all need to get down to the hospital now."

"Lordy, Lordy, I'll bet their trip to the ER was an emotional circus," Dad said with a chuckle.

"Oh, yeah, Gail Freeman was waiting on them at the hospital doors. Donna said that Mom ran ahead of her down that long hall to the CCU in a panic asking, *'Is he dead? Is he dead?'*"

"No I wasn't dead, but I came mighty close. Me and Jesus had more than a few conversations during that time, Son, I'll guarantee you; not because I wasn't ready for heaven, it's just that I wasn't ready to leave earth yet! But God was gracious to me and has given me many more years of life, able to see my grandchildren and two great-grandchildren. It's just that I've had to live these twenty some odd years half-heartedly."

"Half-heartedly?" I reacted.

"The doctor said that the back half of my heart muscle is dead. So I'm living with half-a-heart," he jibed with a curious smile. It wasn't the first time I'd heard him say that. Actually, I think I had heard it at least fifty times before, but I still wanted to hear it again like it was the first time.

"Well, Dad, your half-a-heart doesn't seem to have slowed you down one little bit!"

On the way home from the radiation therapy treatment we stopped for a well-deserved cup of frozen yogurt. Opting not to go through the process of having Dad climb in and out again, we sat in the truck while we enjoyed our sweet treat. In between spoonfuls of cold delight he commented,

"Mark, you've had a couple of pretty serious brushes with fate yourself." I assumed he was referring to a brain aneurysm I had experienced four years earlier. They were able to remove it before it burst, but it was a very scary time for me, and required an extended period of recovery.

"Yeah, anytime they remove a part of your skull and then put it back, it's not a walk in the park," I responded.

"You better believe it," Dad said. "But that's not the only time you've been on the edge of eternity. When you were only six weeks old you nearly died from the whooping cough."

"I remember Mom telling me about it," I said. "But I was obviously too young to remember it."

"I've never seen a baby as sick as you were. You would cough until you turned blue and couldn't breathe. We had to hold you twenty-four hours a day so that when you had a coughing spell, we could toss you up in the air to catch your breath. A lot of babies died from whooping cough in those days, and we were frantic."

"Sorry, I didn't mean to scare you guys so badly," I quipped to lighten the moment. However, Dad was so wrapped up in the story, he never heard me.

"Your mother refused to leave your side for days, but I made her take a break because she was so exhausted," he continued. "Your grandparents and Sadie Thompson and your Aunt Charlotte took turns during the days and nights to allow your mother and me to get some rest, but they were terrified that you might quit breathing on their watch. It was a harrowing experience for all of us.

Finally, a pharmaceutical salesman from Birmingham who knew our situation called me and told me about a promising new medicine their company had just acquired. It was an answered prayer because you were getting worse by the day. That same hour they rushed the order to me, putting the medicine on a Greyhound bus traveling from Birmingham to Columbus, Georgia. I paid a young teenager to jump on his motorcycle and intercept the bus on highway 280 near Goodwater and bring the medicine back to Ashland. Within six hours of your first dose, you were on the mend."

"Wow," I responded, unable to think of anything else to say. Then, scraping the last of the chocolate yogurt from the bottom of the Styrofoam bowl he said,

"Four years ago when you had that brain aneurysm, I sat in the surgery waiting room and remembered your battle with whooping cough fifty something years earlier. I was there with Peggy and your girls putting up a strong front, but deep inside it was like you were my little boy again, and I needed to do something to keep from losing you. I wanted to pay some teenager to jump on his motorcycle and bring back the miracle cure, but all I could do was pray and trust the Lord. I remember thinking that I don't know how I could handle it if you didn't make it through. I was so afraid you would see Marylyn in Heaven before I did. Fathers are not supposed to outlive their children, you know."

Treasures

I couldn't wait to return to The Oaks the next evening. I had in my possession the Bible that Dad had used throughout my childhood. I had seen it in his hands every Sunday as far back as I remember and had watched him use it personally. I remember seeing it on the table beside his easy chair and saw him underlining verses and jotting notes in it countless times. When his eyes demanded reading glasses in his fifties, he began using a more up-to-date translation with a larger type.

The original Bible found a new home on the top shelf in the den. I found it several years later on a visit to home and borrowed it. Because I had chosen to enter ministry, Dad told me to keep it. Now, years later, it represented more to me than a leather-bound King James Version of the Bible. It reminded me of my family's Christian heritage, my father's devotion to Christ, and of the great value, I was taught to place on the Word of God.

Driving on the back road to The Oaks my mind was flooded with memories of my father's faith, and of his powerful impact on every part of my life. From my earliest days as a child, I remember a mealtime custom at the Sims house that has always remained with me. At the beginning of every meal Dad thanked God for the food, and at the close of the meal, he thanked Mom for preparing it. It went beyond that. My brother, sister, and I could not leave the table until we thanked her as well. Conversely, if we ever went out to eat, Mom would thank Dad for the special treat, and we were expected to respond in kind.

Sometimes we failed in fulfilling our duty at mealtime. I recall the times when I would be in a hurry, jump up from the table, only to hear Dad say, *"What's the hurry?"* or *"Wha'da ya say, Son?"* If my response was, *"Oh, yeah, thanks,"* as I selfishly charged out of the room, things did not go down well. But if I stopped and said a simple *"thank you"* from my heart, all was well.

When I was about ten years old I attended Bible School at our local Baptist Church, and for the first time inquired about accepting Christ as my Savior. I remember the Pastor came to my house that night, but it was my father who knelt with me at the couch and led me in the prayer of salvation. It was my father who let me know how proud he was that I was being baptized, and who gave me his total support when I chose to enter ministry as my life calling.

Just as I turned onto the drive leading up to The Oaks I remembered one particular evening when our church pastor came to our house late in the evening. I was already in the bed, but I could hear everything that was being said just down the hall. He had come to let them know that he was leaving to pastor another church. My parents were disappointed but accepted his decision with grace. I don't remember many of the details, but I do remember one thing Pastor Bob Curlee said,

"Coolidge, you have been a very good friend to me here, and I respect you so much. In fact, I don't think I've ever worked with a finer Christian man than you."

Sitting in my truck that evening I recalled the pride I felt as a ten-year-old in knowing that my Dad was considered the best of the best. It had to be so—the preacher said it. Working my way through the halls clutching the Bible he had given me years before, I entered room 138.

"Dad, are you awake?"

"Hi Bud," I heard him say from the bathroom. "It's about time you showed up." Carefully he made his way with his walker out of the bathroom sporting his Auburn cap and matching shirt. "You about ready to go eat supper with me?" We walked together to the dining hall and took a seat at an empty table.

"I'm not real hungry tonight, Mark," he declared. "I think I'll just get some soup and crackers."

"Sounds good. I think I'll do the same, Dad." Waiting for our soup to arrive, I laid my heart bare. "Dad, a lot of people complain about how their parents forced them to go to church against their will. I'm the opposite. I am so grateful that you made church attendance a priority for our family—not a choice."

"Your mother and I knew it was best for our family to be faithful to the Lord, and you can't do that without being a part of a church," Dad responded.

"It wasn't just that, Dad. I was always proud that my Dad was a respected leader in the church—not ashamed to take a leading role. And we didn't bounce from church to church when things didn't go your way. You kept us in a stable spiritual environment."

"Yes, church hoppers always bothered me," he explained. "It's not right to shop churches to get the best deal like it's a car dealership. It's selfish. I think committing to a church family is like marriage—it should be permanent unless someone moves, or experiences something out of the ordinary, not just because they don't like this pastor or the music. That's how I've always felt about it."

"I remember as a kid pestering you, asking if we *had* to stay for *big church*," (In those days there was no children's church service, all kids moved from their Sunday School class into *big church* and sat with their parents.) "but you always said, '*don't ask me that again, or I'll have to spank you.*' We were there almost every time the church doors were open, and I don't resent it one bit."

"You weren't the only one. Your brother and sister went through that stage too. But we didn't let you get your way. If we had have, it would have caused more problems down the road," he postulated. "And you also got in trouble from your mother a few times in *big church*."

"I sure did! Remember the time I got in trouble for laughing at Mrs. Blackstock?" Dad laughed, immediately recalling the event.

"I'll have to admit, I laughed too. You were sitting down front with your Grandma Nichols. Lucille Blackstock, one of the pianists, was sitting on the pew in front of you. The song service was over, but she was just sitting there staring straight ahead. She did that a lot. A little housefly landed on the open hymn book she still held in her hand. She stared at the fly while it moved around on the page, and then suddenly slammed the hymnal shut—crushing the poor fly. You burst out laughing aloud. Mrs. Nichols put her hand over your mouth, and your mother looked your direction with all kinds of embarrassment."

"Oh, I remember the look she gave me. I knew I was dead meat when I got home," I added. Dad was almost teary eyed with laughter.

"I saw the whole thing happen," he chuckled. "It was the funniest thing I have ever seen!" We took our time to relive it all one more time before I returned to our conversation.

"I developed my spiritual foundation at the First Baptist Church. I loved our church, Dad. There were so many opportunities there for us, especially as teenagers. My social life revolved around the church; my best friends were from the church; my best memories are from the church; I was inspired to go into the ministry because of the church. I think I wanted to be a preacher because of Bob Curlee—and I was only eight or nine when he was our pastor."

Dad was not just a church member; he was a "churchman." And being a pastor myself, I respected him even more for it.

Hey Peetey

I showed him his old Bible and called his attention to a couple of the notes he had written in it. One conversation led to another and before long we found ourselves talking about the fear of death.

"When you were young, Dad, do you remember a time when you thought you might die?" I asked candidly.

"Not really, at least not until I went in the army. It was during the Battle of the Bulge, the winter of 1944, the Germans counterattacked and pushed our lines back."

"What happened that was so scary?"

"Some Nazi paratroopers had landed in our area and we were on high alert for over a week. At nighttime, we took turns on guard duty for several hours on a road spanning about a mile. I was scared to death, and it was exhausting. We were soldiers running an army hospital, not infantrymen." Dad slurped a couple of mouthfuls of tomato soup out of the oversized spoon in his right hand, followed by his left hand shoving an entire saltine cracker into his mouth.

"That would send chills up the spine of any twenty-one-year-old!" I commented. Still reliving the moment he took a quick sip of milk and continued,

"There was this one particular night when it was cold, really cold, and I had sentry duty in the middle of the night. I was bundled up the best I could, but I had no gloves. That cold rifle I was carrying made me feel like my fingers were about to freeze and shatter onto the ground. And it was dark that night; so dark, with cloudy skies hiding the moon and stars. Of course, it was my luck to be assigned sentry duty in the eighth of a mile farthest from the unit. The whole time I kept thinking about the report we'd received the day before about an ambush incident not five miles away from us, and Son, I'll tell you now, I was praying like a sinner with one foot in hell." Dad's eyes were fixed straight ahead but focused on nothing particular. He resumed his story,

"'*Who goes there?*' I barked when I thought I heard something in the shadows. I can still feel the hair on the back of my neck standing straight up. 'Who goes there,' I said a second time, squinting at first and then opening my eyes as wide as possible, trying to locate movement in the dark. I remember thinking how scared I was—not feeling the least bit brave.

A few seconds later I heard something—a faint cracking sound, like someone trying to walk lightly on the graveled road, but I still couldn't tell where it was coming from. I just knew that whoever it was could surely hear my heart pounding like a drum. I could feel it too like it was about to come right out of my chest. I imagined a German paratrooper sneaking-up on me, and then pictured in my mind's eye several of them coming from every direction. Then I heard it again, only this time from behind me. I spun around and clutched my loaded rifle, on the cusp of firing a warning shot into the air. 'Stop, or I'll shoot,' I yelled.

'Hey, Hey Peetey!' A familiar voice pierced the darkness. It was too late to stop the adrenaline rush through my body. I felt my once frozen finger suddenly become warm as the blood coursed through my veins and into my hands. There was only one person in the world that ever called me Peetey.

'Johnny Wise, I ought to shoot you! You scared the living devil out of me."

'It's two o'clock, I'm here to relieve you,' Johnny said, clueless of the terror I had just endured.

'I said, who goes there?'—twice!' What's wrong with you, fool!'

'I guess I didn't hear you. I was looking for my cigarettes,' he muttered while lighting up a Lucky Strike. 'You can get some sleep now, Peetey.' Still irritated I fired back,

'Thanks to you Johnny, I've got to go back now and check my britches. And I probably won't be able to fall asleep for days.' I made my way back to my tent and stayed awake the rest of the night."

That night we talked about a lot of things over tomato soup and crackers. Dad explained why he cringes when people call him a hero. He didn't think of himself as a hero, but as a young American doing his patriotic duty.

"We were all the same," he said. "I didn't do anything special. I was as scared as the rest of them." Recognizing his innate modesty, I replied,

"It all sounds pretty heroic to me." We were the last to leave the dining hall. On the way back to the room I asked,

"Why in the world did Johnny Wise call you Peetey?"

"I don't know. He just did. He gave everyone a random nickname. Back in the day a lot of people did that. Granddaddy Sims gave all 13 of his children nicknames totally different from their real names, and a few of his grandchildren too. And some of them stuck for a lifetime, like my cousin—Hop Sims. "Hop" is not really his name."

"Wow. Are you kidding! What's his real name?"

"I have no idea," Dad said with a chuckle.

"A Father is a son's first hero; a daughter's first love."
Unknown

Chapter Seven

Since Memorial Day was approaching at the end of the month, The Oaks scheduled me to give a special talk to the residents about World War II. Most of them were alive during the war and clamored to celebrate their memories.

I taught American history for years at Kingwood Christian School and was glad to volunteer for the task. I planned to make it interactive, asking questions about specific memories, instead of lecturing. I knew that if no one else interacted with me, I could count on Dad. After all, the role Dad played in American history was actually my number one connection to him, as it had been all my life.

As I filled up the truck's gas tank I began thinking about my lifelong desire to make my father proud. I'm sure every dad's son has similar thoughts, but that didn't take away my own struggle to earn his approval. I was never good at athletics, and I didn't enjoy many of the things that he enjoyed with my older brother. I'm sure it wasn't true, but I always felt something lacking in my relationship with Dad.

In my teenage years, I defied his authority in ways my brother did not, and I even challenged him verbally on a few occasions. I assumed some things about him that proved not to be true, and I'm confident that I hurt him in believing them. But the one thing that we were always on the same page about was his service to his country. I had him speak to my high school history classes on multiple occasions, I honored him on Veterans Day at my church, and I even had someone who was returning from Europe to bring me a vial of sand from Utah Beach in Normandy where he landed.

In 2006, on the eve of my 50th birthday, I came up with my big idea.

My Big Idea

For a year, Peggy had been hinting around at what special gift or celebration would be best for my fiftieth birthday. She's a planner so waiting until the last minute to arrange an April 2006 shindig would be out of the question. I usually dream big, so I began to mull over what would be the most memorable way to celebrate the big five-0.

Ever since Mom died in 1999, I had tried to make sure I kept in touch with Dad in Ashland often—with a weekly phone conversation at least. It was during one of those phone calls that I first got the big idea. Dad and I were recounting, as we often did, his time in the army during World War II. It was like he remembered every step he took from the day he landed on a Normandy beach, through northern France, and all the way to Frankfurt, Germany and beyond. I've heard it a thousand times and could almost picture it—almost, but not really.

Eureka! Why not take a short trip with Dad to France—beginning in Normandy and trace his path right into Germany? It would be the best possible 50th birthday for me, and for Dad a way to *show me* exactly what he had *told me* about my whole life. It was one of those *Ah Ha!* moments; an *epiphany* of sorts; a *dream come true* idea—a bonding event for the father I admired so much but had struggled to be close to all my growing up years. It could be my gift to Dad. It was our common ground. I was the history teacher and he was the guy who had lived history. It was perfect!

I couldn't wait to put the plan together and tell Dad about it. I got out the maps and created a 6-day dream trip. Dad was going to be thrilled! He would be beside himself. It would solve any relational problems we had with one another, past or present. I made up a reason to travel to Ashland and tell him about my big idea. And I did. He sat quietly in his favorite recliner as I explained the whole plan to him. Afterward, there was a moment of silence as his eyes wandered around the room. I could tell he was searching for what to say, and how to say it. His reaction was not what I was expecting. Without looking at me straight in the eye, he rambled his way through it:

"Son, that sounds like a great plan, and I appreciate the invitation. I think *you* should go, but I don't really want to go back there. At one point your mother and I talked about taking the same trip, but her health wasn't up to it so we decided against it. I had always told myself that if I couldn't take Marylyn with me, I wouldn't want to go at all.

Besides, Mark, the war was over 60 years ago so I probably wouldn't be able to recognize anything, anyway. I think I'd rather remember it the way it was the *first* time—and it might be a little bit too emotional for me right now.

Son, I have three children, two daughters-in-law, a son-in-law, and seven grandchildren to live for. I think I'd rather spend my remaining time with them, and not with the French. They never seemed to like me anyway. I appreciate it, but the Lord let me survive one tour in Europe, and that was enough."

Dad was right. We can live life only once. Re-living it is impossible. By the way, I stayed home for my 50th. Dad got to celebrate with me, and with all the family—in Alabama.

Honor and Respect

I arrived early enough to make sure Dad was ready for the 10 a.m. gathering. I strolled into the room and there he sat, all decked-out in a red, white, and blue patriotic shirt and a USA baseball cap from Honor Flight. The only thing missing was a fireworks display.

One of the highlights of his retirement years was the Honor Flight trip to the World War II Memorial in Washington. The Honor Flight organization paid for thousands of vets from the all over the country to make the one-day trek to Washington while they were still able. Coolidge Sims proudly stood with other vets from Alabama who were honored for their service to their country.

I will always remember the crowd of baby boomers who gathered at the Birmingham International Airport that day to welcome their fathers and grandfathers home from the well-deserved trip. We all cheered and waved American flags as they deplaned and made their way down the concourse toward us. Dad wasn't the only one shedding tears as they heard us cheering. Later he told the family that it was one of the proudest days in his life. It's something he had never experienced. The honor from a grateful nation was well overdue.

Our planned gathering for the World War II generation at The Oaks was well attended, and the patriotic residents reveled in it. I asked questions like,

"Where were you when you first heard Pearl Harbor had been bombed?" and "Did you lose any friends or family in the war?"

The responses were many and their memories were quite sharp. Dad participated but didn't dominate the discussion by any means. There were plenty of stories and opinions.

One really sharp, well-spoken lady told of special prayer meetings that were regularly held in local churches to pray for our soldiers. It caused me to remember my mom saying that she and her friends in college, and later while working a job, often went to church to pray for the soldiers during lunch breaks. Mom said that first on her list of soldiers to pray for was always Coolidge.

I *did* call on Dad to tell a couple of his stories, and he relished it. There was one that stood out to his peers in the room.

"After my unit landed on Utah Beach, we walked about three-quarters of a mile inland and dug trenches, foxholes, and set up a field hospital—now called M.A.S.H. units. The next day we went into a little French town called St. Mary's Eligse.

You may remember a movie about the D-day Invasion called, "The Longest Day." I believe John Wayne, Henry Fonda, and Eddie Albert were some of the actors that starred in it. There was a scene where an American paratrooper's parachute got hung-up on top of the tall steeple of the Catholic Church in St. Mary's Eligse. The American paratrooper was just hanging there helplessly when a German soldier shot and killed him. Well, that was a true event. I saw the remains of that tattered parachute still flapping in the wind on the steeple at St. Mary's Eligse."

One thing was obvious—those seasoned octogenarians knew their American history, and greatly valued the price of freedom. It's a lesson for us all. I felt pride that my father was one of those. He reminded me that when his time came, he preferred a flag draped casket and the playing of Taps.

Cheeseburgers

After the event, we decided to make a day of it by going out to eat lunch on the way to radiation therapy. Dad craved a really good cheeseburger for lunch, so we made plans to search for best possible burger joint. In Ashland, it would be the Blue and White Barbecue without question. They serve the best cheeseburger and fries in Alabama, but alas, we were seventy miles away from cheeseburger perfection. At the last minute, we settled for the Sonic drive-in, postponing our search for Birmingham's perfect cheeseburger to another day.

Sitting in the little Nissan truck at Sonic we began a random conversation about the earliest memories of life. My earliest memory was seeing Papa Sims' hunting dogs in the back of his truck. I remember being scared silly by their incessant barking.

"Mark, do you remember my father at all?" he asked. "You were really young when he died."

"I remember the dogs in the truck, but not Papa Sims. What I *do* remember is you holding me up to see him lying in a casket. I remember thinking how soft the white pillow looked. I believe the casket was in Mama Sims' house, correct?"

"Yes, it sure was," he recalled. Back then it was normal to have visitation in the dead person's home, with the casket open in one of the rooms. You have a pretty good memory. That was in the summer of 1959."

"I was barely three years old."

"Well, if you remember that, then you probably remember when the Fox Hunter's Club honored Papa Sims with an outdoor cookout. They presented Mama Sims with a trophy that she kept on the mantle in the living room."

"Sorry, but that doesn't ring a bell," I admitted. "When you've seen one cookout, you've seen them all."

"Now I *definitely* remember that cookout," he informed me. "It was one of the most painful days of my life."

"What?" I asked.

"You were toddling around looking at things and I was supposed to be watching you. Suddenly I noticed that you were nowhere to be found. It scared me to death, especially since the cookout was held near a lake. I didn't alarm your mother, but I ran around trying to find you.

When I saw you at the edge of the woods I was so relieved, until I noticed that you were standing right under a hornet's nest! I could see that you had disturbed them and they were preparing to attack. I ran and scooped you up just in time, but I got hit by a couple of those angry hornets—right in the top of my head. I tossed you to Uncle Led who came when he saw the whole thing happening, while I swatted the hornets away from my head, but a third one popped me on the cheek bone."

"Dad, you probably saved my life," I declared. "Multiple hornet stings can kill little babies."

"You'd better believe it," he replied. "And they nearly killed *me.*" That night had to be the most miserable one I've ever spent. My head was splitting, my face was throbbing; I had a fever, and was nauseated all night long. Hell couldn't be much worse than what I felt that night. I couldn't even go to work for a couple of days."

"I guess I owe you," I said to him. "Thanks for saving my life." Dad nodded in approval and then answered,

"Ok, you pay for the cheeseburger, and we'll be even."

"Deal"

Complications

Our trips to the radiology unit at Brookwood Hospital were not that onerous. The treatments didn't take long at all, and I was encouraged at how easy it was. The hardest part was just getting him in and out of the truck without falling.

As soon as we returned to The Oaks, Mike called me to find out the plan for the ongoing radiation treatment. He was mildly concerned that radiation therapy had forced them to take away his Lasix—a daily pill to keep fluid from gathering around his heart. But he also realized that continuing Lasix while taking radiation could lead to kidney damage. It was sort of a, "pick your poison" roulette. He pledged to give Dad's heart doctor a call. It's good having a brother who is a doctor and can translate med-talk into common English. After such an active morning, Dad took a much- needed mid-afternoon nap.

Donna dropped by to say hello even though it was her "day off". That's how it was with us in those days. It was hard to stay away, especially since we lived so close to The Oaks. Mike was three hours away, and a physician, so it was impossible for him to visit as often as he wanted. But we spoke with Mike often. He was our trusted medical expert available twenty-four hours a day, and we took advantage of it. Donna caught up on the cancer treatment plan and then moved on to her own plans for the upcoming holiday.

"Daddy, Allen and I want you to plan to spend Mother's Day with us next weekend." Mother's Day had been difficult for Dad ever since Mom died. I knew Donna wanted to occupy his mind on that day and not let him brood.

"Okay," he agreed softly. I wasn't sure if it was post-nap grogginess or something more ominous. He had displayed a poverty of words ever since he woke up.

"Is there anything you need, Daddy?" Donna asked.

"For what?"

"For anything," she pressed him.

"No, I can't think of anything I really need." His *far away* look concerned both of us. We wondered if the short radiation treatment he had today had adversely affected him. The specialist had downplayed the immediate side effects of radiation, and we knew Dad was not in robust health, but to see such a drastic change from the way he had started the day was disconcerting. Donna let me know she would give Mike a call from home.

The nurses helped us get Dad to bed early that night. Donna planned to return early on Saturday morning to check on him. I could expect a call from her then. We were both apprehensive about what was ahead of us.

Turnaround Saturday

My cell phone rang a few minutes after 8 o'clock on Saturday morning with the distinct *War Eagle* ringtone that told me Donna was calling.

"Hey, Donna. How is he this morning?"

"Well, I'm here with Dad, and he's all dressed up and chomping at the bit for his physical therapy session."

"I'm not sure they do PT on Saturday, Donna. You could ask at the nurses' desk."

"Good idea, I will do that, but I just wanted to call and let you know that Dad slept fine and got up this morning all bright eyed and bushy tailed. He's had his breakfast and we're either going to PT or we're going to visit for a while. Things are looking good." Her happy talk was simply code for, *Hallelujah! It isn't as bad as we thought last night.*

"Okay, great. Today I'm preparing my message for Sunday morning. Let Dad know that I'm using a story about him having to deal with me as a young teenager. Yep, he'll be front and center in the sermon at Kingwood Church this week."

"I'm sure he'll be delighted when I tell him!" Donna asserted.

"I'd love for him to come if he wants, and I'll let him tell the story himself," I offered.

"I'll ask him, no kidding. But I doubt if he'll want to help you preach—unless you want to pay him." We snickered a bit before ending the call.

I decided to drive back to The Oaks later in the day and see if he wanted to be my guest at church on Sunday. But lately, his preference seemed to be to avoid crowds, especially while having to use a walker. I doubted he would take me up on the invitation.

Not-So-Good Morning

Peggy and I dropped by to see Dad late on Saturday afternoon. He adored my wife Peggy from the first time he ever met her. Mom remembered him making the comment,

"Marylyn I sure hope Mark's smart enough to hold on to Peggy. She's a keeper!"

Dad was chipper and glad to see us but declined the invitation to join us at church on Sunday. He loved having company, especially family, but with his recent history of falls he was wary of going anywhere in public.

"I'm so glad y'all came by to see me. I took a nap after lunch, and when I woke up I had no idea where I was or what time it was. I must have dreamed something and woke up a little confused."

"Are you feeling better now," Peggy asked.

"Yeah, I got my bearings after a minute or two. I just sat here in my chair until I could figure it all out. I'm OK now."

"Dad, do you remember last summer when you went to Talladega at 7 o'clock at night, thinking it was 7 o'clock in the morning?" I figured that an interactive conversation might help him focus.

"I sure do." He spoke straight to Peggy as if she was the only one in the room.

"You see, I had fallen asleep watching golf on television and woke up about seven. I felt sort of *stove-up* so I thought I had slept all night in my recliner. I remembered that I had a dentist appointment in Talladega at 8 o'clock in the morning, and I thought I was going to be late. It takes me at least 20 minutes to get there, so I grabbed my billfold and jumped in the car and took off."

"You were headed west, did you not see the sun setting in front of you?" I asked.

"You know, I did think that was a little odd," he chuckled. "I got to Talladega about 8 o'clock, and nobody was at the dentist's office, so I called my sister Gwynnelle to make sure I was at the right place.

Gwynnelle scolded me, *'Coolidge, it's 8 o'clock at night! What's wrong with you? Have you gone crazy?'* I told her I probably had and then laughed for a minute. She thought I would come home right away, but I was hungry and decided to go to the Huddle House and get me something to eat. When I didn't show up when she thought I should, she started calling me. But I left my phone in the car while I was eating."

"Oh yeah," I interrupted. "She called me at home, flipping out. She was sure you had wrecked somewhere between Talladega and Ashland and might be helplessly lying in a ditch in the dark of night."

"And she sent Steve to look for me, too. He can't see at night to drive, much less to look for me." Dad perked up, laughing about the whole experience. Peggy just had to ask the question,

"Now Pop, what did you eat that night at the Huddle House?"

With a sheepish grin, he answered, "A big, fat breakfast, of course."

Greasy Hair, Silly Prayer

Dad wanted to know what story about him I was going to mention in my Sunday sermon. I revealed it, and he was entertained, but then he had a revelation of his own for me.

Here's the story that I shared in my sermon:

The year was 1970. I was 14 years old and needed help with life. Being the shortest kid in my class was hard enough to handle, but couple that with my inability to excel at anything athletic, and anyone will understand why I needed help. The eighth grade is ground zero for male insecurity. Everybody knows that everything matters in the eighth grade-- voice, wit, romance, odor, clothes, and especially HAIR.

In 1970 it was a guy's hair that told his story. The crew cuts and flat tops of the 50's and 60's were history, and guys were finally liberated to look like Jesus-- or at least like the Beatles. The coolest men on TV sported locks of hair down on their shoulders and plenty of facial hair. Add bell-bottom jeans, wide leather belts, and love beads and any guy could possess undisputed <u>coolness.</u>

Unfortunately, I was a 14-year-old shrimp with only a little facial fuzz and very traditional parents who thought long hair was a sign of satanic rebellion. I tried showing Dad multiple pictures of Jesus in my Sunday school quarterly to prove that long hair could be a godly look, but it was of no use. He wouldn't even let my hair creep over my ears, much less flow across my shoulders.

We were able to work out a compromise though. I WAS allowed to wear my hair down on my forehead like Paul McCartney, just so the back was neatly trimmed and the entire ear showed. He didn't like my "bangs" hovering over my eyes, but it was a compromise he was willing to accommodate-- especially when he noticed how many of my friends were actually chasing the Jesus look, while their parents were obviously looking the other way. For me, it was just the best I could get, even though I looked like a clean-cut guy with love beads around my neck and a brown possum resting on my forehead.

One normal Sunday morning as the Sims family was busy getting dressed for church, a crisis erupted in our pink tiled bathroom that ruined the entire day-- and could have ruined my entire life. I was meticulously working to get a thick swoosh of hair to rest perfectly on top of my eyebrows when I heard Mom bellow from the yellow bathroom,

"Where's my Aqua-Net?"

Aqua-Net was, of course, the hairspray of choice for moms everywhere. It was basically shellac in an aerosol can. It was the only way to guarantee that hair would stay in place all day-- no matter what. My mom had a ninety-mile an hour hairdo that lasted a week-- from Friday to Friday when she would again visit Hilda's beauty shop. Between Fridays, it was Aqua-Net that preserved the shape of Hilda's weekly sculpture on Mom's scalp.

"Mark's got it," my 7-year-old sister turned spy announced. That was NOT good news for my Dad to hear. Having been dressed and waiting impatiently for the last hour, Dad freaked out and made a beeline to the pink bathroom. In the mirror, I saw his eyebrows raised high as he barreled in-- man on a mission.

"No son of mine is going to primp in front of a mirror with a can of hairspray in his hand!" My normally cheerful Dad was really upset. "Follow me to my room," he barked jerking the Aqua-Net out of my hand. I obeyed but should have kept my big mouth shut.

"Come on Dad, what's the big deal?"

"If you don't know, I'm about to show you!" he answered without slowing down. I followed him into the yellow bathroom where Mom was getting ready. She didn't say a word as he handed her the Aqua-Net. Then Dad yanked the cabinet drawer open and pulled out a tube of Brylcreem. Brylcreem looked like a tube of toothpaste but was actually something used to slick down men's hair so that a comb could tame it. Brylcreem was an emulsion of water, mineral oil, and beeswax. It looked like lard and made hair look wet and greasy. No! This was 1970! The "dry look" was in.

He squirted a generous amount of Brylcreem into his hand (although the Brylcreem jingle said, "a little dab'll do ya.") and began working it into my scalp!

"No, Dad, please don't!" I begged. He grabbed his comb and began combing my thick bangs straight back across my head. I was mortified! I looked like my 60-year-old school principal. How could he be doing this to me? I could see that my Mom was disturbed. Somehow she knew this would not be good for my self-esteem.

"Coolidge, you don't have to do that," she said calmly.

"Oh yes I do," he retorted. "He's got to learn how to look like a man." Mom slipped out of the yellow bathroom without saying anything else, but her body language was loud and clear, 'Momma's not happy.'

Dad was defiant. "He'd better be glad I don't have scissors in my hand right now or I'd whack it ALL off."

The drive to church was silent. I was teary-eyed and pouting in the back seat with my sister staring at my face the whole way. I would have screamed at her to stop looking at me, but I was afraid to say anything that might make it worse. Mom just stared out the passenger seat window silently feeling my pain. I wished my brother was in the car for moral support, but he was away at college doing who knows what with his hair. Oh, the injustice!

Dad parked the big Buick in the church parking lot, but I didn't want to get out of the car. How in the world could I walk into the intermediate boys Sunday school class and face my friends looking like Conway Twitty? I was ruined. I was done for. I would be the laughing stock of the class today and of the school tomorrow. "Cool" would never define me, and no girl would ever want to 'go steady' with a greaser. But skipping Sunday school was not an option in the Sims household. Deep darkness crept in as I slowly made my way into the church and up the stairs. I hid in the bathroom for a few minutes just to gather my thoughts. I was already late, and at least two dozen of my friends would see me and gasp when I entered the room. Alas! My life was over!

"Oh God, help me!" I prayed in the boy's bathroom. It was a silly prayer to pray,
but suddenly I had an idea. It simply _had_ to work-- there was no other option.

I grabbed a broom from a corner in the men's bathroom and burst into the Sunday school room, using the broom as a microphone, singing,

"You ain't nothing but a hound dog; Cryin' all the time." Elvis had entered the room and they loved it; Brylcreemed hair and all. An insecure fourteen-year old survived because there is no such thing as a silly prayer.

Bathroom Humor

Dad got a kick out of the story. He remembered it, and pseudo-apologized for his strict hair policy in 1970. He had relaxed the rules by 1972. But he got the last laugh when he reminded me of another story that emanated from a bathroom in the Sims household.

"That's funny, Son, but do you remember the time you gave yourself a special acne treatment?"

"Oh yes, I think I know what you're talking about." He was definitely getting the best of me in this battle of the bathroom stories. Addressing Peggy he began his story,

"Peggy, one Saturday night Mark felt the need to give himself an acne treatment. He was about the same age as he was in the tale that he just told on me—maybe about thirteen years old. Like most teenagers, he was dealing with oily skin and clogged pores, and needed to give his face a good cleaning so that he would look really nice for church the next day."

Watching Dad tell that story made me think of the way Andy Griffith told tall tales in Mayberry. Like Andy Taylor on TV, his hands were in full motion and his voice was totally southern country sounding, and his face was fully animated. He was milking it for all it was worth as Peggy gave him her undivided attention.

"Now, there was a new product on the market that I sold at the pharmacy called Sea Breeze that was popular with young people. I don't know if it's still out there, but I sold a lot of it back then. It was advertised as something that would cleanse the skin of excess oil and help prevent acne. It had a glycerin and alcohol base, but also stuff like camphor, clove oil, peppermint, and fragrant things like that. It made your face sort of *tingle* and made the skin on your face feel tight and fresh." He sounded more and more like Andy Griffith as he continued,

"Mark was staring in the mirror working hard to get all that oil out of those clogged pores, justa' digging and swabbing and pampering himself really well. About that time Mike walked past the bathroom door and glanced in at Mark. Then he did a double take, and came and got me. Mike whispered,

'Dad, shhh; come with me. You won't believe what Mark is doing. You've got to see this.'

I followed him to their pink and blue tiled bathroom and peered in. I couldn't believe it either! Mark was holding a Kotex pad soaked in Sea Breeze, wiping it across his face!! He had no clue!

Mike and I started laughing and laughed so hard we could barely breathe. We were rolling on the floor, and poor Mark had no idea what he had done. Marylyn came to see what was so funny. She laughed a little at first, but she felt so sorry for Mark she had to take up for him. Mark said he found it in one of the cabinets and thought the feminine napkin was perfect for applying Sea Breeze.

Marylyn admitted that she probably needed to have a *little talk* with Mark."

I had actually relayed that story to Peggy before, but Dad enjoyed telling so much, I didn't want to stop him. We were especially glad that he was feeling good enough to be his old self and enjoy a good laugh. His discomfort was getting more evident, and he often suffered from exhaustion, weakness, and nausea at night. Happy evenings like this one were becoming more and more rare.

"My father used to play with my brother and me in the yard. Mother would come out and say,
'You're tearing up the grass.'
'We're not raising grass,' Dad would reply.
'We're raising boys.'"
Harmon Killebrew

Chapter Eight

I was anxious to see how things had gone for Dad over the weekend so I made the trek to The Oaks again on Monday morning. My truck's air conditioner was barely keeping up with the heat, and it was only nine o'clock. But there was no time today to have the AC looked at by a mechanic, so I asked God to heal it of its infirmity—and I was not joking. It was already getting mighty hot in Alabama.

Coffee Talk

I found Dad in his room, dressed, and sitting in his still un-reclined recliner. He was perfectly still, head bowed forward, giving me a moment of pause at his lifeless appearance. To reassure myself I crept forward listening for a sound or sign of breathing. My tennis shoes made an eerie squeaking noise on some moisture on the floor, arousing him to my presence in the room. When his eyes finally focused on me, I whispered in a low voice,

"Good morning Sir." Relieved that he was only napping, I feared that the staff had just finished mopping something up—hoping that it was not an indication that Dad's nausea had made an early appearance.

"Hey, Bud!" he whispered. I could tell he had been napping for more than a few minutes. "I guess I didn't get my sleep out, and I didn't get my coffee yet either."

"No morning coffee?" I asked. "Have you had breakfast yet?"

"Yeah, I asked the orderly to bring me a tray in here because I wasn't dressed yet. He did, but then I bumped into it and spilled my coffee on the floor. Poor guy, I caused him a ton of trouble this morning." Embarrassed at his morning mishap, I became his priest in the confessional booth. Absolution was quick.

"That's no big deal, Dad. Did you eat some breakfast?"

"A little bit. And I drank my juice."

"But you need your coffee! I remember you having a cup of coffee almost every morning at Horn's Café with Arthur Junior Hardegree and Clarence Junior Pruet. I'll see what I can do to get you a cup."

(I don't know what it is about the South, but we love to insert the title *Junior* in between the first name and the sir name instead of at the end. As is true about so many Southern things, there is no explanation. It is what it is.)

Drug Dealers

About that time a morning nurse came in to give him his meds. "Mr. Sims, the pharmacist has arrived!" she said playfully. "I know you were the pharmacist for all those years—now it's my turn." Dad countenance lit up.

"Why, I swanny, Mark. My drug dealer has arrived!" She giggled.

"You know, he always jokingly called himself a pill pusher," I announced. "Once we were stuck in traffic while leaving an Auburn football game, and some weird panhandler holding some carnations in his hand came up to our car and tapped on the window. Dad rolled the window down and the guy said, *'Will you buy this flower to help get kids off drugs?'* Dad didn't trust him for a minute, *'Heck no, Buddy, I <u>sell</u> drugs,'* then he rolled the window up on his carnation!"

"Mr. Sims! You are something else!" the nurse erupted. Dad, now fully involved, continued my story,

"Well, my wife was furious at me for doing that. She said, *'Coolidge! What must that man think of you?'* I said, *'Marylyn, I don't give a rats tail what he thinks of me!'*" We all laughed heartily. Dad had perked up; being more like himself. He asked her to get someone to bring a replacement cup of coffee if she could.

"Why sure, Mr. Sims! I'll bring you some coffee if you'll take these pills for me."

"Well that's a deal I can't turn down!" he replied genially. Like a good soldier, he swallowed them all and sent her off to fetch his much-needed caffeine. I kept the conversation alive taking him back to his years at the Ashland Pharmacy.

Pharmacy Fun

"Dad, some of the best memories I have are from being at the pharmacy, especially with Mrs. Richardson. She was one of a kind."

"You know she worked for me for about twenty years. She was a great employee, but she was so much fun to work with. She went by "Peggy" Richardson, but her real name was Enis. She had two sisters—Eunice and Exa."

"Eunice, Enis, and Exa," I commented, "Her parents ought to be whipped."

"Yeah, the girls didn't like their names either, so they all used nicknames. Hers was "Peggy." There was a widower who went to high school with her, named Q.P. McKay that came in the store pretty often. He would greet her with, 'Hello there Miss Enis!' It would irritate her to no end!"

"She was hilarious," I recalled. "I remember a lady coming in the store that wore her legs like parentheses—severely bow-legged. Mrs. Richardson and I were watching her waddle out of the store after she had purchased her monthly supply of laxatives when I asked, 'I wonder why she is so bow-legged?' She quipped, 'Well, it's no wonder, 'cause she's been dodging Metamucil for years.'"

Dad loved talking about pharmacy days. "Mark, do you remember that day Miss Bama Huntley came in to buy some deodorant?"

"I'm not sure." My face expressed curiosity.

"Miss Bama was a woman from up on the mountain who didn't come in often. When she did, she would just announce what she wanted. No talk. No discussion. On that day she said to Mrs. Richardson, *'I want some d'odrunt.'* Once Mrs. Richardson figured out what she was saying, she was thrilled to help her, knowing that deodorant would make an excellent addition to Miss Bama's daily routine. Peggy Richardson showed her several options, including an item that was popular with the older ladies—Five Day Deodorant Pads. They were inexpensive and convenient.

Miss Bama responded, *'Naw, you know I can't hold them thangs under my arms for five days and get my chores done.'"*

That was just the beginning. We spent over an hour talking about life at Ashland Pharmacy, going from one funny story to another, both of us upping the ante with each tale.

"Remember Nellie Hicks?" he asked.

"I sure do. I think she lived up in the hills near Miss Bama."

"Yes, she did," he said. "Of course, I sold all kinds of stuff at the drug store, including a few gifts. Miss Nellie came in looking for something for a Christmas gift for her grandson. I showed her a small battery operated reel-to-reel tape recorder that she might be interested in. (It was before the days of cassette tape recorders.) She bought it on the spot. We gift wrapped it for her and she left happy.

But in early January she showed up again as mad as an old wet hen, complaining that the tape recorder didn't work at all. I examined it and saw that it had no batteries. I quizzed her about batteries, and she shot back, *'Batt'ries? Batt'ries? It didn't say nothing about batt'ries.'* Then pulling a basketball pump out of a paper sack she said, *'I got one of these like it said, and tried pumping it up, but it didn't work."* Miss Nellie had somehow found instructions for using a basketball pump and thought it was for the tape recorder! I gave her some free batteries for all her trouble, and waited until she left before we could laugh out loud."

"Remember that life-sized cardboard cutout you had?" I asked, hoping to jog his memory. "It was the one with the girl in the bathing suit holding a Polaroid camera in her hand?" Dad's eyes lit up and he began to shake his head up and down, chuckling several times before he could say anything.

"Oh yes! Stanley Smith and I put that cutout in the little bathroom we had in the back of the store. We put it behind the door so that it couldn't be seen until someone had closed the door and pulled the light cord hanging from the fixture in the ceiling. Every time a drug company salesman came for a visit and asked to use the restroom, I would take him to the back and point toward the little bathroom. Then Stanley and I would get close enough to hear him holler when he closed the door and turned the light on. It got 'um every time!"

The Ashland Pharmacy was one of the gathering places for the men in town to laugh, tell tall tales, and carry on conversations about everyday things. Any number of men might show up at different times during the day to fraternize. Pete Matthews, Edgar Wynn, Walt Hill, and Everett Willis were the regulars—known as "The Chairmen."

Dad recalled a prank that they played on Mrs. Richardson during one of their random gatherings—one that I have heard him tell countless times. Still, I wanted to hear him tell it again.

"Mark, one afternoon Everett Willis, Walt Hill and I were sitting in those wicker chairs out front laughing and carrying-on when we overheard Peggy Richardson in a friendly conversation with a customer. She was showing off a fancy new wool sweater that she had just received as a Mother's day gift from her son who lived in Florida. She was as proud as a peacock that her son Billy had picked out such a beautiful and expensive gift for her. She admitted that it was too showy to wear to church where the members might

think she was being pretentious, so she wore it to work instead.

The Charimen began teasing her about how high her salary must be to own such an extravagant cashmere sweater. They went on and on about how 'uppity' she looked wearing such a sophisticated garment to work. She laughed and played along beautifully with their joking and kidding, enjoying every minute of it. Meanwhile, I slipped out and went next door the Five and Dime Store where I bought a little bottle of disappearing ink—a gag toy I had heard you beg for days earlier.

'Mrs. Richardson,' I said returning from my secret errand. 'Will you please hold this inkpad open for me while I refresh the ink? It will only take a minute.'

'Okay,' she said curiously as she took the pad from me. I fiddled with the inkbottle for a couple of seconds and then 'accidently' squirted a long stream of blue ink all over her pastel pink and white wool showpiece. She was thunderstruck! Speechless!

'Well now you've done it!' she exclaimed, madder than a mule chewing on bumblebees!

My fake, lame apology attempt quickly morphed into a little grin, and then into a full giggle. She was even more shocked at my odd behavior.

'Coolidge, I don't think there's anything funny about ANY of this!'

'What are you talking about, Mrs. Peggy?' Walt whined as he switched his cigar from one side of his mouth to the other. Incensed, she turned to show him the ink stain, and then noticed that the stain wasn't there.

'Well, I don't see the problem,' Everett confirmed. She was incredulous at its disappearance. A few tense seconds of silence erupted into a cavalcade of belly laughs as I showed her the magic ink trick. She got the biggest kick out of it, and laughed about it all day long. Later she told me,

'Coolidge, you better be glad it was disappearing ink, or I'd a had to kick you straight to Abraham's bosom.'"

Michael Time

Late in the morning, I received a call from Mike that his son, Michael, was on his way to Birmingham to see Dad. Michael, his first grandson, was in medical school in Georgia and wanted to spend a couple of days with his Papaw before his wedding in July. Dad was overjoyed that Michael was coming. It seemed to lift Dad's spirits and lifted Donna's and mine as well.

Dad's issues with balance, exhaustion, nausea, and nighttime confusion had taken a toll on us. Dad's care was requiring more time and effort than the level of assistance that The Oaks could provide in that particular unit, so Donna and I were trying to fill the gap. Michael is much like Dad—witty and conversational. Michael's visit, I avowed, could not have come at a better time.

Dad was taking a long afternoon nap when Michael arrived. By the time Dad woke up, he had forgotten altogether that Michael was coming. Looking wild-eyed and confused, he finally got his bearings enough to engage in conversation. Michael, in true form, knew just how to bring out the best in Dad. Together they decided to take a drive and get an early supper —anything to take a break from the same four walls.

It took forever to get Dad's shoes on and creep down the hall, and finally outside to the car. Michael quickly learned how difficult it is to get a man with balance issues in and out of a vehicle. The hardest thing was figuring out how to collapse the fancy blue walker and get it into the back seat!

"Hey, Papaw, I came up here to see you just so you could tell me some of your best stories of growing up," Michael said as they exited The Oaks property. "Tell me something I don't already know." Dad fumbled around with his thoughts but finally locked in on something to reveal.

"Michael, I know how much you enjoyed playing baseball at LaGrange College. Now I didn't play baseball in college, but I did play in high school. In about 1937 or '38 our baseball team in Ashland took a two-week trip out to Texas, and even across the border to Mexico."

"Were y'all playing in some kind of tournament?"

"No, I think it was just a "reward trip" for having a good season. We called it our "Mexico Or Bust" trip. Most of us had never been out of Alabama in our lives, and certainly not to another country. We rode all the way in a bumpy school bus, and we did it in the month of June, mind you. It was as hot as a firecracker driving through Texas in that oven on wheels."

"Where did you guys sleep? If it was during the Depression, I'm sure you didn't have much money to spend—certainly not on motels and restaurants," Michael assumed.

"No, we ate a lot of pork and beans and Vienna sausages on that trip. We usually slept on the bus, or where ever we could lay down a blanket and go to sleep. Sometimes we asked permission to sleep outside of churches and stuff. One night in San Antonio, we slept on a baseball diamond in their minor league stadium. That was the highlight of the trip." Dad was transfixed as he relayed his memories to Michael. He enjoyed the company immensely.

"And one night," he continued, "I remember us sleeping in an old abandoned house that we imagined was haunted. Coach Ralph Sneed was driving our bus, and he saw the empty house from the road, and so we camped there. We tried sleeping on the floor of the old house to protect us from coyotes, but when it got dark, and we had no light, we all got scared. Half-grown boys screamed like girls at the least little sound. And then somebody said they saw a ghost, and so after that, any chance for a good night's sleep was over. I was never so glad to see the sun rise that next morning!"

Michael and Dad went through the drive through at McDonald's for a burger and then sat in the car to eat. It was too much trouble getting in and out with the walker. Dad's stories continued as they ate.

"Papaw, I guess you really learned to stretch a dollar in those days."

"Stretch a dollar? You better believe it. Some of my friends in high school nicknamed me *"Tight."* I wasn't stingy, I was just frugal." They both laughed.

"Michael, I remember my brother Bremon and his new wife asked me to bring his car from Ashland to where he had moved in North Carolina. I was probably just a junior or senior in high school. I drove it up there, and then Bremon gave me money to take a bus back to Alabama. But I decided to hitchhike home and pocket the money. It took me three days to get home, and I slept a couple of nights on benches like a hobo, but I made it—and had hardly spent a dime. It felt great!"

Upon arriving back at The Oaks, Michael noticed Dad acting agitated. By the time he got him back in his room, he was having a full-fledged panic attack. The nurses said it had been happening frequently—especially at night. The medicine that should have helped him calm down didn't do the job. He complained that his heart was racing, becoming more and more confused and unsure of where he was.

Suddenly, it was as if his grandson was not in the room at all. Michael gave Donna a quick call. She explained it as *Sundowner Syndrome*—a common occurrence in older people who become disoriented, moody, and confused when the nighttime comes. Being chronically ill or in pain usually exacerbates the symptoms. When they finally got Dad in the bed and asleep, Michael was exhausted.

Sunrise, Sunset

The morning brought a happier scenario. Dad hardly remembered the panic attack but was not as perky as the day before. Still, Michael used the opportunity to engage Dad in conversation that transported him back in time. Breakfast together in the dining room provided the perfect atmosphere for their dialogue.

"So Papaw, what about your time in the war? Tell me something else I've never heard you say." Dad rolled his eyes, grinned, and set the bait.

"Have I ever told you about the time I went AWOL?"

"What? Did you go AWOL? That's hard to believe." He had definitely succeeded in grabbing his grandson's attention. Michael only wished that he had brought a pen and paper to make notes.

"It was toward the end of the war in Europe, after we had won the Battle of the Bulge, a buddy of mine and I got a rare seven-day furlough pass. It had been a tough winter so we decided to go to Paris for some R and R. We hitchhiked on troop trucks back across the Rhine and all the way to Paris. My buddy and I, Dunwoody we called him, were crossing the Champs Elysees (the main boulevard in Paris) when we saw one of my high school friends from Ashland—Billy Saxon!"

"What are the chances that would happen?" Michael inserted.

"That's right! Out of two million American servicemen in Europe, I ran across one of my best friends from a small Alabama town of 2000. Unbelievable! And we had the best reunion you can imagine, right in the middle of an intersection in the center of Paris, France. The Arc de Triomphe was on one side of us, and the Eiffel Tower on the other. Billy was an MP and was directing traffic at the time—we're lucky we didn't get run over! Dunwoody and I stayed with him for a couple of days in Paris, and then we decided to go to London. By the time we got across the English Channel and to London, our week's furlough was almost over."

"So you had to turn around and go back without seeing the royal family?" Michael jested in a perfect British accent.

"Well, what happened was this: Dunwoody was a big guy and had a pretty hot temper. He got into an argument with an American MP and got so mad that he punched him in the face and knocked him to the ground." Michael's face lit up with surprise,

"NO WAY! There is no way that happened." Dad relished his reaction.

"Yes, it did! And before the poor guy could get up, Dunwoody started running, with me right behind him. Neither of us wanted to get locked up in the military brig, so we ran like scared rabbits. There was a train station right around the corner from where we were, so we jumped on board just as it was about to leave. During the war servicemen in uniform didn't have to buy a ticket, so we just took a seat and assumed we were heading back to the coast where we could get the ferry back to France. But we found out it wasn't going south, but north—to Scotland!"

"Ah Ha! So that's why you were AWOL!"

"You got it! We decided that since we were already going to be late, we might as well be really late and enjoy it. So we had a great time in Edinburgh, Scotland."

"Papaw, somewhere I've seen an old black and white picture of you in a full Scottish kilt. Was that when it was taken?"

"Absolutely! I'll never forget when that picture was taken. The photographer was outdoors on a windy balcony. My knobby little legs were freezing wearing that man-dress, and it took him forever to take that photo!"

Dad was a clear as a bell that morning, and Michael treasured that alone time spent with his Papaw. Dad had been Michael's guest in Columbus at so many baseball games and sporting events, and now Michael got to be his guest at The Oaks just six weeks before Michael and Misty's wedding day. The time spent with Coolidge's eldest son's eldest son was family bonding at its best.

When Donna arrived she and Michael loaded him up and took him to his scheduled radiation treatment.

Scans showed the radiation was effective on the tumor, but Dad was getting weaker and weaker. Before Michael left for home, he called Mike and relayed his impressions. Mike was concerned that the radiation was becoming too much for Dad, and agreed to consult with Dad's medical team. Michael left enriched and saddened at the same time. All of his memories of his Papaw had been of a strong, active grandfather whose life attitude was tireless. The change was hard to comprehend.

Stressful Days

The next week was like purgatory— waiting and hoping for something to change for the better never came. Dad's bouts with nausea continued, now accompanied by diarrhea. It was humiliating to our father and increasingly frustrating to his caretakers at The Oaks. We knew that it would not be long before he was forced to move into another unit—accelerating the costs and diminishing his independence and comfort. Almost nightly Donna got a call from the nurse's desk that he was displaying a panic attack, inquiring about whether or not to call an ambulance. It appeared to them that it required one of us to calm him down.

He was barely over halfway done with the 10 radiation treatments we had agreed upon in early May. Fortunately, the 14 to 20 they had first suggested had been reduced because of his age. I took him to his seventh radiation treatment that week. It was a very difficult trip. He didn't really want to go at all but went because the doctor had ordered it. In his day, physicians were the final word. What they said had to be trusted without question. We were late for the appointment because he soiled his underwear just as we were about to leave The Oaks.
As I helped him get a quick shower and clean up from his accident, his brown eyes met mine in the bathroom mirror,

"Mark, I'm so sorry you are having to do this. It's not right for you to have to help me like this." I immediately understood what he was trying to say. His words were ones of embarrassment, and of humiliation, but his eyes were saying *"Thank you, Son, for being here with me."*

"Oh, Dad, I'm just repaying you. You changed my diapers plenty of times back in the day." I tried to lighten the moment, just like he usually tried to do in stressful moments, but he was having none of it. His voice was shaky when he uttered,

"It's not the same, Son."

All I could do was nod my head and whisper, "I know, Dad."

By the time I got him back from the treatment, he was totally exhausted. The air-conditioner in the truck was still not working well on this very hot May afternoon, which added to his discomfort. I left him for a moment in the parked truck and dashed in to fetch a wheelchair, usually always available at the assisted living center lobby. He was glad to ride in the wheelchair instead of having to exert energy walking to his room. It was tough getting him from the wheelchair to his easy chair, but with help from a nurse, we got him in his chair and settled. He was in some pain, so the nurse administered pain meds before the pain became too much to control. Usually, he liked the TV on as background noise, but not today. He just wanted to rest.

I felt it necessary to step out and call Mike. He answered my call quickly.

"Mike, remember how you were concerned that Dad might be too old to handle ten radiation treatments? Well, you were right. Since about the fourth one he's been nauseated, weak, confused, and still experiencing pain in his leg."

"I was afraid of that. Michael mentioned it to me after visiting Dad last week."

"I'm confused, Mike. I thought the whole thing about radiation therapy was to shrink the tumor, reduce his pain, and give him a better quality of life—and hopefully length of life as well."

"That is true, and I'm sure there *will* be benefits, but I think right now his body has taken all the radiation it can take," Mike explained.

"And now he can't control his bowels either. It's embarrassing him and taking a toll on his will to fight," I added. "I'm afraid they're going to ask us to move him to another unit soon. The staff can't attend to him as much as he needs. Donna and I are having to tend to him more than we are really able, and still, hold down our jobs."

"I think I'll try and come up there this Memorial Day weekend and see him," he offered. "We three can talk some more then. And in the meantime, I'll call his doctors and see if we can end radiation therapy early."

"That will be great, bro. Thanks."

"Okay, I'll call y'all later and confirm my trip up there. Thanks for letting me know. Love Ya."

Crossing the Line

Donna joined me at The Oaks in the late afternoon. We had to wake him up just to keep him from sleeping all day long— meaning he might be awake and confused all night long. He could hardly keep his eyes open. We tried watching TV, talking, drinking coffee— but he was still exhausted.

For supper, he wasn't able to eat anything more than a few peanut butter crackers and half of an Ensure shake. Donna suggested that he change into his pajamas and asked him to unbutton his shirt while she gathered his bedclothes. Within a minute of her request, he had not even been able to unbutton the first button. He fumbled around with the button for a few seconds and then drifted off.

"Mark, I'm glad Mike is coming this weekend," Donna whispered. "It's hard to describe the difference in his condition over the phone. The last time Mike was here Dad was able to put on a good show, despite his leg pain.

This time I don't think he'll be able to bluff his way through it."

"I agree. I don't think I could bear to take him to even one more radiation treatment," I commented. I hope Mike can work that out too.

Sure enough, the very night of my conversation with my brother, Donna got another call from The Oaks—this time at 2 a.m.! It scared her and Allen to death.

"Mrs. Taylor, your Dad has had another fall in his room trying to make it to the bathroom," the nurse announced.

"Is he OK? Did he break anything?" Donna was startled, expecting the worst.

"Oh no, we got him back in bed. We just wanted you to know because, as you might remember if a patient falls more than three times within one thirty day period, we have to move them to a higher risk unit. Tonight makes fall number three. The next one will require a move."

"Alright. Thank you. I'll check on him first thing in the morning."

Mrs. Teel and Daddy's Girl

Fortunately, we were able to avoid another fall before Mike arrived on Friday evening. Dad had a pretty good day on Friday. Donna was with him much of the day and was pleased that he was trying hard to function normally. Donna had always been a "daddy's girl". She was born after Dad had turned 40, seven years younger than me, and twelve years younger than Mike. Mom had already had two caesarean section births, and having a third at age 39 was risky in those days. Dad struck up a conversation out of the blue.

"Sweetheart, did I ever tell you about the time Mrs. Teel came into the Ashland Pharmacy and spoke to me about something, not long before you were born?"

"Mrs. Teel?" Donna was vaguely familiar with the story but wanted him to tell it again.

"Yes, there was a lady from down near Millerville named Mrs. Teel. She came in the store every once in a while, but I really didn't know her well at all. She had a reputation as a *fortune-teller*. I had heard of people going to her and asking where they could find a lost ring, or whether they were going to get married, or whether it was a good time to change jobs, or whatever. They would pay her to tell them what they needed to know. I never really thought anything about it."

"One day she was in the pharmacy, and had just finished paying for her medicine and was walking toward the door when she turned around and said,

"Mr. Sims, your wife's going to have a little girl, but I'm hoping she makes it." I was stunned. It wasn't a secret that Marylyn was pregnant, that was obvious. But to say we were going to have a girl, and that she *"hoped that she makes it,"* was alarming. Who was she hoping would make it? Marylyn? Or the baby girl? I wasn't sure. I got the feeling, though, that she was talking about Marylyn."

"Did you mention it to Mom?" Donna asked.

"No! You know your mother would have worried herself to death if I had told her about it. It was bad enough that she told me! It bothered me greatly. I'll admit, I was fearful when your mother went to the Clay County Hospital to have you."

"Oh, Mother wouldn't have made it if you had told her. She always worried about it when anyone "got a feeling" about something," Donna surmised.

"No, I didn't tell anyone about it at all until way after you were born," he explained. "But the strange thing was what happened on February 25th, the day you were born. Doctor Beale came out and said, *'Coolidge, you have a healthy little girl, but we almost lost Marylyn.'*"

"It was like a dagger in my chest for a minute. All I could think about was what Mrs. Teel had said."

"What was the reason that Mom almost died?"

"Dr. Beale and Dr. Horn were both working with her in the C-section. They said that right before they lifted you out of the womb, that her blood pressure bottomed out, and they had to cut the cord and work with her to get her back."

"I remember Mom telling me that she was awake during the caesarean, but that she blacked out," Donna recalled.

"Marylyn had blood pressure problems with both Mike and Mark," Dad explained. "They had to take Mark two weeks early because of her blood pressure problems and heart palpitations. Mark's due date was actually in May."

"Dad, don't you think that it was probably an indication that she had had heart problems for a long time and didn't know about it."

"Yes. After Marylyn got diagnosed with an enlarged heart, the doctors assumed it was most likely from a childhood virus."

"Did you ever tell Mom about what Mrs. Teel said?"

"Not for a long time—in fact, it might have been a year or two before I told her. It was the strangest thing, Donna; I was about to spend a lot of money remodeling the pharmacy building and was beginning to have anxiety about spending that kind of money. I thought about Mrs. Teel and decided I might inquire of her about whether or not it was a good time to do it. That's when I told Marylyn about it."

"What did Mom say?"

"She thanked me for not telling her about Mrs. Teel's prediction earlier. And she didn't have a good feeling about me going to Mrs. Teel at all. She asked me to mention it to Brother Bob Curlee, our church pastor first. And I took your mother's advice."

Donna wasted no time with a response, "I assume Brother Curlee wasn't a fan of the idea."

"No. He told me the truth," Dad said speaking with hand gestures that reminded her of a preacher. "He said that fortune telling was not Christian at all and that it played on our worst fears. He pointed out that trusting

God and praying is how we get direction. That was pretty good advice from Bob Curlee."

He had told me the same story years earlier and I had discussed it with Mom and Dad. I am so thankful that Pastor Curlee helped Dad shut that door forever. So many people look for alternatives to prayer for finding God's will. Fortune telling and occult practices try to fill those empty spaces and usurp the Holy Spirit's rightful place in giving us direction.

In one of my many conversations with Dad about it, I quizzed him about this scenario: If he had gone to Mrs. Teel for advice, and then subsequently been successful in his business, wouldn't it have driven him to do it again whenever he had to make another business decision? Dad concurred, seeing what the trap could have been. We were glad Brother Curlee helped him to reject fortune telling, and put *all* his trust in God.

Dr. Mike

Mike's arrival that evening found Dad in pretty good spirits. Donna had reminded him all day that Mike was on his way to visit. He didn't feel much like eating supper, but she did get him to drink some Boost. Mike appeared in the doorway just before dark.

"Hello big brother," Donna blurted out when she saw him easing into the room. Dad was all smiles.

"How is my favorite father doing today?" Mike said as he bent down to hug Dad's neck.

"Your favorite sister thinks that our favorite father has had a really good day," she declared. The three of them talked for a short time before Donna excused herself, leaving Dad in Dr. Mike's care. "I would tell you what to do, but since you have been to medical school, I'll keep my mouth shut and leave you two alone." Mike followed her out into the hall as she left.

"Has he had supper yet?" he inquired?

"He has had some Boost, but that's about all," she answered. "Mike, I have one question before I leave. Why does he still have pain in his leg? I thought the radiation was to shrink the tumor and relieve the pain."

"Well Donna, actually radiation does more than burn tumor cells, it also causes some burning in the surrounding tissue, and on the adjacent nerves. The pain will subside as the tissue around it heals."

"That is good news, Mike. Y'all have a good evening and call me if you need me. I'll see you sometime tomorrow. Mark said he was coming by sometime tomorrow too." With that, Mike gave her a quick hug and headed back into the room.

Sandworms and Bicycles

"Mike, I guess you heard that Michael came and saw me last week. I really enjoyed it, too."

"He had a great time, Dad. And he's doing very well in medical school, too. He thinks he may want to go into surgery." Dad wasted no time responding,

"I hope Michael's half as good a surgeon as you were one day in our back yard with a Frisbee. I was telling somebody about that the other day. I don't even have a scar!" He lowered his head in Mike's direction to prove it. "But I'll have to admit, it sure did hurt!"

"You didn't give me time to administer any anesthesia, Dad." Both gave a quick chuckle. Dad continued,

"Mike, It just seems like yesterday that little Michael was born! And now he's in medical school, and about to get married! Of course, it just seems like yesterday when *you* were born in the hospital in Dothan." He paused for a few seconds. "Do you have any memories of living in Dothan?"

"I don't think so. I was only about three when we moved to Ashland."

"I'm kind of glad you don't have many memories of Dothan. When you were a little guy, barely talking, you got an infestation of sandworms under the skin in your legs. The only way to treat them in those days was to freeze them with a liquid nitrogen spray. Your mother was supposed to hold you down while I applied the liquid nitrogen, but she got to where she couldn't handle it and would go in another room to cry. I had to pay one of my fellow pharmacy employees to come home and hold you down."

"Ohh, liquid nitrogen is really cold, even though it feels like being burned with fire," Mike acknowledged.

"It was the only way we could get rid of them. For three or four months I would come home every evening, and as I walked from the car to the house I would hear you cry, *'Mommy don't let him hurt me! Mommy, don't let him!'* It about <u>killed</u> me to hear you say that every evening, but I had to do it! I did it because I loved you, not to hurt you." It was almost as if Dad was apologizing to his three-year old son for misunderstanding his motivations, sixty-two years after the fact.

"Mike, your mother and I moved to Dothan in 1949, right after I graduated from pharmacy school in Auburn. Marylyn wasn't so keen on moving so far away from Ashland, and neither was I, but it was a job offer and I needed a job! Dothan was in extreme southeast Alabama, and it felt like the edge of civilization to us. The only thing there was an abundance of peanuts. It took us almost three hours of driving to get anywhere!"

"I worked at two different pharmacies in Dothan. The first one just about worked me to death. I worked long, long hours, and we were barely making it, so I ended up with stomach ulcers, and Marylyn about went crazy. She was pregnant with you and I was hardly ever at home.

Then I got another offer from our main competitor in Dothan that was a dream job. Everything changed. We were able to buy our first little house— on Roosevelt Drive, which is where we lived when you were born.

Before we left in 1954, Marylyn would have been happy to stay in Dothan the rest of our lives. I had a good job; we had a good church, good friends, and a wonderful son. Life was good."

"Dad, then why did y'all decide to make the move to Ashland?"

"We were home visiting your grandparents. Dr. Cicero Rudd, who owned the Ashland Pharmacy, mentioned to me he wanted to retire and offered to sell me the store. He had not done very well as of late, and the business had gone down to nothing. I rejected the offer at first, but the more I thought about it, it sounded like an opportunity I might want to take. So I did. We borrowed the money and prayed that we could make a go of it."

"My first memories of life were in Ashland, not Dothan," Mike said. "I do remember our first house in Ashland. We had a parakeet on the back porch, a dog named Bounce, and there was a stump on the side of the house that I crashed into with my bike."

"You sure did! You were about the age of five and had a new bicycle. I was trying to help you learn how to ride, but every time you went downhill, you found a way to run right into that stump! It's like a magnet was drawing you to it. And it wasn't just once, it happened every time you tried to navigate down that hill." Dad was totally into the story, using hand gesture and facial expressions as if he was a comedian on stage.

"You kept saying, 'Daddy, I can't help it!' So finally I tried reverse psychology and told you to aim directly at the stump. I thought maybe then you'd miss it!" Mike let out a loud laugh and asked,

"Did it work, Dad? I can't say that I remember if it did or didn't." Dad rolled his eyes backward and then snickered,

"I don't think so. You spent most of your bike riding time wrapped around that dang stump."

Lessons and Questions

Dad had a decent night's rest, only having to get up twice to use the bathroom. Mike got a few hours of sleep in the recliner. Mike's thoughts went back to childhood; to a troubling exchange, he had had with Dad as a five or six-year-old boy.

As a youngster, Mike couldn't help but notice that his father did not return the usual repartee of *'I love you'* at bedtime like his mother did. It bothered the little guy. Mom said it over and over, responding to *'I love you Mommy'* with *'I love you more,'* to which he said *'I love YOU more,'* and so on and on to the delight of the much-loved son. Dad never played that game with him. Mike wondered why. So one day he crawled into Dad's lap and asked,

"Daddy, do you love me?" He was shocked at his little son's question.

"Sure I do, Mike."

"Then say it, Daddy."

"Say what?" Coolidge asked awkwardly.

"Say you love me," Mike said plainly.

"Of course I love you, Son. I sure do love you."

Mike often wondered why it had been so hard for him to say it aloud. But looking back, he realized the reason was mainly Dad's upbringing. Papa Sims was not a gushy, lovey talker or hugger, and neither was Mama Sims. The Nichols side of the family, in contrast, hugged and kissed you to death— in public—to the point of embarrassment. It was probably just learned behavior on Dad's part.

Deep inside Mike knew that Dad loved him—and he had proven it through his life and actions, time and time again. But his awkwardness in actually *saying* it was a strange manifestation of affection in the eyes of a six-year-old. In every other way, Dad was an excellent communicator and not afraid to speak in public.

My experience and Donna's experience with Dad was not as void of his verbal expression of love as was Mike's. We talked about it together several times and determined that over the years Dad grew in learning the value of verbal affection from Mom, who was the queen of the art. Piecing that together was an important part of understanding exactly how our loving father expressed love.

The following morning Mike went through the normal maneuvers to get Dad ready for the day— helping with his bath, getting him shaved and dressed, and escorting him to the dining room for breakfast. For the remainder of the morning, they spent quality time together outside in the warmth of springtime.

"Dad, I really appreciate the hard lessons you were willing to teach me as I was growing up. Nowadays, many parents don't consider things like *lying* and *disrespecting authority* as a big deal, but you did. And your three children are the better off because of it." Mike has never has been as expressive as Donna or I am, but whenever he is passionate about something, he has a good way with words. His expression of gratitude to Dad was genuine and heartfelt.

"That's what parents are for," Dad responded. "Of course I wanted to be your *friend*, but it was more important that I be your *parent*. Once a person is grown, it's mighty hard to change their character. Do you remember when you carved your initials on the bedpost?" Mike gave Dad a guilty grin.

"Unfortunately I do, although it *was* best to learn my lesson about lying early in life." Dad rehearsed the whole story anyway.

"I saw the MS carved on the bedpost of yours and Mark's bed. I asked you if you did it, and you looked at me straight and said, *'No sir, Mark did it.'* Of course, Mark was only about three years old at that time and had definitely not learned how to write his letters, much less carve them into wood with a knife. I figured that you and your new Cub Scout knife were probably responsible.

'Alright, then I'll ask Mark about it.'

You blurted out, *'I'll ask him,'* as you darted out of the room to get to Mark before I did. I stopped you and sent you to wait in my bedroom. About that time Mark came strolling down the hallway. He must have watched you do it because when I led him to the carving on the bed, he was so proud to give you the credit— *'Mike did it!'"*

"Yep," Mike confirmed, "That was probably the worst spanking I ever got. I remember it well."

"It wasn't so much for carving on the bedpost, as it was for lying. As Barney Fife always said, *'You gotta nip it in the bud.'"*

"And I learned my lesson, Dad, as I hope you remember. Because not too long after that I got in trouble with Robert and Alan for shooting out the windows of the city pump house with our BB guns."

"You sure did! Chief Elliott told me he suspected you boys did it," Dad recalled.

"And when you asked me," Mike continued, "I thought about that spanking I got for carving, and I told you the truth,"

"And if you'll remember, I didn't spank you either. I just made you work and earn enough money to replace the windows."

Making the Call

As rich and wonderful as the morning was, the remainder of the day lacked luster. After a long afternoon nap, Dad woke up fidgety and in some pain. He wasn't as talkative as before and complained of a queasy stomach.

By late afternoon Donna and Allen had arrived, and I arrived shortly afterward. Lindsay and her husband Joel came to visit Papaw as well, with three-year-old Sophia, and one-year-old Grant in tow. Lindsay was six months pregnant with her third child—who was to be

Dad's fourth great-grandchild. Trained in cosmetology, Lindsay had promised to cut Dad's hair and nails while she visited.

We were all loud and talking and barely noticed that Dad was not feeling well at all. Usually very playful and talkative with Lindsay, Dad was strangely reticent, talking softly and barely answering her questions.

Just after Lindsay completed his haircut, he began to breathe heavily, displaying a look of desperation. Donna noticed it at first and asked if he was okay. In a split second he projectile vomited the supper we had coaxed him to eat earlier. Quick thinking Mike caught most of it on a tray, but our delightful family social event came to an abrupt halt. Poor Dad. No matter how hard he tried, his radiation absorption continued to take a toll on his body.

The overnight was difficult, but his nausea finally abated. Mike left the next day, but only after confirming with Dad's doctors that there would be no more radiation therapy. It was time to strengthen and heal as much as possible so that his quality of life would be good for whatever amount of time he had remaining.

"One father is more than a hundred schoolmasters."
Georg Herbert

Chapter Nine

Traffic on highway 52 is always a nightmare, especially when Helena Intermediate let out at three o'clock, so I timed my travel to avoid the congestion. The temperature in May in Alabama is usually very pleasant, but it can also be downright hot on occasion. I rolled my window down since all attempts to fix my AC had failed thus far. Careful to observe the school zone speed limit as I passed the school, I couldn't help but notice how warm and thick with moisture the air was as it swirled around the cab of the truck.

Summer Songs

Safely past any great chance of offending the local police who were surveying school traffic, I accelerated around the right-hand curve and down the hill toward the Cahaba River Bridge. I switched off the radio since the roar of the wind drowned out the sound of the broadcast. Driving alone and thinking of Dad I suddenly burst into a song— a song I hadn't thought of in years.

> *I took a leg from some old table; I took an arm from some old chair;*
> *I took a neck from some old bottle, and from a horse, I took some hair;*
> *And then I put them all together, with the aid of string and glue;*
> *And I get more lovin' from that ole' dummy than I ever got from you.*

The words and the tune took me back to my childhood; to Sunday afternoon drives to and from Clairmont Springs where we enjoyed eating Sunday lunch after church services in the summertime. Our Dad was the consummate entertainer, especially in an automobile. On every trip, short or long, we would ask him to sing for us the folk songs he had learned as a child—the songs that became our favorites. We all joined in the jubilation, as heartfelt as the family Von Trapp in *The Sound of Music*.

Singing Dad's old songs became my fondest memory of traveling anywhere as a child. If the trip was long enough Dad always ended with his all-time favorite—*Paper Doll* by the Mills Brothers:

I'm gonna buy a paper doll that I can call my own,
A doll that other fellows cannot steal;
And then the flirty, flirty guys with their flirty, flirty eyes
Will have to flirt with dollies that are real.

When I come home at night she will be waiting;
She'll be the truest doll in all the world;
I'd rather have a paper doll to call my own
Than have a fickle-minded real live girl.

I was still humming *Paper Doll* when I drove onto The Oaks property.

New Hope

Dad was temporarily moved out of room 138 for the whole month of June and placed in the physical therapy facility at The Oaks. Besides addressing his balance issues, his twice-daily interaction with the friendly PT staff seemed to lift his spirits. We were so glad the radiation was over and we had new hope that, although radiation therapy had temporarily weakened him, perhaps it had shrunk the tumor enough to extend his days and give him quality of life. He had already made great progress in just a week. The further we got from his last radiation treatment, the better he was feeling. Increasingly his chronic fatigue was lessening, and most of the stomach and bowel problems were fading. Some pain remained, but medicine was helping to control it. The plan was to spend thirty days in rehab, and then return home to room 138. It was the best news we had received in two months.

My sister and I took turns every other day visiting him at least once each day, sometimes twice. I actually enjoyed going with him to the physical therapy sessions. The pretty PT technicians seemed to get more out of him than I could.

Walking side by side with him as he crept slowly down the hallway pushing his new, shiny blue walker to the PT room became routine. One particular morning I met him already halfway to the therapy session, and at least 30 minutes ahead of time. Of course, for Coolidge Sims, being late for *anything* was not an option. I spotted him from a distance all decked out in his bright orange Auburn sports polo, navy blue jogging pants, and those cushy white rubber-soled shoes that you're allowed to buy only after you reach the age of seventy. Looking carefully at the floor he didn't see me coming.

"War Eagle," I called out causing him to abruptly stop moving.

"War Eagle," he responded like any Auburn sports partisan would instinctively do. A broad smile greeted me as he looked up through his finger-smudged bifocals. "Oh, it's you! I thought that voice sounded familiar."

"Well don't you look dapper this morning? Aren't you a little ahead of schedule?"

"Am I? What time is it? I thought I was going to be late," he confessed.

"It's only 8:30. You aren't scheduled until 9."

"Well, Traci said they'd see me first thing in the morning. Nine o'clock seems a little later than *first thing*," he countered.

"Well, it's Friday. They don't begin until nine on Fridays," I reminded him.

"What a waste of time! General Patton could have taken half of Germany by nine in the morning." The older he got the more he compared life to his experiences in the war. I've noticed the same to be true for his peers as well—although there are fewer and fewer of them remaining. They were the men of what Tom Brokaw called *The Greatest Generation.* They were conditioned for toughness by the years of the Great Depression and were defined as men in World War II—the largest war in human history. Those who returned from the war were determined to build a safer, more secure future for their own children. Coolidge Sims was one of those grateful survivors.

"Have you had your coffee yet, Dad?"

"I don't remember," he admitted. "The coffee in the dining room is not that memorable."

"Well, I have some really good hot coffee in my thermal mug. Let me get you a cup and we can share it while we wait for your physical therapy session to start. Let's sit in those chairs across the hall." While we sat and sipped our coffee, I noticed something that I had never recognized before. I am exactly like my father in the way I drink coffee— taking short, noisy slurps followed by a slow and satisfied *ahhhh*. The Sims men drink their coffee with gusto—windy and loud.

Stacey and Company

At Dad's insistence, I met the physical therapy staff as they opened the therapy room. He pushed his walker into the room even before Stacey had switched on the lights.

"Mr. Sims, you're here *early* this morning!" Stacey chirped. "You must be ready for your workout!"

"I sure am," he responded. "I felt all stove-up when I got out of the bed this morning. Stacey, you might remember the other day in my room when I introduced you to my oldest son, Mike and his wife Kathy."

"Yes, the doctor from Georgia," Stacy said. "They were a really sweet couple."

"Well, this is my second boy," Dad announced, pointing to me.

"Hello, I'm Mark Sims. I'm with him," I said pointing back toward Dad.

"Okay, I see the family resemblance! Mr. Coolidge has told us all about you and your brother and your sister, Donna. I met her yesterday. The PT staff here all feel like we are already part of your family."

"Well, now you've met all my offspring," Dad affirmed.

Stacey's hair was dark brown, almost black, and pulled back in a tight ponytail. Her trusting hazel eyes sparkled with life, contrasting boldly with her dark eye shadow and liner. About forty, she was fit and visibly strong; sturdy but not bulky. She clearly enjoyed her job, treating each patient as an individual case, not a one-size-fits-all class.

I could see why Dad enjoyed physical therapy so much. As usual, he had charmed them all with his wit, and they had returned the attention—and he ate it up. Some of the old blue hairs accused him of flirting, but I know it is just Dad being Dad.

Stacey sat him in a chair and put him to work doing ankle and leg stretches. Even as other patients showed up for therapy, Stacey and her PT associate kept a conversation going with Dad.

"Mr. Coolidge, didn't you say you are a pharmacist? I'll bet you're an Auburn man, right?"

"Did my orange and blue shirt give it away?" he chuckled.

"No, but the big *Auburn Tigers* written on your cap did! Did you play sports at Auburn?" Stacey asked.

"Me? Are you kidding? I'm 5'4" and have never weighed more than 150 pounds. I was the captain of my high school football team at a whopping 118 pounds. I'm even too short for college shuffleboard!" The ladies giggled, egging him on for more.

"I know you won't believe it, but I played *college* basketball at Jacksonville State." He dropped it right in their laps to see their response. Stacey cut her eyes over at me.

"It's true," I offered.

"Really? Mr. Sims? You played college basketball?" Stacey's assistant remarked.

"I sure did." Dad relished getting to wow them with his true story. "I went to Jacksonville on a basketball scholarship in the fall of 1942. The reason was that World War II had just begun, and almost the entire basketball team had entered the service and went off to war. I was already enrolled at Jacksonville and was one of very few that had high school basketball experience—so they paid my way and we fielded a so-so basketball team. And that's the truth!"

"Mr. Coolidge, you must have been really good! You're probably just being modest," Stacey remarked.

"I don't know about all that. I wasn't very tall but I had a mean hook shot!" Dad quipped. Everyone laughed, even a couple of the sour old timers that had just arrived for therapy. Stacey was busy helping another gentleman get settled on the exercise bicycle when she quizzed Dad again.

"Mr. Coolidge, did you transfer from Jacksonville State to Auburn?"

"Nope. I transferred from Jacksonville State to General George Patton's Third Army. As soon as I was old enough I got called into the service to fight the Nazis. I was only in college for one semester. Within a couple of years from leaving Jacksonville, I was a part of the Normandy Invasion."

I decided to chime in before Dad gave a lengthy day-by-day account of his experiences in the war.

"Yeah, after the war he came home, got married, and moved to Auburn for pharmacy school." Stacey moved Dad to another location in the room. It was time to work on his balance.

"Whew, I'll bet you were itching to get home and get married, Mr. Coolidge!"

"On the boat back from Europe, all the men were bragging about how they were going to get married as soon as they got home, but not me. I told them how I was going to finish college, get a job and save enough money to buy a car and a house—and THEN I would get married."

"Ooooh. You were a smart man," remarked one of the patients, a gentleman who had been listening to the whole conversation.

"Not so fast," Dad responded, "I got home from Europe at the end of May and married Marylyn Nichols in August, and moved to Auburn in September. So much for planning." Everyone in the room laughed aloud. The PT tech clapped her hands together and remarked,

"I'll bet Mrs. Sims was happy you chose *her* over your savings account."

"Well, let me tell you—being a full-time, married college student wasn't easy. The G.I. Bill paid my tuition, but we still had a hard time making it day to day. And I was so busy with school work, I don't think I paid enough attention to my beautiful new wife who worked all day long in a stuffy office for a cranky math professor."

Faux Pas

Again, I felt it necessary to throw-in my two cents. "Dad, tell them about your first Valentines Day as a married man."

"Oh, dear," he mumbled. I knew he was secretly thrilled to get to tell it. As entertainers, I suppose Dad and I always worked well in tandem.

"Oh yes, do tell!" Stacey urged.

"It was Valentines Day, and Marylyn and I had just sat down to eat our supper—pork and beans, Vienna sausages, and soda crackers. Our neighbor next door, Dot Whitfield, busted into our house showing off the red, heart-shaped box of chocolates that her loving husband had presented her for Valentines Day. *'Oh Marylyn, look what Whitt gave me!'*

Oh, no, I thought to myself. I had forgotten what day it was. I quickly excused myself from the room and headed to town to buy Marylyn some Valentine candy.

We didn't own a car, so I hoofed it all the way on foot. I went to every store in Auburn and couldn't find ANY Valentine candy. It was all gone. So I did the next best thing—I bought her a regular box of candy—and not a pretty one at that. It had all been picked over. So when I presented it to her, she was not happy....not at all. Marylyn went on a crying jag that I'll never forget. She honestly felt like I forgot her—that she wasn't important to me. So, every year after that and without fail until she died, I bought her a big, beautiful red box of Valentine's candy." He paused, then finished, "I just wish I could buy her one now."

The ladies in the room wound up in tears, every one of them. Stacey had a new hero, and the blue haired ladies in the room had a new friend. And his story was true, every word of it. I remember my mom getting a large red heart-shaped box of chocolates every year—even when she was far too sick to enjoy them. He spent his life making up for his year-one marriage faux pas.

Friends and Neighbors

We ate lunch together, and then Dad took a nap while I ran some errands for him. When I returned he was up ready to talk.

"Hey, Cowboy." His eyes were bright and cheerful. I assumed he had enjoyed a good afternoon nap. He was fumbling through a stack of something in his lap.

"Got some mail?" I inquired.

"Yeah, it's a nice card from Stanley and Charlotte Smith just checking up on me. They've probably heard from somebody that I'm at death's door."

"Well Dad, Stanley calls me often to check up on you. I've told them how you're doing and what to be praying about. That's ok isn't it?" Dad was not a very private man. I knew that support from his friends back home would do him more good than keeping his situation confidential.

"Sure," he responded quickly. "I don't know what I would do without my friends. You know, Stanley started working for me at the pharmacy in 1962 when he was a student at Auburn. We worked together until I retired, and then he bought the store from me. That's over thirty years of working together!"

"Yeah, I know. I can hardly remember the drug store without Stanley behind the counter." I watched Dad remove his glasses, lift his eyebrows, and cock his head to the side. A wry, playful comment was about to come out of his mouth. I had seen it a million times. I prepared to match his dry wit with an equally sharp response. He saw the half-smile creep across my face.

"I'd have been glad to leave the pharmacy to you or Mike or Donna, but y'all had your own ideas, and didn't want to follow in your old man's footsteps. I don't know what I did wrong."

"You worked us too hard," I jested. "Every Saturday, from early morning until sunset we slaved for you at the drug store."

"Slaved, my hind leg!" Dad mocked, meeting my smile with one of his own. "You got there about eleven, took a lunch break at noon, and were gone by three." Our bantering ended in a hearty laugh. He did require all three of his children to work on Saturdays, but he was more than generous with us—and forgiving as well.

Obviously, as we got older, Mom and Dad had us share in the family responsibilities, not just the family resources. It wasn't just working at the drug store on Saturdays, but Mike and I shared the responsibility of the one-acre of yard that had to be mowed in the summer and raked in the winter. We shared the family car once we learned to drive, and were always expected to tithe.

In return, we received more than we deserved from Dad. He *bought* me a year-old car, a Plymouth Satellite, just before I moved away to college. By my senior year in college, I had saved some money to buy a smaller, more economical car. Dad *bought* back the car from me, (the one he had *given* me three years earlier,) and *gave* the car to Mike who needed a dependable car in medical school. It gave me enough to buy the little Honda Civic. Then, when Mike graduated from medical school, Dad *bought* the car back from him and *gave* the car to Donna, who eventually drove the wheels off of it. Dad even bought it back from her once it gave up the ghost. Our Dad bought the same car *four different times!* That's not a tightwad, that's a father who can't stop giving.

"Any more mail?" I asked, changing the subject.

"Here's a nice card from Becky Hardy and Bill and Rudine Wilson." Just the name *Wilson* elicited warm feelings from any member of the Sims clan. The Wilsons had been our next-door neighbors for over twenty years. The loyal friendship between the Wilsons and the Sims could not be overestimated.

"I was reminded the other day about how my friends and I would play *inside* the Wilson's house while they were away at work," I said causing Dad to react with a chuckle.

"That's not surprising," he added. "None of us locked our doors during a normal day, only at night."

"Cathy Kennedy and I played there often," I continued. "We didn't see it as weird. We just knew they wouldn't mind. Besides, the Wilson's house was the best! They had kid-level cabinets filled with lots of games– not up on high shelves or out of reach– but low and easy for us to access. We played concerts for one another on their piano, and since we knew where the drawer was that held paper, pencils, tape, and glue—we did art projects there." Dad laughed at almost everything I said.

"Did your mother know y'all did that?"

"I don't know, but it was even more than that. Dad, I *cringe* when I recall this– more than once I showed Walt and Lee the long Japanese sword that Mr. Wilson brought back from World War II. It was in the back left corner of the master bedroom closet."

"I *know* your mother didn't know you were making yourselves at home to that extent," he remarked.

"Dad, Cathy and I shared the Wilson's house with *any* of our friends that happened to be visiting, and I even taught Donna how to get in and out. Walt, Lee, Deb, Donna, and Gary *all* enjoyed the Wilson's hospitality. I'm just not sure the Wilson's knew the extent of it."

"My goodness, Mark! I'm embarrassed just to hear you talk about it." Dad was truly incredulous at what he was hearing.

"Honestly, Dad," I added, "we weren't even embarrassed to be sitting there when the Wilsons got home from work. Cathy might have been, but I wasn't. In fact, hearing Mrs. Wilson walk up the stairs from the basement was nothing more than a signal that it was about five o'clock, and almost suppertime. She never acted surprised and never seemed like anything was wrong, always greeting us with a friendly smile and engaging conversation. At least that's how I remember it."

"Poor Bill and Rudine," Dad lamented. "They were probably counting the days until you and Cathy grew up and left home. There's no telling what messes y'all left behind."

"I truly owe Mr. and Mrs. Wilson, Bob and Becky, some *huge* apologies. Of course, we never stole anything from them, nor did we *intend* to do any damage. *One of us did accidentally step on Cheeta's leg one day and broke it. Do you remember Cheeta?"*

"Yeah," Dad remembered. "Cheeta was that little bug-eyed Chihuahua that Rudine worshiped."

"Right," I added. "Cathy swears that I was the one that stepped on his little leg. He was in a cast for weeks."

Dad got deathly serious for a moment. "But Son here's the truth of the matter. They never complained; never called the police; never threatened to sue us, and never locked y'all out—and they certainly could have if they had wanted to. They probably *should've!* The Wilson's were just good-as-gold, salt of the earth folk. They were best neighbors a family could have."

Nicknames

"Any other mail, Dad?" I asked.

"No, just junk mail," he answered as he chunked it into the waste paper basket next to his chair.

"Oh, by the way, Sadie called last night. She wanted me to tell you that she loved you and was praying for you." Sadie Thompson was one of Dad and Mom's friends from childhood. She had always been a constant in all of our lives, serving as a Godmother to my siblings and me.

"Is she doing alright?" Dad asked.

"Well, she's having a hard time driving now that her sight is slowly leaving her. Living alone and not being able to drive really impairs her independence."

"You're telling me!" he countered. "But in a way, I don't really miss it." It was his first and last commentary on having his own driving privileges taken away. A few awkward seconds lingered in the room before I re-lit the conversation.

"Sadie has shed more light than anyone on what it was like growing up with you and Mom." I slid a chair in front of his recliner, mid-sentence, and took a seat. "She's always saying she can't remember things, but her stories about your formative years are incredible. It's part of the reason I ask you so many questions."

"Well, Sadie ought to know. She was in the middle of whatever was happening, especially during our teenage years," Dad reported.

"When I talk to her she usually refers to Mom as *Nick*. Did everyone call her *Nick*?" I quizzed.

"No. Not really. Mostly just Sadie—the nickname queen. Your mom was *Nick* because her last name was Nichols. Harold Browning was *Speck* because he had reddish hair with freckles. And *Speck* married Ruth Moon, who Sadie called *Shine* because of that song, *Shine On, Harvest Moon*. Frank Owens was nicknamed *Sleek*, and Levrett Pace was called *Country*."

"Did anyone ever give Sadie one?" I probed.

"Oh yes. We called her *Lanky*. I'm not sure who came up with that one. I might have been me," he added. "My favorite was M.L. Allen. We all called him *Emmy Doll* because it's what his mother called him. She petted him to death, and he just about died every time she called him that in public. Naturally, it stuck."

"Poor guy," I interjected, "But didn't you have a nickname too?"

He rolled his eyes and gave the slightest grin. "Well, I was mostly called *Little Man*, but some of my friends preferred *Tight*."

"*Tight!* Where in the world did that originate?

"You'll have to ask Sadie."

"Well, you can rest assured that I will! I'll call her tonight." We both chuckled and left it at that.

Entertainer Extraordinaire

I loaded Dad into the pickup and headed toward Trinity Hospital for his six-month check-up with his heart doctor. The two of them had enjoyed a twice a year patient-physician relationship since his heart attack over twenty years earlier. Dad looked forward to seeing Doctor Reeves every time. For him, it was far more social than therapeutic.

With the air conditioning in the truck on the blink, the trip to the hospital was very uncomfortable. Dad had his window rolled down all the way, but the outside temperature just pushed hot air through the window and into the truck. I could hardly hear him over the wind noise as he barked in my direction.

"Mark, are you so tight with money you won't run the air conditioner? It's hot as a blue blaze in here. We need some relief!"

"Oh, I'm sorry Dad," I hollered back. "The AC suddenly isn't working. The mechanic said it was fixed, but it's not blowing any cold air. I'm not sure why."

"Well listen here, Son, tomorrow you take my truck somewhere else and get the AC fixed. Just let me know what it costs. I'll pay for it." He was serious. I nodded my head in agreement to do just as he asked. Nothing else was said until we pulled into the hospital parking deck. Then he spoke up:

"Mark, you reckon they have a walk-in freezer I could sit in for a while?"

"Do what? Dad, are you crazy?"

"No, I'm just *hot*. I'm probably crazy too, but that's beside the point. I'd pay if the cafeteria would let me park my carcass in the freezer for a few minutes to cool down. You think they'd let me?"

"I think they'd have you seeing a shrink instead of Dr. Reeves," I chuckled. We worked our way into the professional building, signed in, and plopped down into adjacent chairs in the middle of the busy waiting room. To avoid disturbing the folks quietly sitting nearby Dad leaned in my direction to talk.

"Bud, did I ever tell you about what happened one Sunday afternoon at the icehouse in Ashland?"

"No sir, I don't even know what you're talking about."

"Well, in the summertime a bunch of us teenagers would get together and ride our bikes on Sunday afternoons. Most often we'd go swimming over at Pace's Lake, and sometimes we'd just ride all over town and have fun.

One really hot Sunday afternoon about six or seven of us were bumping around together on our bikes, trying to decide what to do. Sadie had been bellyaching all afternoon about how hot and miserable it was, so Jack Willis suggested we all go by the icehouse and collect some of the ice chips to cool off." *(An icehouse is where blocks of ice were kept before they were sold and delivered door-to-door by horse and wagon to fill kitchen iceboxes—before the days of refrigerators.)*

"Sadie peddled ahead and reached the icehouse before everyone else. When Jack and I arrived, Sadie was already inside the icehouse looking for chunks of ice. I promptly shut the door and locked it with the wooden pin, motioning to Jack about what I had done. He jumped on his bike and met the others telling them the icehouse was locked. As they passed by I joined them and we left poor Sadie inside the cold, dark icehouse, pounding on the door and screaming. I can hear her now,

'Is that you, Coolidge? I know it's you! It's just like you to do this. Now open this door up right now! Coolidge, do you hear me? It's scary in here, and cold too. Open up. It's not funny!'"

"How long did y'all leave her there?" I asked. Pausing a couple of seconds he clutched his right knee with both hands, rested against the back of the chair, and glibly replied,

"Until she cooled off." It caught me by surprise and I snickered aloud. The fellow next to me—the one reading the Sports Illustrated magazine—covered his laughter with a series of coughs. Then across from us a rotund older man and his wife looked at each other and began to giggle as well. Dad glanced around at the audience he had enjoined. It was a good day for Dad. He was in his element—entertainer extraordinaire.

"You were always the prankster growing up, right?"

"Heck yeah. I was never cruel to anyone, but I did enjoy eliciting a laugh or two every day."

"You still do, Dad."

"Maybe so. But Sadie was not really mad after the icehouse prank. Actually, she was as big a prankster as I was. We were both good at dishing it out, but we were good sports when it happened to us as well. You have to be or you won't have any friends left."

"That's the truth," the older lady across from us added, fully immersed in our conversation.

"I know what an icehouse is," her husband chimed in. "When we were kids the iceman would sometimes throw us a little chunk of ice off the wagon and we would put salt on it and suck on it. It was sort of like a free popsicle."

"Sure. We did that too," Dad responded. "There was nothing better on a hot day than an icicle and some table salt." Several people around laid down their magazines and smart phones to listen. Dad became the storyteller at the center of the room, and listeners of all ages were spellbound by his craft. I kept the production alive with a comment here and there.

"Dad, I always heard Mom talking about Sadie and Dot Riley and their crazy antics."

"Heck, Yeah! Those two were a mess, and kept everyone in stitches! Dot was especially mischievous at school. I don't know how she would get away with stuff, but she did. The teachers seemed to laugh at her as much as they corrected her." By this time, Dad was no longer even glancing at me. He was addressing anyone eager to listen to his stories, all with cheerful faces gazing in his direction.

"I had this English teacher in high school named Miss Dean. She was a short, plump young brunette with a big, bulbous nose. Every time I see Bill Clinton on TV, I think of Miss Dean."

"One day Dot and Sadie snuck bottles of Co-Cola into Miss Dean's class and hid them under their desks. Whenever Dot gave the signal, clearing her throat, she and Sadie would lean down as if they were getting something out of the desk, take a swig of Coke, and then reappear above the desk. They did it several times before Miss Dean secretly caught on to what was happening. Unexpectedly, while writing on the blackboard, Miss Dean gently blurted out instructions to Dot:

'Miss Riley, please see to it that yours and Miss Thompson's Coke bottles make their way downstairs and into the crates where they belong.'

'Yes ma'am,' I sure will,' Dot answered as Sadie passed her Coke bottle to her without saying a word. Dot exited the room but left the classroom door wide open, so that from our desks we could all see what she was doing in the hall. She set the bottles down at the top of the stairs and gave them a little kick. They made their way down the stairs, just as Miss Dean had ordered, tumbling step-by-step with every clink and clang echoing against the walls and reverberating across the high ceiling. Teachers peered out into the hall to see what was making such a racket. Miss Dean leaned forward against the blackboard, covered her face and giggled with the rest of the class. She was as entertained by Dot Riley as any of the rest of us. And those kinds of things happened with Dot and Sadie all the time."

A nurse finally called for Coolidge Sims. The waiting room audience was clearly disappointed that story time was over. They thanked him for his yarns and we bade them all farewell, following the nurse into the hallway.

The visit with Dr. Reeves went well. Dad was no better; no worse; and holding his own. At 89 with a cancer diagnosis and only half-a-heart working properly, it was a victory. Our journey back to The Oaks included a pit stop at the frozen yogurt place, as usual, providing a cooling respite to the hot, half-hour road trip. In between a frozen spoonful of creamy cappuccino crunch and a couple of fresh blueberries I shared an observation with him:

"Dad, you've struggled with health issues the last several months, but you're still the same guy inside that you've always been. I was amazed at how you entertained half of the waiting room at Dr. Reeves office."

"Son, as I'm sure you know the Bible says there's a time for everything—a time to laugh and a time to cry. Believe me, I've had my fair share of crying. I've lost both of my parents, my brother, and both of my sisters. And losing your mother was the saddest thing I've ever experienced. It was hard to shake it off, and in a sense, I'll never get over it. And I never want to, because she was always a part of my life. But I've learned that the only way to cope with sadness is to let laughter overtake it now and then. There's always something you can laugh about. If not in the present, then at least you can go back in your memories and laugh again and again at the things that brought you happiness in times past. You can choose to revisit past sadness or past joys. They're all still in there, waiting to be remembered."

It had happened again—over a bowl of frozen yogurt. It's almost like a ride in the truck punctuated with ice-cold sweetness has a way of opening up my father's deepest thoughts. Perhaps it was the understanding that he had entered life's final inning that allowed him to say the things he's been too busy to say all these years, or maybe it was simply the relaxing pauses that allowed him to think through them—I wasn't sure. But the knowledge of who my father really is was becoming clearer with every passing day, making me feel much more complete. Somehow I knew that it made him feel more complete too.

Pranksters

The ride home was not quite so serious. He was noticeably more alert than usual and was experiencing less chronic pain than he had felt in weeks. I baited him for even more fascinating conversation about his growing-up years in Ashland. He was fully loaded for game.

"Mark, I remember another day in Miss Dean's class that still makes me laugh. Miss Dean was called out of the classroom for something, and Dot promptly jumped up and moved toward the teacher's desk. Miss Dean's fur-collared winter coat was resting across the back of her chair, so Dot elegantly draped the coat around her shoulders and took a seat at the desk, hijacking the attention of the class.

'James Burroughs and Coolidge Sims, come now and take your places at the podium in the front, please.' Of course, we dutifully obeyed her, knowing she had something hilarious up her sleeve. *'Now, it has come to my attention that this class is woefully lacking in Christian virtue and spiritual well-being, so I have invited Brother Sims to lead us in an appropriate hymn, followed by an inspiring sermon by Brother Burroughs' taken from the book of One Eyed John.'*

No sooner had I said, *'Now let us stand and sing...'* than Miss Dean came back into the room. Amused, she folded her arms and awaited our next move. Undaunted by Miss Dean's presence Dot spoke gracefully,

'Well, it appears we have a lovely new student joining us today. Would you please take a seat?' The class burst into laughter, and no one enjoyed it more than Miss Dean."

"Did you lead them in a hymn?" I inquired.

"No, I'm sure I hadn't even thought of one yet. We were flying by the seat of our pants, and just in it for the fun."

"Was Mom in the room?"

"I'm sure she was since we normally had the same classes. But you know your mom. She would laugh and giggle at someone else, but usually was not one to take a dare. I'm sure she was worried about what poor Miss Dean might think."

"She always laughed at you," I reminded him.

"Yes. I think that's why we were sweethearts from the second grade on. She was so serious and needed someone to make her laugh, and I just needed someone to laugh at me—and she always obliged."

"Mom was definitely not a prankster like Sadie," I added.

"No, Marylyn's best friends were always the pranksters and jokesters, but she was mostly a gleeful observer—rarely a participant. She wanted me to make *her* laugh but felt so sorry for anyone that might get pranked or be fooled for even a minute. If I was about to 'pull someone's leg' about something, or tell a joke, Marylyn would say, *'Oh, Coolidge, don't do that,'* – giving the whole thing away! I can't begin to count how many times she spoiled my element of surprise."

Old '97

We shared a light dinner together at The Oaks and then returned to his room. Amazingly, he was still alert and didn't seem to be in a lot of pain.

"Dad, this morning when I was driving over here I literally burst into song, remembering some of those songs you used to sing for us in the car. Some of them come to my mind readily, but others I can't quite remember all the words."

"Did you sing my favorite?" he asked.

"Paper Doll?"

"That's right! The Mills Brothers."

"Yep, I remembered it. In fact, I used to sing it to *my* girls on our trips as well. It's a family favorite. The one I have the hardest time with is *The Wreck of the Old '97.*"

"You know, I think I can remember the first time I heard that song. It was on the Grand Ole Opry radio program when we still lived at Delta, so it was before 1932. Papa Sims had a radio and we used to let folks come to our house from miles around and listen to the Opry on Saturday nights. In fact, it's where I had my first job."

"Your first job? What was it, turning the knob to find the radio station?"

"No. I would buck dance to the music, and they would throw pennies to me," he explained proudly. "It wasn't a bad job for a five or six-year-old to have—making a few pennies on Saturday nights. It was just enough to buy an RC Cola and a Moon Pie at the store. Actually,

Mama didn't like me doing it, but Papa said it wouldn't hurt anything."

"I'm a little afraid to ask, but what's a buck dance?"

"For me, it was just shuffling my bare feet to the music—kind of like a clogger. I'm sure I was nothing but silly entertainment for them, but at least I got a snack out of it."

"Dad, I have a pen and paper here, and I'm finally going to write down the words if you'll sing the *Wreck of the Old 97* for me.

"Ok. Let's see. It goes like this:

Well, they gave him orders in Monroe, Virginia
Saying, "Pete, you're way behind time.
This is not 38, but it's old 97
You've got to get her into Center on time.

So he turned and said to his black greasy fireman
Just shovel in a little more coal.
When we cross that White Oak Mountain
You can watch old ninety-seven roll.

Well, it's a mighty rough road from Richmond to Danville
and a three-mile line on a grade;
It was on that grade that he lost his average
You can see what a jump that he made.

He was a-going down the track making ninety miles an hour when his whistle broke into a scream;
He was found in the wreck with his hand on the throttle
And was scalded to death by the steam.

Now, ladies, you must take warning
From this time now and on;
Never speak a harsh word to your true loving husband
He might leave you and never return."

He sang it for me once, then he helped me get the words on paper, and then we sang it together. That was worth a million dollars to me, and it gave him incredible satisfaction to know it would stay alive after he was gone.

Legacy Visit

Just after supper, Peggy came with Lindsay and Betsy to The Oaks for a special visit with their Papaw. Sophia and Grant came as well. They were his only great-grandchildren, but two more were on the way. In fact, both Lindsay and Betsy were due the same month—August, just a couple of months away. Nothing pleased him more than to see Sophia and Grant come to visit him. He showed them around the place like it was his own house, and passed a dollar bill to each of them.

Coincidentally, Donna's two girls, Elizabeth and Meredith Taylor showed up at the same time, brightening his day even more. Elizabeth had just won a place on her high school dance team and wanted to tell Papaw all about it.

"Papaw, you gave me my start when you danced with me in the kitchen in Ashland when I was just a little girl," Elizabeth said.

"I sure did darling. And I hope you've gotten a lot more training than I gave you. You'll be up a creek if I'm your dance teacher."

"I think she's saying that you were her inspiration, not her choreographer," Betsy chimed in.

"You are both of those things for all of us, Papaw," Lindsay added. "We've talked about it, and one of our fondest memories of going to visit you in Ashland was when you danced with us in the kitchen. We would stand on your feet and you would do all the work, but we felt like we were big time ballroom dancers."

"I remember that!" he said nodding his head. "Now y'all might not have known this, but Marylyn and I were part of a square dancing club in Ashland when the kids were little. We were pretty good at it, too."

"Didn't we have a big square dance one time at Mike and Kathy's in Columbus?" Lindsay inquired of anyone in the room who might know. "I distinctly remember Meemaw and Papaw dancing in western clothes."

"Yes," Dad added, "Kathy threw a big party for Mike's birthday, with barbecue and all the fixings. It was a real square dance with a professional caller and everything."

"Mike's fortieth birthday," I surmised. "We all dressed western style. Kathy surprised Mike with it—and we all showed up to dance!"

"She really did a great job putting that night together," Dad recalled. "It was one of my favorite family get-togethers that we ever had. Marylyn and I felt like young people again."

"Papaw, I also remember you dancing with Meemaw in the kitchen in Ashland," Lindsay said. "Watching y'all dance was so much fun, especially when you did a little move you called, *the dip*."

"Oh, yeah! I was always known as a *big dipper*."

"What about when you taught us to do the "two step?" Betsy added. "It was one, two, back; one, two, side…"

I watched Dad revel in love and attention from his family without seeming to tire. More than anything he loved when young ones were around. They were always drawn to him. Both children and teens always felt at ease with *Mr. Coolidge*.

"Donna, go over to the CD player and put on some of my big band music," Dad directed. "Let's see how well these girls learned to follow in my footsteps."

"I'll dance with you Papaw!" Meredith offered.

"Lindsay and I are *out* on this one," Betsy announced. "We're both way too pregnant to do much dancing tonight."

Meredith and Elizabeth each danced a few steps with their Papaw to one of his favorite Glenn Miller tunes—*String of Pearls*. It wasn't as roomy as the dance floor in the Sims kitchen in Ashland, but the special nature of this gathering was more about following in his footsteps than in remembering how to dance.

Every person crowded into his little room in The Oaks that night had been profoundly and immeasurably impacted by his life. Even then my thoughts turned to what life would be like for all of us when he was gone. What time we had left with our father, father-in-law, granddad, and great-granddad was bonus time indeed. It wasn't just about his life—it was about his legacy.

"*Your legacy is etched into the minds of others and the stories they will share about you.*"
Shannon L. Alder

Chapter Ten

Sadie

    I had told Dad that I would call Sadie Thompson and ask her how he got the nickname, *Tight,* and I did just that.

    Sadie lived alone in her Father's old house just outside of Ashland. Judge Thompson's house, built before 1920, was once a beautiful place on a large farm. The Thompson's had the finest furniture and most beautiful oriental rugs. In the side yard was a large area for entertaining. A brick barbecue pit stood on one end and a huge arbor, covered in wisteria, on the other. It was the perfect place for parties and dancing, and Sadie hosted her share of them for sure. The huge house with a wrap-around porch in the front, and a large kitchen in the rear, was now a drafty old house cluttered with dusty artifacts of yesteryear, and stuff—stuff everywhere.

    Sadie had been Mom's best friend from the beginning. She was the only attendant at my parent's wedding in 1946, and a Godmother to my siblings and me. Sadie never married, but she had once been desperately in love—in high school. Her parents had money during the Great Depression when most people had none. Sadie, the youngest of three, was forbidden to court the young man she loved because her mother considered him from a "lower class" than her daughter deserved.

    Interestingly, my Mom invited Sadie to spend the night at the Nichols house often, just so Sadie and James could secretly be together—chaperoned by none other than my grandmother, Estelle. Grandmother Nichols thought it was a shame that Lula Thompson wouldn't let Sadie court James, so she never told Lula about her secret collusion with the teenage lovers. World War II eventually separated the star-crossed couple. Sadie went to college at Montevallo, and James entered military service. After college, Sadie returned home to Ashland and was "guilted" into caring for her aging father and mother. James lost hope and married another after he returned from the war. Sadie lived in regret for the remainder of her life.

Sadie lived at home on her father's dime, supplementing by teaching private piano lessons, voice lessons, and speech training—which we called *expression class*. She remained a social butterfly by serving as cheerleader sponsor for the school, church pianist for the Baptist Church, drama director for any civic event, and friend of every fun-loving person in town—regardless of age. My sister learned to play the piano under her tutelage, and I took "expression" from her for several years. My love of acting and writing came from her. I even took voice lessons one year, believing I had the talent to sing like Paul McCartney. I was mistaken.

After her parents passed away, Sadie earned a teachers certificate and taught elementary school in Ashland until she retired. She was left with very little money and had no way to fix up the Thompson place. Sadly, she began losing her eyesight and in her latter years retreated into two or three rooms in the vast Thompson house—depending on friends to transport her here and there, and always to church on Sundays. The phone was her friend, though, and she knew how to use it.

Nick and Nubbin'

"Hello," She answered on the fourth ring.
"Sadie, it's Mark!"
"Oh, Mark, it's so good to hear from you." Sadie pronounced every word succinctly and correctly, without lost syllables or country idioms. "I certainly hope you and your family are all doing well. How's Coolidge? Everyone misses him so badly at the Baptist Church."

"Well, he's missing all of y'all too," I responded. Phone conversations with Sadie Thompson could go on for hours—literally. I enjoyed them more than most but still had to be careful to remind her of my time limit, an awareness that never came naturally to Sadie.

"Sadie, Dad told me to call and ask you for the explanation of how he got the nickname, *'Tight'*." There was a pause, and then a hearty cackle. Sadie didn't laugh, she cackled. Not a wicked cackle, but rather a raspy cackle, probably due to decades of smoking.

"Well, Son, your father owned several nicknames. Marylyn only had one—*Nick.* But Coolidge had a variety of them; each with its own story. He earned them all, I'll guarantee you."

"Oh, well, I'm ready to be enlightened," I said with increasing interest.

"The coach of our high school football team called him *'Little Rabbit'* all the way back in the ninth grade. So all of his buddies on the team called him *'Little Rabbit,'* supposedly because he was a very fast runner— I think the fastest on the team. But he was also short and low to the ground, and could quickly scoot through a small opening in the line, so *'Little Rabbit'* fit him perfectly. He didn't mind because Coach Sneed had coined it, and it was really quite complimentary of his skills as a football player." So that's where he got the name *'Little Rabbit'.*"

"I think I've heard him mention that nickname before," I admitted. "But I didn't know exactly why. That makes sense. Thank you!"

"You're welcome. Now let me tell you about his other aliases." Sadie was milking every thing she could out of the phone conversation, and I let her. "I was always taller than both *'Nick'* and Coolidge, so once I tried calling him *'Shorty,'* but Coolidge did not like *'Shorty'* at all. So I tried to come up with another name that would fit him.

It just so happened that my father, Judge Thompson, was checking on his corn crop during a drought, and I overheard him say, *'That's no ear of corn,* that just a nubbin.' A "nubbin" is an underdeveloped, small ear of corn. 'Eureka,' I said aloud, 'Thank you, Daddy, that's the perfect nickname for Coolidge Sims!'"

"Oh, Sadie! That's a new one for me. He's gonna hear that name before the day is over!" I pledged.

"Well Coolidge will probably blame it on me, but that's alright since I'm the one that gave it to him." I kept pressing her for more.

"Now what about *'Tight?'* Where did that one come from?"

"Wait," she interrupted. "First let me finish the *height challenged* category of nicknames he obtained." Only Sadie Thompson could draw this out so long. "So far we have *'Little Rabbit'* and *'Nubbin'* on the list. Let me think. Oh yes, some of his friends started calling him *'Little Man'* as well, and I believe that might have also followed him into college at Jacksonville State where he played basketball at 5 feet, 4 inches tall."

"That makes sense," I commented, hoping to finally push her to answer question number one.

"Now, about the nickname, *'Tight;'* I gave that one to him because he was always trying to bum a ride with me in my car, so he didn't have to spend his own money on gas if he borrowed his Daddy's car! I accused him of being *tight* with his money, but the truth was that I loved it when he and *Nick*, or he and anyone else wanted to bum a ride with me. They were so much fun to be with! I just gave him a hard time with that one."

"OK, that explains it! Wow! What a tale."

"Now Mark, you must be assured— your father was not stingy at all! I'm not saying that. He was one of the most generous people I've ever known. I shouldn't tell you this, but Coolidge and Marylyn have helped me stay afloat many times over the years, and I am forever grateful for it. Coolidge was frugal, and he was thrifty, but after a while, Marylyn broke him of that!" She burst into another round of raspy cackling. I joined in just to show gratitude for the information.

Marylyn Memories

Since I had her on the line, I figured it would be good to press her for more first-hand knowledge of my parents. I broached the questions carefully.

"Sadie, I know you and Mom were very close childhood friends, and you also went to college together at Montevallo. What are your fondest memories of Mom?"

"Mark, where can I begin? Your mother and I played together often as little girls—mainly because our mothers were friends. Sometimes we played at the Nichols house, but usually, we played at my house. One Saturday Marylyn, about ten or eleven years of age, had come to spend the day with me and it was a very stormy afternoon. My mother was terrified of storms and thought every puff of wind and every dark cloud on the horizon was a tornado. So I can remember taking dozens of trips to the storm pit, located in our backyard, just on the other side of the lily pond. To complicate matters, my mother's mother lived with us in her declining years, confined primarily to a wheelchair. Getting her out of the house, across the yard, and into the storm pit was an undertaking of mammoth proportions, but between Mother, the maid, and me, we had a system."

"My mother, Lula, spotted the suspicious cloud on the horizon that Saturday afternoon and sounded the alarm— which meant mother started screaming, *'tornado, tornado'* at the top of her lungs. It scared poor Marylyn to death. I told her to run to the storm pit while we got Mawmaw out of the house. In the midst of pandemonium, Marylyn forgot about the lily pond and ran right off into it. I'll never forget the look on her face as she scrambled out of the algae filled pond, dripping wet and emotionally wrecked. Then she had to sit shivering in the damp storm pit while an impotent thunder-bumper passed by."

"Poor Mom!" I interjected, "She must have been so embarrassed!"

"Not only that," Sadie continued, "But she couldn't swim either, and was petrified of any body of water over a foot deep. I swear it traumatized her for life." Barely pausing to take a breath, Sadie moved on to their days together in college.

"Marylyn and I went to college at Montevallo, along with our best friends Dot Riley and Ruth Moon. Back then it was not the University of Montevallo as it is today, it was Alabama College—for women only. We used to identify ourselves as being from the "Angel Farm at Montevallo," or if someone asked, we said, 'I'm just a nun from dear old A.C.'" Sadie was on a roll.

"Montevallo was just a small town, not much larger than Ashland. There was really nothing to do there, and no boys around campus. All the men were fighting across the Atlantic and Pacific, so sponsoring dances on campus was even difficult. To compensate, the high school boys from nearby Marion Military Institute were invited to special occasions. Dancing with tenth graders was just not the same!

On Saturdays, we could spend a dollar to take the AC school bus to downtown Birmingham—over an hour's drive away. At least in Birmingham, we could shop at Loveman's Department Store or Pizitz, and almost every time we would eat at Joy Young's Chinese Restaurant. It made us feel so 'exotic' and 'cultured.' The long trip back to Montevallo on Saturday night gave us time to sing a made-up song like, *Dads, Don't Send Your Girls to Montevallo.*

We complained a lot, but it was really a great experience. I distinctly remember Marylyn being aghast at the girls who would sunbathe on the rooftop of the dorm in skimpy clothing. She said they did it so the guys flying the military airplanes could look down at them as they flew overhead. She was probably right!"

Sadie complained incessantly about not being able to remember things anymore, but in reality, she remembered things that no one else would ever keep in their memory bank. A unique lady, to say the least, this world is better off because of Sadie Thompson.

Little Prisspot

Mom loved to call my sister "Prisspot," but the term was originally coined by Coolidge for Mom's little sister, thirteen years her junior—Charlotte. Charlotte has known Coolidge as long as she had known Marylyn. He was more of a brother than a brother-in-law to her. Charlotte and her husband Elton Denson made a surprise visit to The Oaks one summer morning. I got word that they were coming a couple of hours earlier, but I let it be a surprise to Dad.

"Coolidge!" Charlotte squealed as the Denson's strolled into his room. Dad was startled but wasted no time with his response.

"Well if it isn't Little Miss Prisspot!" Charlotte was tickled to death at his choice of greeting. The three of them exchanged niceties for a few minutes, catching up on family and health issues. Charlotte was determined to make it a happy visit feeling like it might be their last opportunity to talk with him. She choked back her emotions brilliantly.

"Coolidge, we took a trip to Arizona recently and stayed with yours and Elton's cousin, Bud. Here is a picture we took of him. Who does he look like?" Dad stared at the photo for a brief moment, looked up and said,

"Papa. He looks just like my Papa."

"Yes, that's what Charlotte and I thought," Elton said. "He looks a lot like my Uncle Cecil—your daddy." (Elton and Coolidge were first cousins as well as brothers-in-law.)

"It sure does!" I took a quick look and agreed. We Sims must have strong genes.

"Charlotte, I was telling Donna the other day about how you used to spy on Marylyn and me while we were courting in the Nichols' living room. She looked for any and every reason to come into the room and interrupt. It made Marylyn as mad as an old wet hen."

"Yes, I remember it, Coolidge! I was probably no more than four or five years old, and I loved you so much that I couldn't stand for Marylyn to have you all to herself!" Laughter echoed out of Dad's room.

"Elton," Dad continued, "it was the funniest thing. On one of our dates the phone rang—and the Nichols' phone was in the living room where we were, and Little Prisspot promptly came sashaying into the room to answer it." Dad began imitating her childhood voice and pantomiming her prissy entrance with his hands and body.

"She picked up the receiver and said, *'If you're not calling me, then you better just hang up now,'* then prissed right out of the room." This time our laughter was so loud, nurses came to make sure everything was all right.

After we calmed down, Charlotte added, "I kept peeping through the keyhole to catch them smooching, until Marylyn stuck a wad of chewing gum over the keyhole!" The laughter volcano had a third eruption.

Since my mother had died thirteen years earlier, Charlotte felt that Coolidge was the last link she had to family in Ashland. They enjoyed the visit, but in trying to keep her emotions in check, she wished that she had expressed her love for him in a greater way. I reassured her that he knew very well how she felt. During their drive back to Lakeland, Florida, Charlotte cried all the way as she tapped into her treasure bank of wonderful memories.

Good Times

Donna joined us later in the afternoon. Dad and I enjoyed reviewing with her the Denson's morning visit. It wasn't quite as funny the second time, but Donna laughed along for the fun of it. The conversation somehow morphed into remembering our one really big family vacation— the trip to California.

Mom got the idea from her friend Mary Frances Pruet when they invited us to their home to view slides from their trip out west. Dad was not one to leave the pharmacy for more than a few days at a time, so it took some fancy cajoling on Mom's part, but Dad finally agreed on a two-week adventure. Mom chose the summer of 1968 because it was Mike's last summer at home before moving off to college and because Donna was now age five—old enough to remember the trip.

"Hey, I found the travel log that Mom kept during our trip out west," I announced. "She made notes on everything that happened—including an entry about each day's weather."

"I don't doubt it," Dad remarked. "She was bound and determined to get me out of the drug store and on the road for three weeks, and I'm glad she did. It was a great trip, and if I had it to do over, I would've taken more time away from work and with all of you."

We did not realize it as children, but our Dad was in many ways a "workaholic." Mom struggled with Dad with the issue, and I even remember witnessing a couple of explosions over it, but as a rule, it was a private disagreement between them. Dad was self-reliant and felt gravely responsible for providing for the family, but he was also a guy who rarely said *no* when asked to serve on a committee or board. He felt a strong civic obligation in addition to his church and family commitments. Mom was very proud of all of his accomplishments in the community but kept tension on the line—for his sake.

"Daddy," Donna recalled, "I know I was only five, but I remember when we were at Yellowstone Park and you got really sick. It was a stomach virus or something."

"I was so sick, I can barely remember it. I know we were staying at the Old Faithful Inn—which was right next to the Old Faithful geyser."

"Yes, and Mike started calling you Old Faithful because about every time the geyser went off, you did too,"

I explained as we laughed together. "Mom's journal confirms it!"

"And I also remember trying to make up for some lost time on the interstate, and I got pulled over for speeding by an Arizona state trooper—who came out of nowhere."

Donna chimed in, "Oh yeah, Mike and Mark and I were giggling out-loud in the back seat and made you and Mom so mad—but we couldn't stop giggling!"

"Hey! I was trying to be nice and cooperative with the man so he would not give me a ticket, and y'all kept laughing!"

"We had never seen you stopped by the police for anything! It was just funny," I explained. "And you couldn't yell at us because it would have made you look bad to the cop."

"What I remember, besides you children laughing at me," he remarked, "was wondering where the trooper came from in the first place? How did he even know how fast I was going? So I asked him, and he just pointed up to the sky. I wondered if he was saying that God had told on me, but then I saw the dang helicopter above us—a helicopter for Pete's sake!"

"Did you get a ticket?" Donna asked.

"No, I guess he saw our Alabama tag and felt sorry for us. He just gave me a warning."

Adrenaline Mom

"I don't know if *you* remember this, Donna, but at a hotel in Denver, Colorado, you almost drowned," I recalled.

"Oh yes! We had just arrived at the hotel. Of course, we wasted no time heading straight to the hotel swimming pool. You and Mike were playing around in the deep end while I was splashing around in the kiddie pool. I wanted to swim in the big pool with y'all. Mom said I had to wait until you or Mike came to accompany me. I was impatient and decided to jump in on my own.

I remember going all the way under where I couldn't touch. Mom was sitting in a pool chair talking to some lady, and I could see her from under water, but didn't have a way to scream for help. I kept bobbing up and down taking short gulps of air. Each time I saw Mom in a different pose—first, noticing me, then standing up, then jumping in, and finally she lifted me up. And was she ever upset!" I couldn't help but finish Donna's story from my perspective.

"All I know was that I saw my mother, who couldn't swim a lick, suddenly take a diving leap into the pool. Mike and I were stunned!"

"...And I was rescued!" Donna blurted out. Again, we all laughed as we relived the moment from the summer of '68.

"I had gone to get gas for the car, and when I got back to the hotel y'all were all in the room and your mother was a wet emotional wreck," Dad recalled.

"It was all my fault," Donna admitted with a grin. "Mom made us *all* end our lovely visit to the pool."

"Your Mom was not very athletic," Dad observed, "but when her adrenaline kicked in, she could move!" I noticed how much he enjoyed talking about Mom. Every time he was able to bring up her name in a conversation with family or friends, his affection for his wife of fifty-three years seemed to deepen. When others were present who could share his reminiscence of Marylyn, gladness of heart was more often kindled than melancholy. Dad had come alive, so I threw another memory on the table for discussion.

"There was one thing that terrified Mom more than water."

"Snakes," Donna interrupted.

"Exactly! Sis, I think you might remember this also, but one summer afternoon I heard Mom's car horn constantly blasting from the driveway—honk, honk, honk—and I figured that something was wrong. When I got to the carport door, Mom was screaming, *'Snake!*

Snake!' She had not pulled into the carport yet and was screaming for me not to open the door.

'There's a giant snake right in the middle of the carport!!!!! Don't let it in the house!'

Sure enough, there was a brownish gray snake coiled in the middle of the carport. I grabbed a shovel out of the nearby storage room hoping to surprise the snake, but it struck at the shovel as I was preparing to hit it."

"Yes," Donna interrupted, "I was standing at the door watching. When that snake struck at the shovel, you threw it down and raced back into the house. It's mouth was as white as snow. It was a Cottonmouth Water Moccasin! It scared us to death!"

"Right, and our faithful protector-dog Prince started barking furiously at the snake. The snake actually leaped toward Prince and struck at his furry collar. Prince ran away without getting bit. Then the snake then slithered off into the yard toward the creek.

Terrified, Mom pulled the blue Chrysler slowly into the carport, and then gripping the car door like glue, swung out on it and straight onto the top step, followed by a diving leap into the house. I was amazed at my gymnast Mom who spent the next week recovering from pulled muscles and bruises. But her foot never touched the carport floor at all, and barely touched the top step at all!"

Again, Dad was thoroughly entertained by my recollection, laughing until his eyes watered, but he was not about to be outdone. He brought to the table another humorous flashback.

"Do either one of you remember how Marylyn always had to go to the bathroom so suddenly, and at the most inopportune moments?"

"Do I?" Donna answered without hesitation. "If there was a tornado heading straight for us, with sirens blaring and no time to lose—just when we were about to run next door to the Wilson's basement for cover—Mother would inevitably say, '*Wait a minute, I have to tee-tee first.*'"

"That's right," Dad agreed. "Do y'all remember that time when Mike scared Marylyn to death, and her scream scared the rest of us to death?"

"I sure do!" I recalled. "We had gone somewhere for a few days and Mike had stayed back alone because of summer football practice. We got home right about dusk, earlier than Mike was expecting. He had just got up from a nap, and without turning any lights on went to the bathroom. That's when we came in from our trip, but he was on the other end of the house where he couldn't hear us entering. Mom, of course, was the first one in the house, dashing to the bathroom—also without turning on any lights. Just as she came around the corner in the semi-dark hallway, Mike stepped out of the bathroom and scared both of them.

Although Mom saw that it was Mike, it was too late to stop her letting out a blood-curdling scream! Dad heard it as he was bringing in the suitcases, dropped them on the floor in the kitchen, grabbed a butcher knife out of the knife drawer, and sprinted into the dark hallway. Mike was trying to calm Mom down when Ninja Dad arrived on the scene, wielding the knife. Donna and I huddled in terror in the kitchen until we heard calm, familiar voices from the opposite end of the house. It was a thirty-second, Sims family adrenaline fest."

Dad's days in the rehabilitation wing had already paid dividends. It appeared that he had come back from the brink. Although his future prognosis had not changed, he was no longer dreading each passing day. It mattered more to me than ever to discover everything I could about this man I called Dad.

*"My father didn't tell me how to live; he lived,
and let me watch him do it."*
Clarence Budington Kelland

Chapter Eleven

Getting to The Oaks was much less difficult since the summer holiday had begun and schools were no longer in session. Still battling with the air conditioner, I chose to lower the windows and feel the rare, relative coolness of a June morning blowing through the truck. My hair would be a mess when I arrived, but I knew it wouldn't really matter to anyone there. I hurried to get to my destination.

The doctors had ordered him to wear compression stockings on his legs, and he usually needed help in getting them on. One of the residual effects of the radiation had been some swelling in his legs. The lymphatic system was having a hard time recovering from the damage that occurs during radiation therapy. The stockings helped relieve the discomfort and were especially beneficial during his physical therapy workout.

By the time I got to my destination, Dad was already in the PT room hard at work. He was entertaining Stacey, as usual. I walked into the room just as I heard her say,

"Mr. Coolidge, you don't have to show out this morning. We know you can do it, but just don't *overdo* it."

"Good morning, all," I broadcast to everyone in the room. I got a few friendly nods from people I had never seen. "Dad, are you showing out again?"

"He certainly is," a PT tech named Jennifer responded with the same warmhearted personality as her boss. Stacey had faithfully replicated herself in her associates, and the patients were the beneficiaries. In the short time, I had accompanied Dad in the therapy room, I noticed that even the most acidic soul moderated after just a few days with the friendly PT staff. We regularly bragged on them to the *powers that be.*

Family Secrets

Each day that Dad visited the physical therapy team, he got a little stronger, while the PT crew learned more and more about Coolidge Sims. He was an open book, more than I had seen him in years. I stood next to Dad as he was busy on the adjustable incline board. Stacey decided to direct a question to me rather than distract Dad while he reasserted his balance skills.

"Mr. Mark, did Mr. Coolidge ever get frustrated with you, or were you a perfect child?"

"Oh, I was the perfect child!" I jested.

"Lightning's about to strike at any minute!" Dad inserted, rolling his eyes toward Stacey. Everyone laughed.

"Let me answer that honestly," I begged. "I had a… *unique* way of pressing Dad's buttons. There were certain things I did that drove him crazy."

"Like what?" Jennifer inquired.

"Well, whenever I got distracted or forgot to do something I would hear Dad sarcastically say, *'Breathe Mark, breathe.'* Dad immediately broke into a wide grin and repeated the phrase with feeling,

"*Breathe Mark, breathe.* Poor little fellow, sometimes we had to tell him every move to make. He wasn't being disobedient on purpose, he just didn't know HOW to listen. I'd say, *'Son if you don't learn how to listen, you'll have to be told every move to make just to survive. Am I going to have to tell you every breath to breathe?'*"

"Mr. Coolidge, I think that's called ADD, or ADHD," Stacey said as she helped another gentleman to his next exercise.

"No," Dad responded, "Most of the time Mark wasn't hyperactive, he just wouldn't pay attention. He always made really good grades, so it wasn't an issue with his schoolwork."

I decided to chime-in in my own defense. "Dad might say, *'Mark, go brush your teeth and hop into bed, it's* bedtime.' I would dutifully head toward the bathroom with every obedient intention, but would almost always get distracted by something like—the old antique trunk in the hallway. In a split second, that old trunk would become a pirate's treasure chest containing gold coins and jewels beyond my wildest dreams. It would steal away all of my attention.

The next thing I knew Mom would be pinching the fire out of me demanding why I hadn't done what Dad had commanded. I was stunned that she would think I would want to disobey Dad."

"Yep, his excuse was always, 'Mom, I just forgot.' It used to drive me crazy," Dad explained. "Pretty soon we started saying 'Breathe Mark, breathe' regularly, just to get his attention.

When we'd send him outside to feed the dog, 'Breathe Mark breathe;' or to take out the garbage, 'Breathe Mark breathe.' But he eventually grew out of it, and turned out to be a pretty fine guy."

"Ohhhh. That's so sweet, Mr. Coolidge," Jennifer sighed.

"It used to hurt my feelings when I heard it," I admitted, "but I heard it at least a thousand times before I was twelve years old, so I got used to it. Dad was the one who crafted the phrase—I give him all the credit!"

The PT ladies were thoroughly entertained by the Sims family sagas and begged for more, so naturally, we obliged.

"Well, as you have already heard, Dad was a very competitive athlete. He was small but fast and tough. My brother was very much like him. But not me; I wasn't the athletic one at all. I remember being strongly encouraged to play little league baseball as a kid—something I didn't want to do. I preferred playing in the creek next to the house or reading the encyclopedia. No kidding."

"That's true," Dad said. "He loved to read the encyclopedia. He was weird like that."

"I wasn't a top notch baseball player, for sure. I could hit the ball pretty well—I had good eyes but was not interested in the game at all. I played right field, which is, of course, the least active position on the field, and actually *shared* playing the position with a kid who had a patch on one eye, and he was a better player than me. I spent all my time squatting down playing with ants in the dirt. I never even saw the baseball coming in my direction! I'm sure that frustrated Dad for his son to be so inept at sports."

"He might not have been great at sports, but he was a really good drummer in the band," Dad added.

"Well, thank you Dad!"

"You're mighty welcome."

"So sports wasn't your thing," Stacey postulated.

"Actually I love *watching* sports, but I just wasn't good at sports and didn't want to make a fool of myself in competition. There were times I was afraid of failure, so I wouldn't even try. That drove Dad crazy, right Dad?"

"Okay, Son. Why don't you tell them about when I tried to help you learn to ride a bike," Dad said. "Talk about frustrating!..." The entire PT room was all ears as I stood next to Dad and told the whole story. He was re-living it with me as I explained.

"Well, I had been an excellent tricycler and had easily mastered riding a FOUR-wheeled bicycle as well. Thank God for training wheels! As long as I could graduate to a larger bike with larger training wheels, I was fine. But Dad refused to get me a new bike as long as I depended on training wheels."

"He took me to the backyard regularly to teach me to ride my bike without them, but I balked every time.

'Daddy, I can't. I can't keep my balance,' I would argue. He got so tired of taking the wheels off to train me and then putting them back on when I failed to learn, that he finally threw them in the garbage can. That'll teach him, he thought. But it didn't. I just quit riding my bike." The whole PT staff began feeling sorry for me.

"Why feel sorry for Mark?" Dad protested, "What about me? I was the one having to deal with his stubborn fears." He chuckled and motioned for me to continue.

"So day after day that summer Dad forced me into the backyard to try again. A soft, downward grassy slope in the backyard appeared like a plunge off the White Cliffs of Dover to me as Dad tried to coax me into gliding down the slope. He ran behind me holding on to my bike over and over until he was out of breath.

But Dad's right—I was fearful and stubborn. A couple of times he tricked me, letting go of the bike after promising to hold it. But whenever I looked backward and saw that he wasn't holding on, I freaked out and crashed to the ground in tears. I finally quit trusting him."

Jennifer let out a loud sigh of pity. *"Poor Mark."*

"Poor Mark? No, poor me!" Dad declared. Ignoring his comment, I resumed my storytelling.

"Finally Dad reached his breaking point, ordering me to sit down on the grass and stop crying. Then he called my brother, Mike, to stop what he was doing and ride his bike around the back yard.

'Mark, don't you dare take your eyes off of him!' Dad barked. Then he commanded Mike to ride all around me and not quit until I was willing to ride without training wheels! At that point Dad was mad and frustrated and went inside."

"My brother Mike was none too happy with me. Each time he rode near me he issued threats and berated my stubbornness. Eventually, I got as mad as a hornet, jumped up, and walked my little two-wheeled bike to the top of the slope. Mike, sensing my frustration suddenly turned sweet and offered to help me.

Within a few minutes, I was gliding down the hill alone—proud as a peacock. Dad and Mom came out and cheered me, and praised my brother for his role. I never looked back. From then on, bike riding was part of my daily existence." Stacey clapped her hands and bellowed,

"Bravo, bravo for your brother, Mike!"

Dad laughed, then declared, "You know, they never gave me credit for that one, but it WAS my idea!"

"Mr. Coolidge," Jennifer inquired, "You've told us all about your sweet wife who passed away several years ago. Did you ever consider marrying again?"

Stacey quickly interjected, "What she's asking is, 'Do you have a girlfriend?'" The staff and Dad laughed aloud, and the rest of us in the room cracked a smile at the least. I delighted in watching him think of a witty way to answer the question.

Adding to his momentary deficit of words I added, "Yeah Dad, DID you ever think of marrying again?" I winked at him while I said it. He blathered around and finally found the words.

"Yes," he paused, "and no." His eyes glanced from me to Jennifer to Stacey and back to me before he continued. "Yes, I have a girlfriend, and no I never really considered marrying again. But I do enjoy a special friendship with a classy lady back home named Miss Ayler. She's a widow, and pretty too, so we enjoy spending time together and going out to eat and courting a little."

"And getting some sugar, too," Stacey added, "Right, Mr. Coolidge?"

"Well, that's for me to know and you to wonder."

Another Realm

My father had spent fifteen years caring for our mom after she was diagnosed with congestive heart failure. The last three years of her life had been quite taxing on Dad as well. His heart wasn't 100% either, having lost a portion of the heart muscle twenty years earlier. But he was a devoted husband, waiting on her hand and foot.

The last week of Mom's life looms vividly in my memory. She had come back after a brief stay at the hospital, always preferring to be at home. I had driven down to Ashland to help him get her from the hospital back to the house. It appeared to us that she was growing weaker and weaker by the moment.

All day long she had lingered between heaven and earth, talking to God one minute and to us the next. She whispered about some of the people she saw, and the beautiful music she heard. There were moments she was in another realm, the realm of the Spirit, and then she would be totally with us again in the earthly realm.

That particular night she was resting in bed with Dad hovering over her, checking her breathing periodically and giving her comfort as she slept. I stood at the foot of the bed, noticing how her feet were already a pale blue color. Feeling that the time was growing near, Dad climbed into bed with her to be near.

"Is that you, Coolidge?" she asked.

"Yes, Darlin' it's me. I'm here." She was very weak but perfectly lucid. He watched her closely for a couple of minutes. Then leaning on one arm and speaking gently to her he said,

"Marylyn, I want you to know that you're the only woman I've ever loved, and the only one I've ever been with. I love you." He kissed her softly on the cheek. To my complete surprise, Mom opened her eyes and responded to him in a faint voice, just above a whisper,

"And Coolidge, you're the only man I've ever loved, and have ever been with. I love you."

"Whenever the Lord calls you home, Marylyn, it's okay. You go on. I'll follow before too long," Tears coursed through the pleated furrows on his face.

That moment was surreal. I could hardly believe that I was standing in the room in such a holy moment. I said nothing. I simply cried silently, waiting for her to take her last breath.

Dad gently caressed her forehead with a damp washcloth while we waited. Her eyes were closed as a few silent minutes passed, silent enough to hear the tick of the clock in the next room. Suddenly, she opened her eyes and looked hard into Dad's eyes, preparing to say something.

"What is it Marylyn? What do you need?" Dad whispered.

"I need to tee-tee." Lifting her head up from the pillow Mom said, "Coolidge, help me get on the potty, I've gotta go!"

I had to laugh. Dad did as well. Her journey into eternity was put on hold, at least for the time being. How typical of Mom to have to go to the bathroom at such an important juncture in her life. As I walked out of the room I heard her say,

"Coolidge, I think I need a milkshake."

"Mark," he ordered as I was exiting the bedroom, "Marylyn's milkshake from the Dairy Queen is in the fridge. Bring it in here, please."

"Sure thing, Dad." By the time I got back to them with the milkshake, I met them coming out of the bedroom. She was weak but was walking. She had decided that she wanted to drink her milkshake while watching the Gaither's Homecoming Concert videotape in the den.

Amazingly, she sat in a chair next to me for almost an hour watching a video of her favorite music, holding and rubbing my hand, more alert than I had seen her in many days. It was the second surreal moment of the evening for me. I will never forget her touching my hands that night, in perfect peace, humming her favorite hymns along with the Gaithers.

May 25, 1999

Within two days, she was back in the hospital needing oxygen. I came back to see her just after she had been admitted. Walking into her hospital room, I heard her speak her last words to me,

"Look, there's my boy."

We all knew that she couldn't last very long, but she had surprised us before. About ten years earlier her heart output, normally 60 or 70, had gotten as low as 12. She should have been bedridden by then, and the doctors did not give much chance of surviving very long.

But Mom believed in Jesus the Healer and she sought earnestly for His intervention. After being prayed for by a healing evangelist, her heart output went from 12 to 24 in one day. She lived another decade with very good quality of life. Mom's faith in God was always strong.

Mike, Donna, and I had taken turns staying overnight in the hospital room with her before so that Dad could get some sleep and be with her during the long days. They both realized that their turn to spend time with her could be their last.

I volunteered to stay with her the night of May 24 along with Mom's sister, Charlotte. Early in the evening, Mom was in the realm of the Spirit again, talking to God and describing what and whom she was seeing.

Before midnight, she was unconscious and never regained consciousness. Late in the morning on the 25th of May, she peacefully passed into eternity with Dad holding her hand. I was with her, as was Charlotte, and Dad's sister Gwynnelle.

Lonely Days

The days and months after Marylyn's death were at times unbearable. On any day, without warning, grief overwhelmed him like an ocean swimmer caught in the undertow. Sometimes it felt like he couldn't breathe. But then, like the ocean tide, it would finally recede and let him catch his breath. For a while, he received an unusual amount of homemade pies and cakes from eligible widows in the community, but he never questioned their motives.

Other friends were kind to help him stay busy, and he buried himself in church activities. But being the constant caretaker for the love of his life had imprinted him to her presence, and being without it was harder than he thought.

My brother, sister, and I tried to help him adjust by inviting him to visit us, and the grandkids at every opportunity. Their involvement in sports and school activities gave us an easy excuse to keep him busy. He rarely turned us down, able to change plans at the drop of a hat—something that had been impossible to do for a long time while Mom was sick.

Mike and Kathy were always ready to invite him down to Columbus. It gave Michael, Hope, and Keith a special way to bond with their Papaw. He burned a trail to Georgia often for the boys' baseball games, and was Hope's special guest on the night she made homecoming court. He thrilled her that evening when he said,

"Hope, you may not have won tonight, but you're *my* homecoming queen for sure!"

Donna's husband Allen kept him busy playing golf and helped him with his retirement investments. He trusted Allen's insight and honesty. Allen admired his father-in-law and enjoyed his company.

Just a couple of months before Marylyn died, Allen offered to fly Dad to Jacksonville, Florida, in his private single-engine plane. Marie, Bremon's wife, had passed away and Dad wanted to be there for his brother's sake. But Mom was requiring around the clock care, so Dad saw no way he could make a 10 hour drive to Florida. Fortunately, Donna offered to stay with Mom for the day while Allen flew him to Jacksonville and back.

Dad was thrilled with the flight, and even got to "fly" the plane for a few minutes in the co-pilot's seat. It didn't take long for him to give the controls back to Allen— too stressful. While flying across the vast Okefenokee Swamp in south Georgia, Coolidge asked,

"Allen, what if someone had to make an emergency landing while flying over this mess? What would they do?"

"Well, Pop, they'd be in a world of trouble, I suppose."

"I'll say! There's more than a few gators and snakes down there. I'm looking forward to seeing some solid ground," Dad said with his unique blend of jovial sarcasm.

Still, the flight was not without a final wrench thrown in for good measure. On their approach to the Jacksonville Airport, the cockpit light confirming that the small plane's landing gear was locked in place did not appear. Allen had to circle the tower close enough for a visual confirmation that the landing gear was set before touching down on the runway. After that everything went smoothly.

Especially helpful were his golfing buddies—Shotgun Giddens, Don Fulbright, and several others who enjoyed yearly golfing trips to Myrtle Beach. He looked forward to their big trip together every year. Dad referred to it as his annual "hunting trip," where he spent a hour after hour hunting for his golf ball on the fairway.

Working part-time in the Clay County Hospital pharmacy dispensary also helped, but we still had phone conversations with him that revealed deep periods of despondency. I remember this call in particular:

"Hello."

"Hey, Dad! It's Mark. How was your day?"

"It was alright I guess, Markle." He wasn't very convincing. "I didn't have to work today so I've been piddling around the house a bit." I spent the next few minutes of phone time bragging on his grandkids—which always gave him a lift. Then he described a most revealing moment.

"I didn't sleep really well last night. The strangest thing happened. I woke up when I thought I heard something. I didn't have my glasses on, but I could have sworn that I saw Marylyn in the corner of the bedroom, not far from the foot of the bed. I kept squinting my eyes to try and see her better, but it didn't help.

I said, *'Marylyn, come over here where I can see you better.'* But she just kept looking at me and smiling.

'Why won't you come over here and talk to me?' I asked, 'I've missed you so much.'

Son, It was so real to me. I know now that I must have just been dreaming, but it's left me sort of feeling down all day long."

I was glad that he didn't believe Mom was somehow actually appearing to him. Sometimes loneliness leads people to take leave of reality, and believe the strangest things. But on her last visit to Ashland, Donna told me that Dad had hung several portraits of Mom on his bedroom wall, and all around the house—pictures that Mom had put in closets years ago. It was very odd to suddenly fill the house with so many of her pictures.

The one he loved most of all was her high school senior portrait in oils, hanging in the very corner of the bedroom where he had imagined Mom standing. It was a gorgeous portrait of a seventeen-year old Marylyn Nichols wearing a blue dress, with her hands gently folded in her lap, looking straightforward at the camera. He later disclosed how seeing it every night as he crawled into the bed brought him a measure of comfort and a feeling of closeness with her.

Deep down, my siblings and I were very concerned that he was stuck in the grieving process, and hoped that he could soon move forward. It was a very tough year for Coolidge Sims. It was uncharted territory for him. He appeared normal in most ways, but for nearly a year, to look in his eyes was not to see the buoyant father we had always known. Inwardly, we couldn't help but ask the question, *"Is that you, Coolidge?"*

Rebound

The phone call I received from him was similar to the one my siblings also received. It was the only conversation I think I ever had with him in which he was asking for *my* permission.

"Hey there, Bud. It's your old Pa."

"Oh, hello, Dad. I'm always glad when you call." He beat around the bush for a few minutes, informing me of meaningless things, trying his best to appear off the cuff. Finally, after a pause in our back and forth verbal shuffle, he got to the issue at hand.

"Son, I want to ask you what you think about something. I want to know if you might have any advice for me." Wow, was this strange or what! Totally curious, I let him spill the beans.

"I've been thinking about asking a widow lady that used to trade with me at the pharmacy to go with me to a Housing Authority dinner next week. I'm just wondering how you would feel about that, Mark?"

Fortunately, I had prepared myself for this conversation. I had actually prayed to the Lord that Dad would find companionship after grieving. He couldn't see it, but I broke out in a big grin before I answered.

"Dad, I think that is an excellent idea!"

"You do? You don't think I'm out of line?" Like a schoolboy asking to use the family car, he sought and got permission. Dad would never do anything to deliberately cause consternation in any of us. It was important for him to cover his bases and do what was right. I was honored that he asked.

"Of course not, Dad. You were loyal and loving to Mom all of your life, and there is nothing disloyal about what you are asking. Dad, Mom is gone and nothing you can do will bring her back. But you have a lot of life ahead of you, and you should move forward. This is a good way to begin."

"Son, I loved your mother with all my being. I've loved her since the second grade, and I love her still. But she's not here anymore, and memories don't exactly bring her back."

"I'm really glad to hear you say this, Dad."

"She's a really nice lady. I call her 'Miss Ayler' *(pronounced EYE-la, with only the faintest hint of an R at the end.)* She lives on a nice farm down near Corinth

Baptist Church. She used to be a nurse, and her husband, Forrest Caldwell, passed away several years ago after a long fight with heart disease, just like Marylyn, so we have that in common."

"I knew Forrest, and I think I have preached at that church before," I recalled.

"And Mark," he added, "She's an Auburn fan too!"

"Of course, Dad. You wouldn't have it any other way! How old is she? About your age?"

"No, she's a little younger than me. She'll turn thirty next year," he announced.

"Thirty!!!!" I bellowed. "You've got to be kidding!" He was laughing before I even got it out of my mouth. I could see glimpses of the real Coolidge Sims again.

"I AM kidding, but *I got you* on that one, Son! I wish I could've been there to see your face." I quickly joined in the hilarity. Still snickering he clarified, "Naw, she's only about eight years younger than me, that's all."

We spent the next few minutes talking about a variety of things—and Dad sounded like a different man. He assured me several times that he wasn't falling in love, or wanting to get married. But he was definitely looking forward to building a friendship with a classy lady like Miss Ayler.

I recalled something Mom had expressed to Dad as her health was declining. She actually mentioned it to him several times. She told him that she wasn't against him remarrying after she died, as long as it was after a respectable amount of time had passed. Mom even made predictions that he would, but she always ended the conversation by saying,

'Coolidge, all I ask is that you not embarrass my children.'

Miss Ayler

Dad never intended on remarrying, and neither did Miss Ayler. Although they lived apart, they enjoyed spending quality time together. They attended two different Baptist churches, had extended families of their own, and saw no reason to attempt an awkward blend at this stage in life. Going out to restaurants, playing dominoes, watching the Atlanta Braves on TV, and taking long walks on the farm were just a few of the diversions they shared. Their special companionship lasted for twelve years.

My siblings and I quickly began seeing Miss Ayler as part of our clan, always inviting her to family celebrations and big-events. She was there for the birth of Sophia—my first grandchild and Coolidge's first great-grandchild. She was Dad's escort at the weddings of both of our daughters, and there was a gift under the tree for Miss Ayler every Christmas—from each of our families.

For a while, Ayler took daily care of her mother—a classy southern matron in her nineties, living with Ayler until she passed away. "Mama" loved it when Coolidge joined them for supper, and Dad certainly loved Ayler's cooking. A couple of times a week he would call Miss Ayler and make this proposition:

"Ayler, what if I brought three nice, thick pork chops by your house tonight? Do you think you might find something that could go with 'em? I'm sure your Mama and I would appreciate it."

"Well, Coolidge, you just bring those pork chops on down here. I just happen to have some turnip greens and potatoes on the stove right now. And Mama was quite fond of the cobbler I cooked last night. She was wondering if you might like a taste of it as well?"

"You know I do! Tell Mama I'll be there in less than an hour!" Thrilled, Dad would hop into his little Nissan Frontier pickup (the very one I drive to visit him at The Oaks) and show up at Ayler's house in less than thirty minutes.

Teenagers Again

Miss Ayler's was home beautifully situated next to a broad pasture where several horses grazed. The horses belonged to her neighbors, but Ayler fed them regularly. She called them her "babies." Just across the pasture was a small creek at the base of a picturesque mountain. One afternoon, not long after their first date, and late in the Autumn season, Dad and Ayler decided to hike to the top of the little mountain--- just for fun. Holding hands they helped each other across the creek and made their way slowly up the hill.

About halfway up the slope got steeper and the fresh leaves on the ground got thicker. Without warning, Dad's feet went out from under him and he toppled over. Ayler held tightly to his hand in an attempt to steady him, but she lost her balance as well. Together they began sliding down the steep hill, rolling and tumbling in the leaves until they finally came to an abrupt stop near the creek's edge. Once they had determined that there were no injuries, they began to laugh at what they had just experienced. Then helping each other up, they made their way back to the house.

That night I called to check on him. Dad was so excited to tell me of their most recent mishap on the mountain hike. It was like he was seventeen again, recounting to me every detail. There was a new spark in his eye, and a new spring in his step. Everyone noticed it.

Ayler accompanied Dad to banquets, dinners, and church events. They played Rook and dominoes with Dad's friends and especially enjoyed going to Auburn sporting events together. Similarly, Dad drove her to visit with her two sons in the Carolinas at least once a year. Their families grew to love "Mr. Coolidge" as well.

There was one conversation I had with my father about Miss Ayler that I will never forget. It was before he moved to The Oaks. He had just bought a new car in Birmingham, and we were driving it to mine and Peggy's house for dinner. He let me do the driving since it was rush hour in Birmingham. Miss Ayler came up in our conversation.

"How's Miss Ayler doing, Dad?" I inquired.

"Oh, pretty good," he said. "We picked the biggest, prettiest blueberries you've ever seen yesterday. She said to tell y'all to come down and pick some before the season ends and the birds get 'um."

"We love blueberries. That sounds like a good idea."

"Her Mama is a mess," he continued. "She wants to know everything Ayler is doing at all times. She hardly lets Ayler get out of her sights."

"Is she sick, or just nosey?" I asked.

"Both. I'll tell you something, Mark. You're grandmother Nichols was about the same way. I loved Mrs. Nichols to death, but when Marylyn and I were dating, Mrs. Nichols was *always* around. She volunteered to chaperone every dance, every church social, and every party. Marylyn and I would race to get a seat together on the back of the school bus for a school outing, and sure enough, Mrs. Nichols would end up on the bus with us. And Marylyn was too nice to ask her mother to not be so.....so.....so...." Dad was looking for the right way to say it, so I helped him.

"So *present*," I offered.

"Yes, so *present*," he chuckled. "That's secretly the reason your mother and I got married at the Baptist preacher's house, instead of having a big, formal wedding ceremony."

"Oh, that's interesting," I commented. "I never knew that. I did know you had a private wedding, and Mom said she got married in a brand-new wool suit that she and Grandma bought in Montgomery. A wool suit? In August?"

"I have no idea. It was probably on sale. Mrs. Nichols looked for bargains." Dad assumed. "But Marylyn sure did look beautiful in that wool dress. She wore it sometimes to church for several years afterward."

"If Grandma Nichols didn't get to go to the wedding, at least she got to buy the dress."

"Well, of all things, I'm back in the same conundrum with Miss Ayler and her mother. I could hardly get shed of my girlfriend's mother a half-century ago, and now I'm eighty something years old, and I'm STILL having to deal with my girlfriend's mother! I can't even steal a kiss behind the refrigerator without Mama saying,

'Ayler, where are you? What are you doing?'"

I laughed heartily, feeling that he was exaggerating a bit. Then I ventured into unknown territory. Almost without thinking I asked him something I had privately wished to know for a long time.

"Dad, do you love Ayler? Are you in love with her?" There was a long, silent pause. I glanced at him, not sure if he was going to answer at all. Looking straight ahead at the highway in front of us, he spoke very plainly.

"Yes. I do love her." There was another thoughtful pause, and then he turned his eyes to meet mine. "But not like I loved your mother."

Thought-Pegs

My 14.8-mile journey back home from The Oaks in the late afternoon was a blur. I was absorbed in an array of thoughts about the day's conversations and my own adjacent memories. I hardly noticed the pink and white crepe myrtles in full-bloom that greeted me earlier in the day or annoying orange cones that marked the road repairs at Shades Crest Road.

Like an atheist beginning to seriously contemplate the existence of God, I strained to slip my odd-shaped thought-pegs into their correct holes. Rarely had I ever peered so deeply into my father's soul as I did that day I drove his new car home from Birmingham. He had become uncommonly vulnerable about his loves, and I never brought it up again since that day—to anyone.

Looking back, I gathered that for the first time he was verbalizing his feelings for Ayler that day. Did he regret revealing his heart to me? Should I have even asked? Did he ever reveal his feelings to Miss Ayler?

Feeling the familiar bump onto the Cahaba River Bridge, an odd-shaped thought-peg suddenly lodged into its proper place. Dad had not revealed to me a flaw in his character. No wrong had been done; there was no regret to be had. My mother had been gone for over a decade, and their marriage had truly been a picture of love and loyalty. It dawned on me. I was indeed grateful that Dad had not lived his last years imprisoned in grief, but had continued to experience the richness of life and love—of which he had so much to give.

Suddenly, another peg in my mind found its proper place. I had always sought to build a perfect image of my father—not a human one. I always idolized him as a war hero, while he called himself a "bedpan commando." I looked for pedestals on which he could perch— even a few that were out of my own reach. For some reason, it had been important for me to have an ideal father, not a real one. There was no doubt that my father was in every way honorable and noble. But he wasn't perfect.

As a young boy of about ten or eleven years old, I remember being at a high school football game in which my brother was a participant. We were the visiting team playing Wedowee, Woodland, or Winterboro. (I just remember the team logo was a W.) As a family we attended all of my brother's games, rarely missing even one—for years. Until I was old enough to be in the band, my usual place was behind the bleachers playing any number of childhood games with my friends, usually tag.

I'll never forget that night when one of my classmates randomly ran up to me and announced,

"Mark, I just saw your dad drunk in the bathroom." My friends heard his announcement and turned eagerly to me for a response.

"That's not true!" I said dismissingly. Another of the boys gathered around me suggested,

" Aren't you gonna go check?"

"No way!" I asserted. "That's impossible. My Dad doesn't drink." I knew my Dad's integrity, and even at a young age knew him well enough to know how crazy the accusation was. There couldn't be anything more opposite my Dad than a penchant for alcoholic drink. He was so dry he had to prime himself to spit. But now I wonder what it would have been like for me if my father *did* have weakness for such a vice. Would I have ignored it, denied it, justified it, exploited it?

Our tendency is sometimes to not allow our heroes to be conflicted about anything. It requires willful blindness on our part. Am I one of those hero worshippers? As my father's life heads to the finish line, am I more inclined to protect him than to know him? Had I created my father in my preferred image? Or did I know the real Coolidge Sims? There was one thing that over the years had caused more tension between my father and me that was still not resolved— only glossed over. I needed a resolution for myself. I needed to know:

Is that you, Coolidge?

"My father always said that money doesn't grow on trees.
Well, time doesn't grow on trees either."
Richelle E. Goodrich

Coolidge and baby Mike 1951

Gwynnelle, Coolidge, Gail and Bremon

Marylyn and baby Mark 1956

Mike, Donna, and Mark 1963

The Sims men
1956-1957

"Nick" and "Nubbin'"

Tavia Cunningham

Mr. Coolidge
The Medicine Man

Sadie Thompson

Charlotte and Elton Denson

Meemaw, Papaw and grandson Michael

Lindsay's catch with Papaw

50th Anniversary Celebration 1996

Papaw and Betsy
One step, two step...

Watermelon on Mt. Cheaha with Keith and Hope

Shouldn't it be yellow?

Four Generations: Papaw's first great grand

Sophia sharing 1st birthday cake with Great Grandpa

Elizabeth, Meredith and Donna visit Papaw on his 89th Birthday

Feeding the horses at Miss Ayler's farm

Coolidge and Ayler Caldwell

Papaw and great-grandson Grant cooling off at The Oaks

WWII Veteran "Honor Flight"

Michael and Misty's Beach Wedding

Kingwood Church 2012 "Salute to Service"

Juliette Grace arrived August 23, 2012- the same day Coolidge arrived in Heaven

Coolidge's namesake, "Asa Coolidge Sims"

Born December 26, 2013 to Michael and Misty

Proud grandparents Michael Coolidge and Kathy Sims with Asa

Mike and Kathy Sims;
Michael and Misty Sims;
Asa;
Keith and Anna Sims;
Hope Sims;
Inez Deakle

Mark and Peggy Sims;
Lindsay and Joel Sims
Sophia, Grant and Juliette;
Betsy and Nathan Smith
Charlotte and Dalton

Donna and Allen Taylor;
Elizabeth and Meredith

Chapter Twelve

We saw progress every day that Dad spent in the rehab unit. Physical therapy was helping physically and emotionally. Despite the swelling in his right leg and the residual leg pain, he was clearer than he had been in almost a year. His balance was getting better, but he finally welcomed the blue walker to be a permanent companion. He was okay with it, slowly mastering its ins and outs.

Visits from a stream of Ashland friends and other family encouraged him regularly. He was overjoyed each time Lindsay brought his two great-grandchildren to visit. Sophia was fond of him, but Grant was too young to have a clue. Lindsay was only eight weeks from delivering another little one.

Betsy, due in six weeks, came by to inform him of the name that she and Nathan had chosen for his third great-grandchild—Charlotte Elizabeth. She would be named after Aunt Charlotte and Marylyn, whose middle name was Elizabeth. That news brought tears to Coolidge's eyes.

Yogurt Run

It was my week to check on Dad twice daily while Donna's family took a week of vacation. Having a slow week at work, so I took advantage of my time with Dad. Rather than sharing it with the PT staff, I concentrated on our alone time. Transporting him to an appointment with Dr. Reeves, his heart doctor for the past quarter century, gave us a golden opportunity to share time and naturally, frozen yogurt.

I couldn't help but laugh as I remembered our most recent visit to Dr. Reeves' office several months earlier as

Donna and I both accompanied him. After taking seats in the waiting room, I quickly spotted a man with a major mullet haircut sitting to my right. As far as mullet hairstyles go, it was spectacular. From straight on it appeared to be a regular flat top. But from any other angle, one could see that his short hair stopped abruptly two-thirds of the way down his skull, where a thick mop of blonde hair, at least a foot long, extended down his back.

I strolled over to the magazine rack and snapped a stealthy cell phone photo of the mullet masterpiece from the side. Donna hid a laugh as I did my deed. I sat down to send the pic to my daughters who were always on the hunt for any live spotting of a stupendous mullet. While I was typing the message on my phone, Dad looked over at my phone and asked aloud,

"What's a mullet?" The waiting room froze. Donna started a violent fake-coughing spell and exited, while our fellow waiters stared at the floor, feigning invisibility. I shut my phone down and pocketed it, ignoring Dad's question. The elephant was loose in the room.

The meeting with Dr. Reeves was one I'd rather not have had. He lamented having to take Dad off of Lasix during radiation therapy but saw the necessity of it. Consequently, Dad's lymphatic system was having an increasingly hard time draining bodily fluids. The swelling in his leg was a result, and his heart had weakened noticeably since his last visit. Dr. Reeves could do very little for him anymore and basically released him. Still, he directed the nurse to schedule another appointment for December.

A couple of months earlier Dr. Reeves had made an ominous prediction to Mike—that Dad's heart would get him before the cancer did. The good doctor shook hands with Dad as if it was their final meeting. I could tell that Dr. Reeves was not truly expecting an office visit from Coolidge Sims in December.

The drive home included the obligatory stop at the frozen yogurt shop. Again it was chocolate, vanilla, and strawberry yogurt for Dad, amplified with fresh sliced strawberries and dark chocolate chips. I ventured out with an unusual mixture of watermelon sorbet, coconut ice, and blueberries in honor of Flag Day.

"Red, White, and Blue—you're looking mighty patriotic over there, Mark."

"Yeah, Thursday is Flag Day. You know me, I don't forget that day," I uttered.

"So you're still collecting flags?" he ribbed, "You probably have a thousand of the things by now, eh?"

"Not quite that many, but I *am* a full-fledged vexillologist. There aren't many of us, you know."

"You're rare, Son, that's for sure," he quipped, "in more ways than one. My hobby was playing golf; yours was collecting flags. Do you still have that flag I got for you?"

"Are you talking about the Nazi flag you brought back from the war?" I asked.

"No, the one that flew over the Capitol building in Washington," he spoke with an air of surprise. "Do you not remember that?"

"Oh, of course, I do! That was my thirteenth birthday present. It was a brilliant idea, Dad. And you got me a sixteen-foot flagpole for the yard, too. Best birthday ever. I was in heaven."

"Getting the American flag from Washington wasn't as tough as getting that Nazi flag back home from Germany, that's for sure. Did I ever tell you how I got it?"

"I don't think so, but I'm all ears!"

"My unit, the 180th General Hospital, had followed in support of Patton all the way across France, across the Rhine, and into Germany. When we arrived in Frankfurt, the city had just fallen, and we moved our hospital unit right into the nicest hospital in Germany—the huge, state of the art Luftwaffe Hospital. The Germans had abandoned it, leaving the incapacitated patients in their rooms.

We evacuated them as POWs and started using the hospital for our own wounded being shipped back from the front lines. It was like we moved into a Holiday Inn compared to the tent hospital we had been using."

I had heard that part of the story before, but I relished every moment of listening to it again. Dad was so engrossed in the story that he hardly remembered to take another spoonful of his frozen yogurt.

"Our superiors told us not to leave the hospital compound because there were active snipers and pockets of insurgents still in Frankfurt. But me and my buddy, Dunwoody, didn't pay them any attention and decided to snoop around in some of the abandoned rows of houses next to the hospital compound and look for souvenirs."

"Souvenirs?" I questioned. "Who looks for souvenirs in a war zone?"

"Everybody!" he answered. "One of my buddies said he was going to find a way to take home a jeep as a souvenir, but you're getting me sidetracked." He was eager to tell me how he came upon the Nazi flag that I had played with all of my life. Dad had my attention. I had never heard this part of the story.

"It was late in the afternoon when we went into this narrow, three story brick house, typical of city dwellings in Frankfurt, and began looking around. I found the Nazi flag on the floor of an open closet and picked it up. There was no electricity, so it was kind of dark in the house.

Suddenly we heard someone talking. We both froze in place to figure out where the voices were coming from. It was below us, so we assumed that whoever was talking was in the cellar. Trying not to make a sound, we made our way to a door that was cracked open, with stairs leading down into a room where there was an obvious flicker of candles. When we peered in, we saw several men in German uniforms talking around a table, looking at a map and planning something. My heart started pounding in my chest. Neither of us had even brought a gun! I was scared half to death, and praying like a sinner with one foot in hell."

I chuckled at his description momentarily, but then he began to half-whisper, as if I was Dunwoody, and we were both trapped again in the Frankfurt house.

"It was getting darker outside, and we were trying to figure out how to sneak out without being discovered when we heard what sounded like a person coming up the stairs. I glanced at Dunwoody, and he looked straight at me, and then like someone had fired a starting gun at a horse race, we scrambled to our feet and shot like a cat with its tail on fire, out of the house and making all kinds of noise in the process. While we were running, we heard them scrambling too—but in the opposite direction, and probably out the rear of the house. They were every bit as terrified as we were, and just as happy to get out alive."

"And that's how you captured the flag."

"Yeah. Somehow I escaped still holding on to that dang souvenir. Dunwoody had something in his hand too, but he dropped it in all the confusion."

"Well, from now on I'll show a greater appreciation for that souvenir of yours," I admitted.

"That's right! You better. And when I'm gone, you keep that flag and tell that story to your grandchildren."

"You better believe I will! That's awesome, Dad."

"I guess it fits you since you like history and war stories and flags. I remember how you designed Ashland's city flag, and another one too, I believe," he recalled.

"The Clay County flag," I reminded him. "They adopted it, but I'm not sure they fly it anymore."

"Well, the city definitely flies the Ashland one. I usually notice it when they put it up. It makes me proud."

"Thanks, Dad."

Just Like Family

We spent most of the day together, and I ate dinner with him at The Oaks. He barely ate anything, just a half a bowl of soup and some crackers. I figured the sweet treat in the afternoon had robbed his appetite, so I didn't push him to eat more.

Several months earlier, when Dad was still in Ashland and not doing very well, I had come to help officiate a funeral of someone who was very much a part of my family—Tavia Cunningham. Tavia had worked as a domestic housekeeper for our family for as long as I could remember. I was told that she came to work for us when I was just learning to walk.

Tavia was African-American, but was like a second mom to me and to my siblings. She worked for the Sims for over thirty years. Tavia died in her nineties, having suffered from dementia for almost a decade. There aren't many photos of Tavia because she ran from anyone who had a camera. No one could fry chicken like Tavia, and her cornbread was the best in the world— crusty on the outside and moist on the inside.

She had no children of her own but helped raise her husband Jack's children after his first wife died in the 1940's. We loved Jack and Tavia with all of our hearts. Our conversation that evening, with a dinner spread of soup and crackers, turned to Tavia's funeral. Dad brought it up.

"Mark, tell me how that funeral for Tavia Cunningham went. I really regret that I didn't push myself to go. You know, she came to the funeral home when your mother died. It really meant a lot to me. Did many people attend her funeral?"

"Yeah, the little church was full. Everyone loved Tavia. I was one of three preachers that spoke that day, and then we all ate a big spread of homemade veggies and fried chicken at the church. They buried her in a little country cemetery right next to Jack. I was honored to be a part, and I offered my words on behalf of you as well."

"I'm glad they asked you to be a part. She was really a part of our family, wasn't she?"

"Yes, and I had a hard time finding words that could do her justice. She meant so much to all of us."

"She was just like family," he acknowledged.

Deep Divide

I helped get Dad ready for bed before heading back home. During my drive, I couldn't help but think of the place that Tavia and Jack Cunningham filled in my life and the love for them that all of us shared. Dad and Mom had always been very good to Jack and Tavia. They paid her a very good salary, and also her social security so she would have something when she retired. I remember when Mom and Dad bought them their first TV, and how they always allowed Tavia to get whatever she needed from the drug store without cost—just like our family did.

Mom often asked Tavia to join us at the family table for the noontime meal, but she always refused, saying that it wasn't her *place*. At our house, she preferred to eat alone in the den and watch *As the World Turns*. That always seemed kind of sad to me. Still, when it came to Jack and Tavia Cunningham, the Sims family was colorblind.

But I honestly wasn't sure how genuine that attitude was from my father. I knew that he would never be cruel to anyone, but something wasn't right with his view of "race" as a whole. We had clashed vehemently over it during my teen years, but eventually just ceased talking about it. It was a sore spot with me, and we had never resolved our deep divide over the raw issue of race. He was my hero in every area but one. Dare I even try to discover his true feelings? Dare I bring it up after finally probing so deeply into the real Coolidge Sims? Did I want to know the answer? Was I better off just rewriting the story of his life with a feel-good ending?

I was a history major in college and had studied the burden of southern history for years. When the American Civil War ended in 1865, the southerners that had the hardest time with the new order of society—the freed slaves—were not the former slave owners, but rather the poor whites who suddenly found themselves in competition for survival, for jobs and for land. Many poor whites refused to see themselves as equal to the former slaves, developing a deep resentment and class bigotry toward them.

During the war, many resented fighting for a state government controlled by the wealthy slaveholders, for the sake of the slaveholders' interests. But during the more than ten years of Reconstruction, the poor whites were the ones who suffered the most under the corrupt Carpetbagger government of Alabama. Suffering caused them to shift their ire toward the newly freed blacks, eventually reinstating the deep divide between black and white through the infamous Jim Crow segregation laws after the Carpetbagger government finally ended.

Historically, our Sims clan who lived primarily in the foothills of the Appalachian Mountains did not supply the Confederacy with many sons for battle. Tucked away in the hills, many spent the war eking out a living. After the war, they became hostile toward the freed slaves who began to move around the South in search of land and employment. The competition became the enemy, and showed itself in feelings of racial superiority, even though their economic status was virtually the same.

My father was born into that world, just sixty years after the Civil War itself, and at the very height of Jim Crow power. He was raised during the time when the black minority was legally prevented from enjoying all the privileges of the white majority. There were separate public bathrooms, separate water fountains, separate entrance doors into public buildings, separate schools, separate eating arrangements—and yet they all lived in close proximity to one another, knowing each other well, even developing close friendships while legally "different."

There was a story about Papa Sims, often told in jest, that conveys the folly of the era. Allegedly, he was backing out of a parking space on the court square and backed right into a pickup truck belonging to his friend, Zeb—a local black man. Papa got out of his car and said,

"Zeb, didn't you see me coming?"

"Yes sir, Mister Cecil, I sho' did."

"Well, then why in the world didn't you get out of my way?" It wasn't funny to me; it was embarrassing. I always hoped it wasn't true.

I can remember in my childhood before the Civil Rights movement changed Alabama, the days when blacks could not sit at a table in a local white-owned café. They had to get take-out orders at the rear door. I remember the "white only" water fountain in the Clay County courthouse. Our little movie theater in town had a separate door labeled "colored," that led to the balcony where blacks were allowed to sit. Most black families in our town lived in an area called the "colored quarters."

I am honest in saying that it always bothered me. There was a conflict in my soul. I remember asking my mother why the "colored people" had to sit in a different waiting room at the doctor's office. She had a hard time explaining it, saying things like,

"That's just the way things are, Mark," or "They are more comfortable around their own people."

That didn't make a lick of sense to me, nor did it to Mom while she was saying it. Tavia was in our house every day and we treated her like family. She and Jack could sit on the couch and talk with us anytime they wanted. We didn't keep them in a separate room from us. They were not required to use separate bathrooms in our house. My mother was conflicted about the social order of things, much more than was Dad. It's probably because of her upbringing.

Courage and Grit

My Mom's family, the Nichols, didn't show any favoritism concerning race. In fact, my grandmother had best friends who were black and had no problem pushing the boundaries of the Jim Crow laws. Grandma Nichols was different from her contemporaries.

She would have been perfect to play the part of Skeeter in the movie, *"The Help."* She was truly color-blind, in the symbolic sense. She was gifted in mercy, compassion, and generosity—for black and white alike. I stayed with her on Saturdays while my parents worked in their retail business. We would spend much of our Saturday distributing leftover lunchroom food to needy families; checking on elderly persons in their homes; visiting patients in the nursing home and cooking for folks who were sick. Black, white, or green—it made no difference to her. Compassion was shown to anyone.

Grandma Nichols, or Estelle as her friends knew her, was a "lunchroom lady." In fact, she was THE lunchroom lady, in charge of the entire lunchroom mechanism for the local public school. Even before the Civil Rights era, she gladly hired workers of both races. Where most hired minorities so that they could pay them less, relegating them to the back room washing dishes and peeling potatoes, she promoted any deserving worker to the "front serving line," and paid everyone the same regardless of race. She was sharply criticized on occasion, but it made no difference to her.

One day she received a threatening letter from the regional grand dragon of the Ku Klux Klan who lived in a neighboring town, but she refused to be intimidated. After reading his threatening letter, she stormed into her bedroom and locked the door behind her, mumbling under her breath all the way. A short while later she reappeared holding a sealed envelope in her hand. Without saying a word to anyone, Grandma Nichols grabbed her purse and keys, climbed into her 1956 Chevrolet, and headed toward town. It was assumed that she went to the post office, but there was no way of knowing since she refused to talk about the incident ever again. For almost twenty years she was silent about the letter.

But then, as Grandma Nichols aged and became childishly fond of reminiscing about old times, the truth came out. She revealed that she had read his ugly letter. Then, wasting no time, she shot off a terse response letter of her own.

With a fiery pen, she informed him that the lunchroom ladies were well aware of the many illicit affairs he had carried on with women in the county and that publishing the details in the weekly newspaper would be no problem for them. She dared him to bring it up again. She never heard another word from him. (Of course, Grandaddy Nichols might have had something to do with it. Talmadge Nichols was a principled man who was a fierce defender of his family. He wouldn't tolerate threats, especially from a grand dragon.)

Spending most Saturdays as a child with Grandma Nichols gave me a first-hand experience in color blindness. Her best friend in the world was Mary Ballard. I spent many Saturday afternoons visiting in her house in the "colored quarters." Ironically, Grandma Nichols came from a family with rich Confederate military heritage and a number of former slave owners but still raised my mother without any racial bigotry.

Mom felt a deep connection to Tavia far beyond the employer-employee relationship. They were friends; loving, caring friends.

Years later, when my sister moved to a job in Birmingham, Mom brought Tavia with her to help Donna get settled in her new apartment, and to see where Donna would live. Peggy and I joined them for lunch at Wendy's. Tavia tried to sit alone, but we all insisted that she sit with us at the table. It felt good that day to proudly share the table with Tavia.

Mixed Messages

I grew up with mixed messages in a changing world. I began school in an all white elementary school and did not have African-American students in my class until the seventh grade. While my parents' generation echoed George Wallace's calls for segregation, another message resonated from people like Martin Luther King, Jr.

As I grew older, the ideals of Dr. King made more sense to me, especially since I was a Christian. It was confusing to me how Christian people, including my own kin, could share a worldview that made one race superior over another. My own experience with black friends at school clashed with that ugly worldview.

It didn't make sense to me. My Dad had many individual black friends to whom he always showed respect and compassion. Yet, at the same time, he verbally identified with the political ideology of disdain for the black race as a whole. It was thoroughly confusing. At times he would verbalize things that he would *never ever* say to Tavia and Jack, or to his own black friend Banny. As a young teen, I judged it as gross hypocrisy, and it caused me to gradually lose respect for my hero-father.

One of the earliest crisis points was in 1969 at a high school pep rally on the square in Ashland. My sister, age six, was enjoying the pep rally with her first-grade classmates, imitating the cheerleaders as all the little girls did. Donna was standing between two black classmates, holding hands and cheering wildly. After the pep rally, we climbed into the family car to go home and I remember Dad saying,

"Donna, why can't you play and hold hands with some of your little white friends?"

At age 14, I was stunned by his comment. I remember my frustrated Mom quickly responding,

"Coolidge, there's no need for you to say that! None at all!"

"I'm just asking her a simple question, that's all!" he said, equally frustrated.

His comment stuck in my craw and began to fester. Did he mean what he said? How could he have said that? Was it really how he felt deep in his heart or was it because of social pressure from his own peers? I imagined that a busybody had seen Donna and her friends and brought it to Dad's attention, somewhat embarrassing him. But I wasn't sure. Whatever it was, it didn't fit into what I thought I knew about my Dad.

Big "O"

The pep rally incident alerted me to something about my father that made him less than perfect in my eyes. Given my tendency to speak first and think later, major clashes with him loomed on the horizon. The first of many manifested itself on New Year's Day, 1972.

As a family, we had been invited watch the Sugar Bowl football game with the Wilson family next door. Auburn was matched against Oklahoma in a clash of two highly ranked teams, but Oklahoma jumped out to an early lead and never relinquished it. We were all disappointed, but Dad was especially frustrated. Our Tigers seemed to be unable to do anything right.

One of our best running backs, James Owens—also known as "Big O"—fumbled the football just as it looked like Auburn might make a comeback. "Big O" was the very first African-American football player ever to play on Auburn's team, and Dad let out his frustration with the player's untimely fumble.

"I *knew* he would do something like that!" Dad said with gritted teeth. "Why did they give *him* the ball, of all people!" Right in the middle of dipping a potato chip into some luscious French onion dip, I foolishly lobbed a verbal grenade into the room.

"Oh, you don't like him just because he's black!"

Everyone froze. Mom covered her eyes with her hand. I instantly looked up at Dad and began to apologize,

"Oh, Dad, I'm so sorry, I'm so sorry!" His furious eyes made contact with mine and then he ordered me to step outside.

It was the longest walk of my life on that dreary, chilly New Years Day. I feared the worst. We walked silently out through the Wilson's kitchen door, down the brick steps, and into the back yard. He stopped abruptly and turned me around to face him. I looked shamefully down at the ground during the long pause.

"Son, look at me." I obeyed instantly. "Mark, do you really believe what you said to me in that room?"

"No sir," I whispered. My heart was pounding with regret.

"I hope not," he said powerfully. "I wouldn't know what to think if I felt you really meant it."

That was it. It was over. We never spoke of it again. Truthfully, I regretted saying it, but deep inside I still felt that it was true.

Scary Times

My mid-afternoon ride to The Oaks the following day allowed me to make mental plans to ask Dad a few questions about how he processed those days when we clashed so badly. I didn't want to bring him stress, but I wanted to have some sort of resolution. I prayed for God to open the doors widely if it was the right time.

Dad had just finished his afternoon nap when I arrived. I strolled into his room as he was trying to put on the tight compression stockings.

"Hello, Dad!"

"There you are, just in time to help me get my stockings on," he said cheerfully. I proceeded to begin the process as I had done several times before. Out of nowhere I threw out a question for him,

"Dad, do you remember that Sunday morning when we heard about the bomb that killed those four little girls at that black church in Birmingham?"

"I sure do. It was right in the middle of all that trouble in Birmingham— back about the time Donna was born," he recalled correctly.

"Yes, it was in 1963, only a few months before Kennedy was assassinated," I said. "To the rest of the nation and the world, Birmingham became known as *Bombingham.*"

"It was just terrible!" he acknowledged. "I can't imagine how anyone could stoop to that kind of hatred. The country was really divided back then. It was a scary time. We had just had the Cuban Missile Crisis with Russia, and the Civil Rights movement was starting. I wouldn't want to go back to those days, that's for sure."

I knew that Dad would *never* have thought the incident in Birmingham was anything but a terrible wrong. Still, I was glad to hear him say what he said next.

"Mark, I remember telling your mother that day that a line had been crossed, and that I felt like it would cause a lot of regular folk like us to rethink our attitudes toward civil rights. I remember Brother Curlee saying the same thing at a deacons meeting not long after that."

"Had you ever seen anything as cruel as that happen while you were growing up?" I asked as I finished helping him with his compression stockings, and began tying his shoes for him. He sat back in the chair and thought for a moment as I worked.

"Did I ever tell you about the murder of Miss Mary Webster Garrison?"

"That name sounds familiar, but I can't place it," I answered.

"She was an old maid who lived with her parents, Judge and Mrs. Garrison. They lived over at the big house where Clarence and Mary Frances Pruet lived while you were growing up. Mary Webster had been home alone one afternoon. When her mother returned from a church function, she found her daughter dead on the basement steps. She had been viciously murdered. The main suspect was a black man who had been hired as a gardener. They figured it was him because she had been killed with garden tools."

"Oh, my! That will shake up a small town like Ashland," I remarked.

"It sure did. The men of the town gathered at the courthouse with their guns and divided up to search all over town for the killer. Papa Sims and I both went up town with our guns too."

"How old were you?" I asked.

"Oh, about 16, I guess. There were a lot of real firebrands in the bunch declaring how they were going to shoot him on sight, and some wanted to take him alive and string him up on the big tree next to the courthouse. The black folk in town didn't dare come out of their houses.

I remember thinking, *'I don't want Papa and me to find him. I don't want to see my Daddy kill somebody.'*"

"So you were afraid," I conjectured.

"You better believe I was. I wasn't so scared of the killer. He probably didn't have a gun. I was just scared of the angry crowd. I knew it could get ugly."

"So they found him?"

"Yeah, within a couple of hours someone found him—bloody and hiding in an old shed, not far from Judge Garrison's house. They hauled him to the town square and then things got crazy. Before long an angry hothead had thrown a rope with a noose across a tree limb and a group was clamoring for a public lynching.

Unexpectedly Judge Garrison himself appeared on the courthouse balcony and addressed the crowd. He ordered them to remove the rope, demanding that things be done orderly and according to the law. He directed the sheriff to take the killer to Talladega and keep him in jail there until trial, for his own safety."

"That's amazing! What a prince of a judge! What ever happened to the murderer?" I asked.

"Oh, he was eventually tried and sentenced to death. But it was all done legally, according to the letter of the law. No doubt Judge Garrison desired immediate justice for the man who had just murdered his daughter.

But he believed in justice, not revenge. I've always admired Judge Garrison for what he did that night."

Collision Course

We sat out on the patio together just before dinner talking sports, politics, and grandchildren. There was no guiding train of thought, only an array of rabbits being chased wherever we chose to chase them. A resident in a power chair made his way onto the patio and joined us for a few moments. The old guy was primed to talk and engaged Dad in a strange conversation about which car was better, a 1947 DeSoto or a 1948 Studebaker. They exchanged opinions and stories, but never exchanged names with one another. Dad was no longer keen on making new friends. He preferred only family to keep him company.

While he and the bald man chatted, I ruminated on one uncomfortable memory that had stuck with me like a bad cough all my adult life. It was a set of serious clashes that I had with Dad when I was around sixteen.

Being a veteran, Dad was very sensitive about the anti-war protests that enveloped the early 1970's. He was proud of his military service and of his country, having little tolerance for the outspoken critics of our troops in Vietnam. To heckle American soldiers as "baby killers" was beyond the pale.

"Peace signs" that showed up *everywhere* in popular culture unnerved him the most. It wasn't that he was against "peace," he just considered it weakness—anti-military—kowtowing to communism. He was not alone. Millions of his fellow vets felt strongly about it as well, especially in the South.

I was a very patriotic guy, and proud of my father's service in World War II, but as a sixteen-year-old, I had no zeal for the prospects of serving in Vietnam. I wasn't a *peacenik* but was certainly praying for Nixon to bring the Vietnam War to a close. Actually, my Dad was too. He was glad my older brother had received a military deferment by attending college—especially since his number was 7 in the draft lottery— a sure sign that a draft notice would soon arrive.

I was a drummer in our high school marching band. We were a small school, but had a really good band, winning awards regularly in band competitions. Our show that year involved the pop song, *Age of Aquarius* by The Fifth Dimension. It was one of the theme songs for the young hippy generation, especially the "give peace a chance" crowd. It was a really up to date, cool selection for our show. At the end of the song, in unison and right on cue, every band member on the field gave the crowd a salute with the culturally popular, two-finger *peace sign*. It fit the song perfectly.

When my Dad saw us perform the song at a football game, he was incensed at the "political statement" made by our nifty display of the *peace sign* during the band performance. That night when we returned home after the game, it became the center of conversation.

"Mark, I can't believe Bill Locklear had the whole band shoot a *peace sign* during the performance tonight. It was a political statement, and unnecessary."

"Dad, it just matched the song we had played," I argued. "Besides, it's not the same thing as giving the bird finger. You don't *shoot a peace sign*. It's a common greeting, not an insult."

"No, it's a political statement and an affront to all the men serving our country. I'm going to mention it to Mr. Tate," he forewarned.

"Oh, Dad, please, please don't say anything to him. He's not a political guy. It's not what you think!" I was petrified that he would say something to Mr. Locklear, and embarrass the mess out of me. I begged him not to.

"Okay. I won't talk to Bill, but *you* will not participate in it. I better not see you shooting a *peace sign* to the crowd."

"You can't ask me to do that, Dad!" I protested. "You're asking me to deliberately refuse to do a requirement for the show! It will reflect on the whole band!"

"No, I'm telling you that you cannot participate in making a political statement. Let the chips fall where they may. Blame it on me; I don't care. But I don't want *you* to do that on Friday nights in front of the whole town. Do you understand?" He had made up his mind, leaving me no wiggle room.

"Yes sir," I muttered. He nodded agreement and began walking out of the room. "But I still don't understand," I jabbed.

Dad spun around and squared up. "Mark, am I going to have to spell it out for you?"

"No sir," I wilted.

"Breathe Mark, breathe," he shot back just to get under my skin.

That sort of clash came more often than it should have. Part of it was his stubbornness, part of it was my smart mouth, and the remainder of it was just culture. *"Times, they are a changin'..."* Bob Dylan sang, and at the Sims' home, it was no joke.

My parents hadn't had the same challenge with my brother. I'm sure he had plenty of questions, but Mike wasn't as enveloped in drastic cultural changes during his high school days as I was. Hair was still short then, and the media was still conservative. More importantly, he didn't have a "smart mouth" like I did.

But even my brand of Christianity brought clashes in our home. The Jesus Movement of the early 1970's was in full-bloom and I was very much involved. Our theology challenged the status quo of our local church. It wasn't just Charismatic practices like exuberant worship and speaking in tongues that caused a stir. It moved beyond religion and clashed with deeply held traditions of the church.

Later, I chose to enter the ministry, but not within my parents' denomination. That change caused tension even after I had graduated from college, but it was the clash over racial attitudes that caused the deepest rift in my relationship with my father. In some situations, it even led me to question his faith. That was, of course, a bridge too far.

The Inquisition

At the time I was a leader in a student prayer and Bible study group that met in different homes on Tuesday nights. Some of us would meet again on Thursday to go "witnessing." Sometimes it was door to door, and other times it was making special, personal invitations to friends to join us at church on Sunday. Looking back, I also had an air of spiritual pride that was probably easy for others to see, but not me.

One Thursday night upon returning home from "witnessing," Dad drilled me on where I had been. I was defensive and gave some vague answer. He pushed for more detailed information.

"Son, where did y'all go tonight to invite people to church?" he pressed.

"Over in the quarters," I answered reluctantly. I knew by the look on Dad's face that he already knew the answer. He was already agitated. Obviously, someone had called and reported seeing my car at a house on the "black" side of town. He called me into the living room to talk.

"Why do you want to cause trouble in our church? Aren't there plenty of white families who need the Lord? Are there not some colored churches in town trying to evangelize their own?"

I was furious on the inside. I couldn't believe what I was hearing from Dad, a deacon in the church. I refrained from saying anything because I couldn't think of anything to say. My heart was beating out of my chest. I saw Mom standing in the door with both hands covering her mouth.

It was her typical way of reacting to bad news. Finally, I eked out an answer:

"I didn't think souls came in black or white."

"Mark, I don't doubt your compassion for souls, but I do doubt your wisdom and judgment. You're just not old enough to understand." He didn't shout at me, but he spoke with fervor. His words were meant to be calming, but they infuriated me even more.

"No, *you* don't understand what the Bible says! Jesus said to go into all the world, not into all the *white* world. You're just prejudiced!"

"I'm not so sure about that," he said in a crescendo. "Are you sure you're feeling compassion for souls, or are you just using your black friends to prove a point to our church!" The turmoil inside of me turned to tears as Dad spoke, but before I could say anything he made one last plea.

"Son, for the time being, will you *please* not go visiting in the quarters?" He waited for my answer, but I just stared at the carpet and said nothing. My heart was set to explode. I felt a strange mixture of anger and isolation, of confusion and regret. Finally, he walked out of the room without saying another word. Once he was gone, I leaned against the wall and began to sob. I heard Mom enter the room, walking across the carpet toward me.

"Mom, he's so wrong!" I shouted in a whisper. "He can't pick and choose who is worthy to hear about Jesus!" She moved beside me, grabbed my hand, and spoke through her own tears,

"Yes, your Daddy *is* wrong, but *you* are just as wrong."

"What? Mom, what does that mean?"

"It means that you and some of your well-intentioned friends are causing trouble that you don't even know about! And your Daddy is bearing the brunt of it," she exposed in a teary huff.

"No, Jesus is the one who's getting shafted," I alleged. "I'm going to bed."

I quickly moving into the hall and straight to my bedroom. Inside my room, I cried, prayed, and fussed half the night. In my mind, Dad was a pawn in the hands of church leaders swallowed up with prejudice against blacks. They were blind to the plight of those who were lost without Jesus and only cared about preserving the whiteness of our church. I considered it all the work of the Devil. My attitude of self-righteousness bordered on extreme as I drifted off to sleep.

Fortunately, I awoke the next morning with a less-combative mindset. Dad was off to work early, and I made my way to school without bringing the subject up to Mom at all. But for the next couple of weeks, I actually stepped-up my witnessing forays into the quarters. I was convinced of my crusade. Together our prayer group worked hard at school to evangelize our friends— blacks and whites alike.

It happened on a Sunday night. Two of our African-American friends, a guy, and a girl showed up at church and sat with the youth group. I felt a sense of delight, regret, and impending doom at the same time. I expected an incident.

But alas, the walls of Jericho did not come tumbling down, nor did an ugly race war break out in the aisles of the church. Only a couple of marginal church members stormed out of the church when they saw our guests walk down the aisle. When I got home from church, I was stunned that absolutely nothing was said to me about it. Dad and Mom were normal. I kept my mouth shut. The crisis just went away—albeit unresolved.

Forty years later I ask myself, "Did I truly have compassion for souls, or was I using my black friends to prove a point?" Perhaps it was actually some of both. After dinner, Dad and I made small talk until I got him readied for bed. I felt all right about bringing up our clash over the peace sign. I decided to make it humorous instead of heavy. In reality, our verbal fist fight decades earlier was just a small skirmish in the overall war between us.

"Dad, do you remember that time you got up in arms about *'shooting a peace sign'* during the band show?" I gave him the two-fingered peace salute, to which he immediately gave me a wide grin.

"I sure do," he said with his eyebrows raised. "I really acted the fool, didn't I?" I paused before I answered. I certainly didn't want to say *'yes you did'* to his question, so I came out with a sheepish,

"Didn't we all."

"I remember your mother raking me over the coals about that one. She told me I was unfair to make you look bad to your friends. She got me to modify my rule if I remember correctly."

"Yeah, I asked her to intercede for me. You gave me permission to *'shoot the peace sign'* at our competitions, and at the Lineville rivalry game since they were really important," I acknowledged.

"I guess I was too proud to back off totally. That wouldn't have done either of us any good."

I really wished he had settled that with me forty years earlier, but I felt a bit childish to have remembered it so vividly for all these years. I guess *I* was the one who was too proud to back off. I was more like Dad than I wanted to admit. At least we both got to laugh about it in retrospect.

"Speaking of remembering stuff, do you remember the time you brought me up to your church to say a few words about being a veteran, and you gave me a little bottle full of sand from Utah Beach in Normandy?"

"Yes, I knew that would be special to you, especially since we had decided not to try and make a visit to there."

"I want you to know, that really meant a lot to me. It choked me up, and I could hardly say anything." I could tell his emotions were surfacing again. "That little vial of sand meant the world to me," he whispered. I gave him time to wipe his eyes with his handkerchief.

"Dad, the Fourth of July is right around the corner. It's on a Wednesday this year. On that Sunday the first of July, we're having another service where we honor the vets and active service men and women. I want you to join me that day. I'm not expecting you to say anything, but you being there would mean a lot to me and to our church. You know there aren't so many World War II vets left."

"That sounds good. If you'll come get me, I'll be there."

"Deal."

"Being part of a family is less about being born, and more about being loved."
Earl Hamner, Jr.

Chapter Thirteen

Divine Appointment

My phone rang early on Saturday morning showing a number I wasn't familiar with. Out of curiosity, I answered after the second ring, and I'm so grateful that I did.

"Hello?"

"Is this Reverend Sims?" asked the lady on the line.

"Yes, it is."

"This is Desiree Hill, Banny Heard's niece from Ashland. You might remember my Uncle Banny."

"Of course I do!" I said.

"I'm planning on bringing him up to see Mr. Coolidge today if that's okay. He stays in a nursing home in Anniston, but he asks about Mr. Coolidge all the time. Would this be a good day?"

"Absolutely. Dad will be so excited to see his friend. What time do you expect to be here?" I inquired.

"Around noon if that's alright with you. Banny is going down fast, and he wanted to be able to talk to Mr. Coolidge one more time," she explained. "I put the address into my GPS, and will be leaving in a few minutes to pick-up Banny in Anniston—and then we'll be on to Birmingham."

"I can't wait to tell Dad! He will be thrilled! I'll look forward to your arrival."

Ever since they were young teenagers, Dad and Banny Heard had been friends. Banny, an African-American, wasn't allowed to attend the same school as Dad, but they became close friends while working together as teens at the Woco-Pep service station on the courthouse square. Later they were both drafted into the army during the Second World War, and eventually returned to Ashland, where they remained close friends.

I could hardly wait to get to The Oaks that morning and tell Dad about Banny's noontime visitation plans. He was beside himself with the good news, taking extra time to bathe, comb his snow-white hair, and put on one of his "good" shirts. He made sure I was prepared to get a picture of them together, and that his room looked tidy and smelled clean.

Banny arrived in a wheelchair, dressed up and sporting a special WW2 Veteran cap on his balding head. His round wire rim glasses rested loosely on his nose. Banny was always thin but appeared frailer than I had ever seen him. I'm sure he thought Coolidge looked every bit as frail, if not more so.

"Is that you, Coolidge?" Banny said as he spotted Dad seated in a wheelchair just inside the room. The two of them greeted one other with wide smiles and a firm handshake. I had to strain to understand Banny's words. His voice was not as strong as it had once been. A couple of times Dad leaned forward to make sure he didn't miss what Banny was saying. They exchanged pleasantries for a moment, but it didn't take long for them to do what they had always done best—laugh. Dad started the tomfoolery with a simple question.

"Banny, do you remember the joke we played on Junior Riley when he came by to use our bathroom at the Woco-Pep station?" Banny immediately started laughing.

"Which time, Coolidge? We wuz always messin' with him."

"Yeah, but this time was a dandy! Junior came in to "borrow" our facilities. As soon as he went into the little one-seater bathroom and closed the door, I got a can of WD-40 oil and slipped the spray nozzle under the bottom of the door. I gave it a quick squirt and you struck a match to it—pssssssst— a stream of fire shot like a flamethrower into the bathroom. Junior started hollering and next thing we knew he was charging like a bull out of there with his britches down around his ankles!" They both howled like school children. If they hadn't been in wheelchairs, they would have probably been plotting a trick on the nurses' station. Next, it was Banny's turn.

"Coolidge, did you ever know how I got my name, *Banny?*"

"Seems like I heard you tell it before, but I don't rightly remember," Dad answered.

"Well, we wuz playing baseball, and I wuz the pitcher, and I threw it hard and it hit the boy to where it knocked him down on the ground. He started talking out of his head, saying, *'Oh banny oh banny oh banny.'* His name was Gene Rollins. That ball hit him hard. I don't know if it was a curve, or a straight throw or what, but it knocked him down flat on the ground. And after that everybody just called me, Banny." Right away, Dad was ready with another comment.

"You know something, Banny? You're problem was—you fell in love too often." Banny bent over laughing at Dad's observation. "I'm serious, Banny. You'd tell me you had a girlfriend, and then by the time I saw you next, you'd already swapped her for another one. You should have just found one and stuck with her like I did!" By the way they laughed, there *had* to be more to that story. Still, Banny greeted Dad's insight with a nod and a big grin. Soon, their bantering blended into more serious talk.

"Coolidge," Banny said with emphasis, "Do you remember when you and me took that truckload of tires to Anniston?"

"Banny, we took *a lot* of truckloads of tires to Anniston!" Dad responded.

"But this one was different. We unloaded those tires and then we got hungry, so we decided to get us a hotdog and an RC cola. I followed you into the café and the man hollered at me, warning me to get my hide out of his café before he called the police. And you took up for me, Coolidge. I'll never forget how you took up for me and made him serve us both our hotdogs."

"Yeah, Banny, I remember that day," Dad said humbly.

"You didn't have to do that, Coolidge, but you did. That man could have kicked you out too, but you took up for me. I was so proud standing up there beside you, Coolidge. You're about the best friend I ever had."

"And Banny, you're probably my best friend too." Dad and Banny exchanged a few more compliments, and I took a couple of photos with my phone as Banny's niece prepared to roll him down the hall and back to Anniston. Dad thanked him for his visit and thanked him for being his lifelong friend. I could see that Dad's eyes were beginning to water as he concluded.

"Banny, the next time we see each other will be in Glory. We'll both be well and healed having a wonderful time together."

"That's right, Coolidge," Banny quickly responded. "It won't be long and I'll see you again in Glory."

It was another sacred moment for me. This meeting that I had witnessed between my father and his best friend, Banny Heard, had surely been a divine appointment; arranged by God, Himself. It had been *for me,* not just for my father— for me to more clearly see the *real* Coolidge Sims.

Ah Ha! Moment

I had a long talk with my family that night about the final meeting of two amazing friends. It brought tears to all of our eyes. My youngest daughter, Betsy, recalled a conversation she had with Papaw a couple of years earlier, during a visit to Ashland to see Dad. It was right after we had all gathered at Red's Catfish Cabin for dinner. Miss Ayler was there as well. Dad had told a couple of off-color jokes at the restaurant, making all of us uncomfortable with his use of racial stereotypes. My son-in-law Joel had heard him tell a racially charged joke the very first time he met him. Fortunately, I had anticipated that possibility and warned Joel ahead of time.

My brother Mike privately told Dad after the meal at Red's how uncomfortable it made us feel, and how it wasn't good for the grandchildren to hear. Dad recognized it and apologized profusely.

Betsy's visit with Papaw happened not long after that event. Their conversation stood out in her memory.

"Betsy, I 'm ashamed of some of the attitudes I have had in the past about black people. I have told jokes and said things that I'm ashamed of. I was wrong, and I've slowly come to realize it. I was raised in a different time with a different set of social norms. They were wrong, but I grew up thinking they were normal. But, still, that's no excuse. I'm not a racist and I don't think I'm better than anyone else in the world, black or white. I'm just sorry that it took people like me so long to see it. I acted more out of ignorance than malice. I've struggled with it, but I think I see it all more clearly now."

Betsy's recollection was an "Ah Ha!" moment for me. Everyone struggles with things. There is a constant striving we have all experienced between good and evil. None of us are exempt. Dad's struggle with racial attitudes was a battle he fought inside his own heart for decades. It was a gradual victory, but thank God he fought the good fight, and finally won.

Return to 138

The month of June had been marvelous for Dad. His balance was better, his pain was reduced, and his enjoyment of life seemed elevated. Once his thirty days of rehabilitation was up, they moved him back into room 138 in the Lodge. The thing he was most grateful for was his easy chair. There is something about a recliner that makes me think, "father." Dad had one at home in Ashland with an indention in the Naugahyde that corresponded exactly to his 5' 4" body shape. Anyone else who sat in it was made naturally uncomfortable. It was akin to wearing someone else's shoe—it just didn't fit.

Early Sunday morning on July 1st, Peggy and I made our way to The Oaks to help get Dad ready for the special "Salute to Service" day at Kingwood Church. When we arrived at room 138 he was already up and dressed for the occasion. His white khaki pants and red, white, and blue patterned shirt, and white shoes looked sharp, for sure! He was standing in front of the mirror, just finishing-up with his hair when we greeted him.

"Good morning, Pop! You look dashing this Sunday morning," Peggy said.

"And good morning to you, too, Darlin'," he chirped. carefully parting his hair with the tip of his comb. His concentration forced a pause in his sentence. "I've been up... since the crack of dawn. My hair's not exactly doing what I asked it to do this morning, though."

"Let me help you Dad," I offered. He handed me the comb, hoping I could tame the rooster tail that stood tall at the back end of his part. He continued staring at my attempt in the mirror.

"I wasn't sure what time you said you were coming, I couldn't quite remember, so I got up and had my breakfast first thing." The rooster tail settled down nicely.

"Did you sleep well, Pop?" Peggy asked.

"No, not really. I tossed and turned all night long. I felt my heart racing a couple of times and had to sit up for a minute or two. I thought about getting up and moving to my recliner, but I was afraid I might fall again, so I just stayed in bed and fought with it."

"I'm so sorry, Dad. We'll go to church this morning and then to our house for lunch. Peggy has fixed us something delicious to eat. I think the kids are going to join us for lunch too."

"That sounds good. I think I better take my walker, though, don't you?" he asked. "Just in case I get dizzy or weak...."

"Yeah, let's do that. We have a few minutes before we have to leave if you want to sit down and rest for a little while. I'll put these clothes away that the laundry brought back." He made his way to the recliner and plopped down gently.

"Now I might not stand during all the song service at your church this morning. Y'all tend to stand for a long period of time, and I might ought to sit a while and preserve my strength." Dad had always joked about how long our praise and worship segment lasted. He was used to a hymn or two followed by the worship leader motioning with his hand as he announced, *'You may be seated.'* Still, he loved music, especially gospel music.

"That'll be fine," Peggy confirmed. "You remember, we're not very formal, and especially today with our patriotic holiday emphasis. There will probably be plenty of people today in shorts, and nobody in a suit and tie. Good thing, since it's going to be so hot again today." We were in the midst of a *warming trend*, according to James Spann, the trusted local weatherman. Lately, it had been more of a *blazing hot* trend than a warming trend.

"Dad, did they give you your bath yesterday, or this morning?" I quizzed. He didn't have a freshly bathed smell about him—that was for sure.

"No, I didn't feel like getting up for it yesterday morning when they came to help me bathe," he admitted. "Do I stink? I used deodorant this morning."

"No, you don't stink, Dad. Why don't we bring your shaving kit and this afternoon I'll help you with a bath at my house?" I offered. "It'll help you feel a lot better."

"That's a great idea, Mark!" he said without hesitation. "I don't really like those boys that help me with my bath. They're kind of rough at times."

"Ok, we'll bring your toiletries and an extra pair of underwear." It was a good plan.

We took our time driving from The Oaks to the church, making small talk all the way. He asked more than once of what was expected of him at church. I reassured him that he would not have to say anything at all. It was just our attempt to recognize our veterans as a group. He looked sharp, but his mind wasn't as sharp as I had seen for the last month. I attributed it to his lack of sleep.

The Father in the Room

The Kingwood Church *Salute to Service* meant a great deal to Dad. When his branch of service was called to the front, he stepped out without his walker. The cheers from the congregation brought tears to his eyes, but when he put his hand over his heart during the National Anthem, he could not sing at all. My eyes were locked on him the whole time. When I saw his bottom lip trembling, and tears cutting streams across his cheek, I couldn't hold it back anymore. I openly wept, revering not only the flag in the room but even more, the father in the room.

After church, we made our way back to the Nissan truck in the parking lot. It was as hot as Hades by noontime, and even the short walk to the vehicle seemed to tire him. Only living two miles from the church, we were at my house before the air conditioner in the truck had hardly reduced the cab temperature. Even with windows down, the heat and humidity felt oppressive. Dad seemed unusually weak to me.

Betsy and Nathan and Lindsay's family of four joined us for lunch. Dad's spirits lifted when he got to see the great-grandchildren, Sophia and Grant, playing around him. Lindsay and Betsy always enjoyed being with Papaw, as did Joel and Nathan. Dad spoke highly the guys, feeling that his granddaughters had each chosen their best possible mate.

"Papaw, are you going to Michael and Misty's wedding next weekend?" Lindsay asked. "You know they're getting married on the beach."

"I hate to miss it, darling, but I don't think I can make a trip like that anymore. It would be a lot of trouble if I got my walker stuck in the sand, now wouldn't it?"

"I know Michael and Misty would love for you to be there," Betsy added. "But you won't be the only one missing— I won't be there, and neither will Lindsay. We're too close to delivering these babies."

"Hey, if either of them went into labor on the beach, now *that* would cause some trouble," Joel remarked.

"But at least there would be a couple of doctors right there, ready to deliver!" Nathan joked. Dad got a big kick out of that exchange.

"I know that's true, and I hate to disappoint Michael," Dad lamented. "But I *did* get to meet his little bride several months ago down in Georgia. Misty is a really sweet girl. I think she'll be perfect for him."

"I do too," Lindsay expressed. "I know you'll be missed, Papaw. I was so proud to have you and Miss Ayler at my wedding, but I know Michael will understand."

Just before we ate I asked Dad to say grace over the food. He did, but not without an emotional choke-up. We all were a bit emotional about it ourselves.

Peggy fixed a classic Sunday dinner—tender roast beef with potatoes, carrots, and lima beans. Dad bragged on her cooking and enjoyed fellowship with family. Naptime came for the children, so Lindsay and Betsy kissed us all goodbye and went home. I used the afternoon as an opportunity to help Dad with a much-needed bath. Unlike his baths at The Oaks, I was able to let him take his time, without pressure. He emerged from it feeling refreshed, but sleepy.

In the heat of the afternoon, I loaded him up for our trip back to The Oaks. I had offered to let him nap at my house and have some watermelon, but he declined. He was eager to get back to his easy chair. The AC in the truck could not keep up with the heat, so we rolled our windows down most of the way. I had it in the shop the week before, but they had obviously not fixed it. Dad got very uncomfortable and began feeling nauseated. He even complained of heart palpitation, but he was not in a panic. He was so weak when we arrived that I was forced to fetch a wheelchair from the lobby to take him to his room. I was so thankful to get him back in the cool air of room 138 without a major incident.

Panic Button

The beach wedding on the Gulf of Mexico was awesome! While we were in attendance, Betsy and Nathan checked on Dad daily. Betsy reported that he was doing okay, but was not his usually spry self. Nathan had offered him a trip to Cracker Barrel for lunch to celebrate Michael's wedding *in absentia*, but he didn't want to get out into the muggy heat. Still, Betsy made sure Papaw saw the photographs from the wedding as soon as Peggy posted them on Facebook. He was pleased to see them so promptly.

We certainly missed Dad's presence at the wedding, but he *did* find a way to make his presence known anyway. During our two-day stay in Panama City, the sitter called Donna's phone concerning Dad's panic attacks, and whether or not the paramedics should be called. Donna calmed him, but he was most afraid of being alone in the evenings.

Things were better once we all arrived back in town, but still, there were issues. Dad ate very little and began to prefer drinking a Boost supplement shake to dinner most nights. He had good days and bad days, but we saw him slipping day by day.

A couple of weeks after Michael's wedding, Mike's son, Keith, came to spend a whole day with Dad. It thrilled Dad to have Keith visit. Keith's presence gave him a special lift. They talked about everything under the sun. Keith asked questions and Dad entertained him with stories.

Early in the afternoon, Keith saw a box of Boost shakes in Dad's refrigerator and offered one to Papaw— who was not interested. Instead, Dad offered to give Keith all the Boost shakes he wanted to drink, and any he wanted to take home as well. Dad joked that it would fool Donna into thinking he'd been drinking them all along.

"I'll tell you, Donna's a slave driver when it comes to Boost. Every time she comes to visit me, she sticks one in my face and says, 'Drink it!'" They both laughed at his exaggeration. "Keith, you take the chocolate and vanilla ones. I'll keep the strawberry. They're the only ones I can half-way tolerate."

"Papaw," Keith asked, "Since Boost is out of the question, would you like to eat supper tonight in the dining hall, or do you want to go out to eat?"

"What are you hungry for, Keith?"

"Oh, it doesn't matter, Papaw. Whatever you want."

"I've got a good idea," Dad proposed. "Why don't you go over to the Blue and White and get us a couple of cheeseburgers and fries? They have great cheeseburgers. Best in the land."

"Sounds like a plan, Pop," Keith answered.

"Ok, let me give you some money, and you go pick them up. I don't think I want to get out tonight. My walker is so much trouble. We can eat and watch the Olympics or something."

"Where do I go? What's the name of the place?" Keith inquired as he grabbed his keys. Dad used his hands to give directions.

"Just go out of here to the end of the driveway, and go right until the road comes to a T; then turn right, and go down a couple of blocks, and turn right again, and you'll see it right there on the highway, on the right side of the road." Keith couldn't keep up with the directions but noticed that it was basically a long series of right turns. How difficult could that be? Besides, he could use GPS if he couldn't find it."

"Papaw, what's the place called, again?"

"It's called the Blue and White Barbecue," Dad affirmed.

Keith followed Dad's directions to the best of his memory, but there was nothing that he saw that in any way resembled what Papaw had described. When he entered *Blue and White Barbecue* into his GPS device, the destination appeared—but 73 miles away!

Meanwhile, in room 138, it dawned on Dad that he had sent Keith on a wild goose chase since the *Blue and White Barbecue* is actually located in Ashland!

"What have I done?" Dad thought. "I guess I'm crazy. How could I have done something so stupid?" Since he didn't have Keith's phone number, all he could do was call Donna for help.

"Hello? Daddy? Is that you?" She recognized his number on her phone.

"Donna, I have done the stupidest thing. I have sent Keith after a couple of cheeseburgers, and for some reason, I thought I was in Ashland, and sent him to the Blue and White! I don't know what to do now." Donna couldn't help but laugh, but she certainly didn't let on that she was amused.

"Daddy, don't worry. I'll call Keith. Elizabeth and Meredith both have his number."

"I declare, I'm a terrible grandfather to send my grandson off to the wrong place," he repined.

"Daddy, Keith's a big boy; he won't get lost. Don't worry, we'll call him and let him know."

While Donna was talking to Dad, Keith was calling me on the phone.

"Uncle Mark, this is Keith. Papaw sent me to pick-up some cheeseburgers from the Blue and White—but isn't that in Ashland?"

"Oh, Keith. He's confused tonight. It would take you three hours to get to Ashland and back. That's a long way for a couple of cheeseburgers."

"That's what I thought," Keith said. I'll just stop at McDonald's for the burgers. It's not as good as the Blue and White, but a whole lot closer."

July Recess

The entire month of July saw deterioration in the solid progress that had been made during the month of June. Sundowners Syndrome crept back into the picture as his sleep patterns were disrupted. Waking in the middle of the night with an urgent mission to repair the bedpost, or obsessing over the position of the blanket on the bed became more commonplace. During daylight hours he was less confused, but almost always sleepy.

A list of close friends from Ashland made trips to The Oaks to see him, knowing his time was short. A visit from Stanley Smith, his longtime friend and fellow pharmacist from the Ashland Pharmacy meant the world to him, but he struggled to be himself during the visit. Close friends like Pete Phillips and Don Fulbright, men with whom he had shared time on the golf course, in civic work, and in leadership at church were brokenhearted when they saw his steady downward spiral.

The attending physician at The Oaks, the gerontologist through whom his daily meds were regulated, met with us to evaluate where we were in Dad's palliative care protocol. Dad sat with us for part of the consultation.

"Mr. Sims, how are you feeling?" the young doctor inquired.

"Well, Doc, it's sort of hard to put my finger on that." As was happening more and more, Dad had a hard time spitting out the words he was trying to say. Often he would say the wrong word, recognize his mistake, and then unsuccessfully try to correct it. We had also noticed a change in the way he spoke. It wasn't paralysis, but he talked with his lips semi-pursed rather than with his voice, hardly opening his mouth. It was a drastic change from the man whom we knew to be an engaging public speaker. Nevertheless, Dad pushed through and continued his attempt to answer the good doctor's question.

"You see, I suppose I'm sort of depressed. Doc, I lost my wife of 53 years, and then my father, my mother, both of my sisters, and my only brother—all together at the same time, and it's been very difficult for me to handle this loss in such a brief time." Donna and I both showed facial reactions to his bizarre timeline of their deaths. The doctor saw it and acknowledged with a gentle nod without interrupting Dad's explanation.

"I had a heart attack a few years back, and my youngest sister died of cancer. I also had surgery for cancer in my leg, not too many years after I got discharged from the 180th Hospital Unit, attached to Patton's Third Army during the Second World War, and these sort of things." The doctor gently interrupted, deftly moving Dad's attention to another place. Dad respectfully followed the doctor's lead. Later, the doctor told us privately that Dad was simply rambling through life memories, attempting to tie them all together in a way that made sense—a common but frustrating pattern in an older person with deteriorating health.

In one of his more together moments, Dad and Donna and I were trying to recall an old song we sang together on long trips in the car when Dad suddenly thought to remind us of something important.

"I want you both to know that back before Marylyn died, I made a cassette tape of me singing all the old songs, and I put it in the black safe that's in the den closet at Ashland. It's not professional, but at least you'll have a way to remember them and pass them on down to your grandchildren after I'm gone."

Donna responded, "Oh Daddy! That's wonderful. Thank you! But we'd rather hear you sing them live!"

"Oh, and there's one more thing in that safe—in the same place I put the song tape. I also made a cassette tape of my life story. Not that my life was so heroic, but just so all of my grandkids and great-grandchildren will know some stories about their Papaw."

"Dad, that's a treasure! Your *memoir!*" I applauded. As quick as a flash he looked up at me,

"*Parlez-vous Francais?*" he questioned with eyebrows raised. Donna and I giggled. We had heard him say that all of our lives. It was the only French he ever learned, despite his long army stint in Europe. Donna teased him,

"Mom used to say that you left with straight hair, and came home with a little wave on the top. She blamed it on the French girls!" Dad responded with a chuckle of his own. Again, he had taken a serious, sad-like moment and injected humor.

"Mark, I don't know that it's as fancy as a *mem-waar*. It's more like a brief outline of my life. It's in my safe. I just wanted y'all to be aware of it."

Dad enjoyed some good days and endured the bad ones. *Sundowners* didn't show up every evening, but increasingly so. By the end of July, we were paying sitters to stay the night, just to keep him from getting up in the middle of the night, confused and risking another fall. A broken hip would be devastating.

Last Kiss

By the first week of August, we were considering hospice care. We knew that it was inevitable and that it might be sooner rather than later. Mike promised to come see Dad soon and help us figure out our next steps. Things felt better when we all three could meet face to face.

I was getting a morning TV update from the London Olympics when my cell phone rang.

"Hello, Don," I answered after the first ring. Caller ID told me it was Dad 's buddy, Don Fulbright.

"Hi Mark, it's actually Jo, because Don is driving the car. I just wanted to let you know that we are on our way to Birmingham see Coolidge this morning, and Ayler Caldwell is riding up with us. She really wants to see him, but we won't stay too long. Just a brief visit." Jo always spoke with calm reassurance, encouraging even the most despondent person. I knew Dad would be thrilled to see them, especially Ayler. They had talked on the phone, but had not seen each other but once since he moved to The Oaks.

"That's wonderful Jo. I'm sure it will make his day. I'll see y'all there." I called Donna to inform her of their plans, knowing she would want to speak with them as well. But Donna was iffy about what Dad's reaction would be.

"Oh, Mark. I'm not sure Dad will want Ayler to see him like this. If you remember, he was apprehensive about the visit from Don and Pete a couple of weeks ago, and even mentioned to me afterward that he didn't want any visitors for the time being except family. I don't know. Although if there is anyone that qualifies as 'like family,' it's those three."

"Well, the die is cast," I contended. "They're on their way, and I don't think we should tell them to turn around and go home. He might enjoy it more than he anticipates. What do you think? Should we even tell him they are coming, or should we let it be a surprise?"

"I agree that Ayler especially needs to see him again, so she will understand what's happening. But I don't want him to have a panic attack over it," Donna reasoned aloud. "Maybe we should tell him about ten minutes before they arrive; that way he won't worry himself into a dither, but it will be too embarrassing for him to refuse them."

"That's not a perfect plan, but I can't think of anything better," I conceded. "I'll call Jo and ask her to call just before they arrive. She'll understand." Donna agreed, and we determined what time we should rendezvous in Room 138. Donna wanted to get there early enough to make sure Dad looked nice.

They arrived around 11 am. Donna broke the news to him as they were driving onto The Oaks property. They had agreed to take their time getting to his room. As

Donna predicted, he was initially disturbed. But the gentleman in him determined to make the best out of what he saw as a humiliating presentation of himself. I was sure Jo and Ayler could change that impression.

After a gentle knock on the door, Don peeked in for permission to enter. Dad and Don locked eyes immediately.

"Is that you, Coolidge?"

"Yeah, it's me. Come on in, Don," Dad mumbled.

"Coolidge, this time it's not just old ugly me; I brought a couple of pretty ladies to see you." Jo made her way in with a happy countenance, with Ayler just behind her. Ayler looked especially beautiful, and her big smile greeted him with obvious emotion.

Donna and I stayed in the room long enough for the assurance that he was okay before we left them alone to visit. In less than thirty minutes, Jo and Don joined us in the lobby.

"I tried to prepare Ayler for the change in Coolidge's condition," Don offered. "She put on a good front, but I could tell that she was emotional."

"She's a nurse," Jo remarked confidently, "And she knows exactly what is happening with Coolidge. But she had to see him for herself. It's part of her grieving process."

"Was Dad emotional?" I asked.

"His eyes were," Jo discerned. "He didn't say very much, mostly answering our questions with as few words as possible. Don did most of the talking."

"Silence is awkward, right Mark?"

"Yes, Don, and you and I are cut out of the same mold," I chuckled. "There was a time Dad would have been in there right with us." Ayler joined us in the lobby with a tissue in her hands and tears in her eyes.

"He thanked me for coming, and we told each other goodbye. I just leaned down and gave him a kiss on the forehead," she whispered.

Like Banny Heard a few weeks earlier, Ayler knew that it was the last time she would see him. According to Don and Jo, she was very quiet and subdued during their ride home. The three of them were the last visitors Dad ever hosted in room 138. Their visit confirmed to us all that very soon the story of Coolidge Sims would no longer be punctuated by a series of commas, but with a final period.

"My friend Banny (G.P.) Heard, friends since 1935"

"A great father is one whose children look up to him rather than away from him."
Richelle E. Goodrich

Chapter Fourteen

Unpredictable

Donna and I returned to room 138 to find Dad quietly sitting in his chair. He was somber, although we tried to lighten the load. We knew that in his heart he preferred friends remember Coolidge Sims, as they had known him, not in his present state of confusion and decline. Our 5' 4" father sought all of his life to stand tall, and he did. He was always a giant in our minds.

Suddenly appearing at his door was my daughter, Betsy. Standing only 5' 2" and fully nine-months pregnant, she waddled into the room.

"Hi, Papaw! I just ran into Miss Ayler when I was parking out front." Dad suddenly came to life again. If there was anyone who could rouse him to life, it was Betsy. She enjoyed visiting him often, interested in everything he talked about. She was a second-grade school teacher who especially loved history. Once she dressed in a World War II era WAC uniform. It was the year Dad spoke at the Kingwood Salute to Service. He thought that was the greatest thing in the world, and he had us take their picture together. Betsy was known to even take notes of his many stories, and she loved to hear him sing his songs. Of course, Papaw ate up the attention from Betsy.

"Yeah," he garbled, "Ayler, Don and Jo were just by here checking on me. We had a good time together." He said the right words, but his delivery betrayed him. He was visibly despondent. Donna and I excused our selves into the hallway to let them talk for a few moments. We figured Betsy's arrival was a timely blessing.

"Papaw, guess what tomorrow is?"

"Probably the day your belly explodes," he said, trying hard to be upbeat. Betsy giggled.

"Well, you're sort of on target. I'm going to the hospital tonight to be induced. So sometime soon our little girl will be born, probably in the morning. Wanna come with us?" Papaw gave her a sheepish grin.

"I don't think so. That wouldn't be my place." He paused for a moment. "What are you naming the baby?"

"Charlotte Elizabeth," Betsy revealed, although she had already told him more than once.

"That's right. Charlotte Elizabeth. Named after sis....sist....sisters." He now had difficulty spitting out certain words. It was so unlike him to ever stumble over them. It embarrassed him. Betsy knew it and hurried to cover him.

"Yes, for Aunt Charlotte, and for Meemaw's middle name."

"Marylyn Elizabeth," he said. "And your real name is Elizabeth too, right?"

"It sure is, Papaw." Betsy noticed how he engaged in brief conversation and then moved into periods of silence, where he stared at the TV or out the window. His moods were becoming more unpredictable. "Well, I have a lot to do yet, so I better go. Be praying for us tomorrow, Papaw."

"I sure will, sweetheart," he promised. She leaned down to give him a quick hug and a kiss. She ambled to the door and turned to look one more time.

"I love you, Papaw. I'll try and bring the new baby to see you when I get out of the hospital."

"No, that's ok. You don't need to do that," he said surprisingly. "Don't do that." Betsy smiled and left confused, unsure of what he meant. What she *was* sure of was that he was in rapid decline, behaving less and less like the Papaw she remembered. She whispered to Donna and me outside the door,

"He's not doing very well today, is he?"

"No, this has been a tough day, and the days ahead will probably get even tougher," I predicted. "But Mom and I will be sitting on go, tonight and tomorrow, waiting for our new little girl to arrive."

"I'm so excited for you, Betsy," Donna said. "Don't worry, the Taylors will come visit after little Charlotte makes her appearance."

Charlotte the Third

Peggy and I were ecstatic at the birth of our third grandchild, Charlotte Elizabeth. She arrived on Thursday just before noon with only one hitch—on her way out she decided to do a cartwheel and presented herself breech. A caesarean section solved the problem and the third Charlotte in the family was born. She was a beautiful little girl with a perfectly shaped head, thanks to the caesarean. My mother's sister had a granddaughter and now a great-niece as namesakes. We spent the day at St. Vincent's Hospital with Betsy and Nathan—adoring Charlotte. I waited until Friday to check on Dad.

"Good morning Great-Grandpaw!" I gushed as I entered the room. He was sitting in his chair, properly dressed, and clean-shaven. "Looks like you cleaned up well this morning."

"Hello Markle!" he responded. "How's the new grandfather feeling this morning?" I was amazed that he realized what had transpired since I saw him last. It was the best emotional and mental state I had seen in a week. He had good days; he had bad days. I was so glad that today was a great one. They had become too rare.

"I'm as proud as a peacock, as you can imagine. Peggy is going back up to the hospital this morning. I'll join her later. Now, let me show you some beautiful pictures of Charlotte." I took my time showing him photos on my phone screen. He made over each one like it was a showstopper.

I couldn't help remembering how overjoyed he was when his each of his own grandchildren came into the world. Lindsay was their first grandbaby. They drove from Ashland to Birmingham as soon as we told them Peggy was in labor. It was a Sunday morning, and Dad put the "pedal to the metal" all the way. An Alabama state trooper pulled them over about ten miles out of Ashland. When the Trooper asked *'Why are you in such a hurry?'* Dad wasted no time telling him that his very first grandchild was about to be born, and he couldn't help but be in a hurry. Dad won him over with his honesty. The lawman only issued a quick warning and sent him on his way. Two days later, Dad closed his pharmacy early so he and Mom could drive to Birmingham and see Lindsay again!

Final Resolutions

Dad was perfectly lucid that Friday. I took advantage of his mental clarity by initiating a light conversation about our stressed relationship in the past. I did not want to rub salt into any wounds but felt that time was of the essence. I still had a couple of questions left to ask, and a heartfelt apology to make. I sensed an unusual warmness between us and knew the Lord had answered my prayer for an open door. Dad actually pushed the door open.

"Want a Co-Cola, Bud?"

"No thanks, not this early in the day," I explained.

"What about a Boost? I'm trying to get rid of them before Donna gets here."

He was *on* it today; he was in rare form. His peeved snicker was contagious, and I had to chuckle out loud. His mind was clear, but he was frail, and he still had difficulty spitting out his words. "What's on your mind this morning, Bud?" he inquired. I wasted no time getting to it.

"Dad, you and I had a conversation way back when I was about sixteen, and I told you and Mom about feeling called into ministry. Y'all were always very supportive and paid a lot of money to send me to Samford for my education. I remember you telling me that it might be better if I majored in something other than ministry so that I could fall back on something if things didn't go well." He was ready with his response.

"And you told me you didn't want to ever have to fall back on anything. You were convinced that you were following the Lord's will, and after you told me that, I was convinced too." I felt my throat tightening up—about to cry.

"Dad, I'm so thankful for the way you and Mom stood with me, and for the bucks, you spent on me for my education."

"It's been worth every penny, Mark. You've done real good with your chosen occupation," he said convincingly.

"Dad, do you remember when I took the job at Kingwood during my senior year at Samford, and you and Mom advised me not to? I know you weren't happy that I had changed denominations, but do you still think I did the wrong thing?"

"No, not at all," he spoke. "We were creatures of habit, like most people. I couldn't imagine you being anything other than a Baptist preacher like we've always known. But as I said, you and Peggy followed God's will and I'm really glad you did. I like your church, and your mother always did too. She got to where she believed just like y'all do."

"Yeah, she did," I admitted.

"But Mark, you never really caused us much trouble; Mike and Donna didn't either," he conceded. "You never got involved in drugs, or alcohol, or things of that nature. You were honest, married a great girl, raised a fine family, and turned out pretty good." Again, I was on the brink of tears.

"Dad, I owe you an apology for the disrespect I showed you during those years when I made it hard on you as a church leader. I was pushing an agenda, and didn't understand why you would say something like, 'Don't go visiting in the quarters.' It didn't sound right to me. And I don't think we ever resolved it." He sat quietly for a minute, looking for the words.

"Son, I'm not the same person I was in those days, but I wasn't against what you were trying to do for the Lord. I was just in a tough situation, that's all."

"Why did you forbid me?" I asked plainly. "Mom said you were bearing the brunt of my actions. What did that mean?"

"Son, a few of us on the deacon board knew that it was a matter of time when integration would hit the youth group—because whites and blacks were in school together. It was inevitable. But there were some that wanted to fight it and split the church. So, I was chairman of the deacons at that time, and I was trying to work with the Pastor and some of the leaders so we would have a plan in place that wouldn't let the hot heads cause a scene."

"And I was pushing hard before you were ready," I realized. "I didn't know that Dad! Why didn't you explain it to me?"

"Because you were headstrong and proud, and you would have run your mouth and ruined everything."

"Dad, I'm so sorry. You were working for Jesus too, and I was too blind to see it. I should have trusted you more than that."

"I had mixed feelings myself, and I said a lot of things that were wrong in those days. I'm sorry too. I grew up with the wrong mindset, and it stuck with me way too long. Remember, God is patient with us. Sometimes it takes us a lifetime to finally get it right."

That had reminded me of a verse from the Bible; one that I had used in a recent sermon from Romans 2:4.

"*Or do you show contempt for the riches of his kindness, forbearance, and <u>patience</u>, not realizing that God's kindness is intended to lead you to <u>repentance?</u>*"

Dad was right. God is good, kind, and *patient.* It was the strength of Coolidge Sims' relationship with the Creator that finally won the war. I saw it in his eyes. He was ready.

Taking Turns

By lunchtime, he was slipping back into lethargy. Eating very little for lunch, he took a long nap in his easy chair. When he finally woke up, he was dazed, confused, and complaining about his swollen ankles and legs. Donna joined us and we tried to watch some of the London Olympic Games together, but we watched most of it without him. He nodded-off, taking micro-naps much of the time. Donna stayed with him until the sitter arrived at bedtime. I took leave and went home.

The next day was the same except that my sister and I switched roles—she came early, I stayed late. It was a pattern we kept going for the next week, adjusting who came early or late by the demands of our schedule. We called it our "crazy routine."

On Thursday, Mike called Donna and confirmed his plans to drive up from Columbus and visit on Saturday and Sunday. Donna and I were always strengthened by his visits, but this one would be especially helpful considering his rapid decline in the last two weeks. He could help us determine if the time had come to arrange hospice care. As it was, we were paying sitters for nine-hour stints during the overnight night hours—solely for his safety.

That Thursday night, around ten o'clock, I got a phone call from Donna.

"Hello Donna, Is everything all right?" I asked, fearing another nighttime catastrophe.

"Oh yes," she reassured. "I'm leaving The Oaks right now; the sitter's there, and Dad's in bed. But I had to call and tell you about an eye-opening conversation I had tonight with a lady in the dining room. There's a tall, kind lady in a wheelchair that sometimes sits at the same table as Dad. You probably remember her."

"Yes, I know who exactly who you're talking about. She has a really sweet, calm voice."

"Right. Well, I was having a hard time getting Dad to even take a bite. He wouldn't even open his mouth. I was begging him to eat and drink something for nourishment sake. He kept saying, *'I can't, I can't.'* I was so frustrated and decided to roll him back to the room and try to get him to drink another Boost. When I excused us from the table, the lady motioned for me to come to her. She said so calmly, *'Let him die. He's ready to go, please let him die.'* That's all she said to me." Donna's voice trailed off into a whisper, and tears welled in my eyes.

"Donna, it makes sense," I admitted. "She must have lost her husband, or she was a nurse or something. It sounds like she is aware of what's happening to him, and we're not. We've never done this before."

We Three

Mike's visit on the weekend confirmed our inclination that it was time for hospice care. Donna made the necessary phone calls and set things in motion. Dad was becoming more weak and frail by the day. Even standing while leaning on his walker was no longer possible. He had to be physically held up to shower, to use the restroom, or to brush his teeth. For a fiercely independent, self-reliant man, the result was the humiliation of being helpless.

My brother noticed it during his two-day visit with Dad. He tried to engage Dad in as many conversations as he could, but they usually ended in Dad's frustration at not being able to express what he was trying to say, or in nodding off to sleep. Much of Mike's time was spent just watching him sleep, and remembering the vibrant father that had been his mentor. He was proud to have Coolidge as his middle name.

Mike had always been a respectful son and had idolized his father in so many ways. As a teenager, Mike guarded his tongue and didn't clash with Dad the way I did. He had a tougher time with Mom, who was quick to scold him when he was a minute over curfew, or when he did something that was the least bit dangerous. I learned from his mistakes—I learned what *not* to tell Mom.

Dad and Mike shared a lot in common—medicine, sports, faith. He was the oldest, and a great student of our father's good character.

When Mike left Sunday evening for Columbus, he knew that there was a great possibility this visit would be his last. The three-hour drive would give him plenty of time to unpack his feelings in private and to thank God for the blessing of knowing Coolidge Sims.

Donna and I said goodbye to Mike and together got Dad ready for bed. I agreed to come in the Monday morning, and Donna would again take the evening shift before the sitter arrived. All that would change once hospice came on board.

God Encounter

When I arrived Monday morning, August 13, Dad was dressed, but asleep in his easy chair with a woven blanket tucked tightly around his legs. I woke him up, and at first, he didn't know who I was. Eventually, some of the brain fog lifted, and he addressed me as Mark. He was not interested in breakfast, or even in morning coffee, and I knew better than to offer Boost or Ensure. Something was going on with him as he sat in the brown recliner. It reminded me of when Mom was at the very edge of death, lying in her bed enjoying visions of heaven and discussions with angels.

He was breathing heavily and groaning a bit. His lips moved like he was talking, but I couldn't understand any of his words. He mostly kept his eyes closed, but randomly looked upward for a moment, and then closed his eyes again. I risked asking him what he was experiencing.

"Dad, what are you thinking about?"

"I'm thinking about home." Then he began to sing something. The only word I could recognize was the word,

'Jesus.' It was like he was dreaming. His whole body trembled strangely, but not violently.

"What's Jesus saying to you, Dad?" I ventured to ask. He responded with more singing. This time I understood his words and the melody was clear. *"Welcome home, Son, welcome home."* He became calm again and was awake, but he didn't say anything afterward.

Whether it was a dream or a vision, or a "halfway there" encounter with Jesus, similar to the ones Mom experienced, I don't know. But it happened spontaneously in room 138 as he sat in his easy chair, and I know that it was real.

Shutting Down

The Oaks allowed us to get twenty-four-hour hospice care for his final days. It was a great relief to Donna and me, as we had been unable to leave him alone in his condition, even for a moment. The hospice nurses were a blessing, treating him with the utmost respect and kindness. He slept most of the time, sometimes in his easy chair but most of the time in his bed—especially at the end. Donna's oldest daughter, Elizabeth, visited Papaw several times during these days, but he seemed confused, often calling her Marylyn, or Gwynnelle, or Donna.

Early on, the hospice nurse saw my sister's frustration at Dad's refusal to drink his Boost supplement. She pulled Donna aside and instructed her,

"Your father is not going to die because he's not eating; he's not eating because he's dying. His body is shutting down and doesn't want nourishment." That was the day Donna understood what that lady at his dining table was trying to say to her,

"Please let him die." It had sounded harsh then, but now it made sense.

For the next week, Donna and I planned to continue our "crazy routine," but neither of us could stay away. We both showed up in the morning, and again in the evening—all the while, a hospice nurse was in attendance, too. Mike got a daily report from us by phone at least once a day. We got the word out to our extended family that his time was short. Dad slept a lot and barely ate anything at all, although they brought him a tray at every meal. There were a couple of "good days," but that was a relative term—it meant that he didn't sleep most of the day, or that he carried on a brief conversation with someone.

On Monday morning, August 20, Donna made her way to room 138 expecting to see him still in the bed, as he had been most of the weekend. Instead, he was sitting in his brown recliner, freshly bathed and dressed.

"Hello sweetheart," he spoke in a feeble voice. Donna was thrilled to hear him acknowledge her. Unfortunately, those were the last words he spoke to her. His energy left him, and he spent most of the day asleep.

Peggy and I brought Lindsay to visit him the following day. He was asleep in his bed and never acknowledged any of us. Lindsay sat beside his bed and held his hand, quietly sobbing. Nine months pregnant and planning to have the baby on Thursday, she knew it was possibly her last time to see him. Saying goodbye was tough.

We brought Betsy on Wednesday to say our goodbyes. Betsy stood quietly beside him and then kissed him softly on his cheek before she left, whispering in his ear, *'I love you, Papaw.'*

Hoping that he could hear and understand, Peggy expressed to him how much she loved him, and thanked him for being such a wonderful father-in-law. Next, I stood silently beside him for a moment, and then leaned over and whispered in his ear,

"I love you, Dad. I hope to see you tomorrow."

Donna met us out in the hallway before we left the building. "Now Mark, tomorrow Lindsay is having the baby, so you are *not* to come up here at all. We'll be fine. My family will visit Dad tomorrow. Tomorrow is about Lindsay and Joel and the birth of your fourth grandchild. I'll call you if anything happens."

Peggy and I agreed, thanked her, and headed home. Tomorrow, August 23, was going to be a great day!

Oh, Happy Day

Beautiful little Juliette Grace was born at around noon on Thursday, August 23. Having two granddaughters born in 21 days was amazing. The month of August already a month of celebration for our family— Charlotte's birthday (2nd), Nathan's birthday (4th), mine and Peggy's anniversary (22nd), Peggy's parents' anniversary (23rd), Juliette's birthday (23rd), Mom's birthday (24th), Dad and Mom's anniversary (24th), Peggy's brother's birthday (25th), and Sophia's birthday (25th). August is one big party!

Celebration was in order on this Thursday as we welcomed Juliette's entry into the world. Her arrival brought smiles to all of our faces. Her eyes were dark, just like her mom's—a beautiful little girl. We spent all afternoon and evening at the hospital, taking turns holding her, watching after her two siblings, and loving on her proud parents. Finally, we made our way home, grateful for such a happy day.

At around nine o'clock that evening I received a phone call from my sister.

"Mark, hospice just called me. A little while ago, Dad passed away peacefully in his bed. I'm sorry it had to happen on such a happy day for you and Peggy." Pausing for a few seconds, I was philosophical in my response,

"Oh, it's *still* a happy day for all of us, especially Dad. It was just a few hours before his and Mom's anniversary and Mom's birthday. He always preferred to arrive somewhere a little early, and he did."

"I'm about to call Mike and Kathy now," she said with a shaky voice. "Then Allen and I are headed to The Oaks."

"Ok. I'll meet you there shortly."

I drove the all too familiar path to The Oaks in silence. My mind flooded with thoughts and emotions of every kind. I wasn't surprised that he died without any of us being present. He had spent his life protecting us from pain, and I was certain that he preferred to spare us the grief of watching him take his last breath.

It brought to mind the song he heard God singing, *Welcome home, Son, welcome home.* I envisioned what it must have been like to instantly feel strong and vibrant and fully healed. It was a beautiful irony that Juliette was welcomed into this life on the same day her Great Grandpa was welcomed into the next. In God's Kingdom, life begets life.

I picture his arrival at a real place called Heaven. It was not entry into some blissful ocean of the mind or a vague, mystical fog bank. It's a place more real than anything Coolidge had ever seen on earth—a place of eternal light, and of reunion with familiar faces. I can only imagine his response after hearing a familiar voice ask...

..."Is that you, Coolidge?"

"Our fathers never leave us. Ever."
Brad Meltzer

Chapter Fifteen

We located the closet safe and the cassette tapes Dad had told us about earlier. Next to them was a sealed envelope containing his wishes for a memorial service. Most of them were easy to fulfill, but several of his choices for pallbearers had preceded him in death.

Weeks earlier, I had gotten permission from my siblings to pen his eulogy. We chose a local pastor, Ben Rosser to read it, especially since I knew I could never get through it without falling apart. The word *eulogy* means, "good words." It was my first attempt to pen my thoughts about our father, Coolidge Sims. [See the full eulogy text in the Epilogue.]

That day, the Baptist Church was filled with mourners and admirers, but one person was strangely absent—Sadie Thompson. Later we got word that she was too physically ill to attend, but deep inside we knew that she was unable to handle the deep emotion of losing her last link to yesteryear. Mike, Donna, and I paid her a visit a couple of weeks later, bringing a measure of comfort to her aching heart.

We were so appreciative of the outpouring of love and affection for our father from the community. Dad had been an icon in Ashland, and we were blessed by the stories of his influence in the lives of his fellow townspeople. In a small town, life leaves a clear footprint, and death leaves a very deep crater.

Grandkids Remember

Gathering with all the family at Dad's house after his burial was cathartic for us all. The deep respect and love for Dad that Peggy, Kathy, and Allen felt for their father-in-law was obvious. Peggy noted something we all recognized as true:

"We could always expect a call from him where he sang *Happy Birthday* to us—the whole song, not just part of it. I'll miss that on my birthday in a couple of weeks."

Allen remarked, "Coolidge took me in as a part of the family from day one, treating me with respect and love at the same time. Watching him fill the role as a leader in the church inspired me to do the same. He taught me that real men can be spiritual leaders in the home as well as in the church."

I watched how the grandkids clustered together remembering Papaw through the stories and jokes he told them over and over. It was a raucous time as they laughed and celebrated his life. I knew that if he could, he would have been right in the middle of them, cutting-up and enjoying the moment more than any.

"He always walked with us up town, to get a cone of ice cream at the Dairy Queen," Hope recalled. "One day Keith and Betsy and I begged him to let us go alone. We knew the way and wanted to do it ourselves. He finally agreed, but before we got halfway there, we saw Papaw coming behind us. Meemaw had freaked out, fearing that we would get lost, or kidnapped or something."

"I remember, Hope, we *were* lost! At least I was," Keith chimed in.

"I'm glad he did!" Betsy added. "I remember some dogs started chasing us, and he picked up some rocks and blistered their hides!"

"Do y'all realize how in Ashland people always say they are going *"up town"* instead of *downtown?"* Michael inquired. "I asked Papaw why, and he said, '...*duh, because you have to go up a hill to get there.*'"

"Do y'all remember his favorite joke?" Keith asked. "The one about the Wilson's little dog that ran out of gas?" Everyone laughed heartily recalling how Dad told the long version before popping the punch line.

Meredith spoke of trips with Papaw to Ayler's farm, where they fed the horses and rode on the four-wheeler. "I was the youngest, and never remembered Meemaw. Miss Ayler was like my grandmother from Ashland," she revealed.

"A couple of years ago," Betsy recalled, "Papaw was in the hospital getting his pacemaker fixed. We were all in his room after the procedure when he asked Uncle Bill Carpenter, *'Bill, will you do me a favor? Will you drive over to Ashland and feed my little dog. I forgot to get someone to take care of him for me.'* We all looked at each other like he was crazy. He didn't have a dog! Uncle Bill had a weird look on his face but agreed to do it. Then Papaw said, *'Bill, you won't have to do anything but feed him and give him water. And don't call him, because he won't come—he doesn't have any legs. But if you don't mind, please take him out for a short drag.'* The room exploded in laughter. It was so typical of a Coolidge Sims moment.

Elizabeth remembered, "Every time we drove by that graveyard on the way to Red's Catfish place, Papaw would say, *'Do y'all know who's buried in that graveyard?'* We would say *'no'*, then he would say, *'Dead people.'* He did it every time, and we knew what he was going to say, but we laughed anyway!"

"Keith, do you remember empty pill bottles that we played with in Meemaw and Papaw's den?" Elizabeth asked.

"Yes!" There were hundreds of them that Papaw brought from the pharmacy for us to use as building blocks. I remember building high towers and then crashed into them, scattering the blocks all over the place."

"We have a picture of it somewhere," Meredith added. "Playing with them was so much fun. Papaw kept them in a box next to the piano, just outside the laundry room."

"Exactly," Betsy agreed, "and I have that pic somewhere at home."

Michael threw another memory onto the table: "Papaw sometimes took us fishing at a catfish farm where it was impossible *not* to catch fish. There were so many fish in that small pond, we would catch them about five seconds after putting our hook in the water."

"We thought we were such great fishermen," Keith admitted, "because he told us we were." Michael also recalled the small cardboard container of six Coca-Cola drinks that always sat on the floor, just outside the kitchen. He told how he and Lindsay wanted to drink them so badly but were afraid to ask.

"Papaw told me that he never missed a day of school from first grade through twelfth grade," Hope said. That seems impossible, but Dad said it's true! He has the certificates to prove it."

"I have a crazier fact than that," Keith added. "Papaw was a legit, every-morning school bus driver from the time he was seventeen-years-old. Can you imagine that nowadays? A minor driving a school bus full of kids?"

Betsy reminded everyone of how Papaw and Meemaw enjoyed taking them swimming at the Riley's house next door. Once when Hope and Betsy were enjoying their swim time, a brief rain shower began. Papaw scared them to death when he hollered, *"Hurry,* girls! Get out of the pool! It's raining, and you might get wet!"

Meredith deepened the group conversation when she recalled a Sunday afternoon visit with Papaw at The Oaks.

"Elizabeth and I were asking Papaw how he was feeling, and he said, 'I'm tired all the time, and I think I just want to go home.' We thought he was talking about moving back to Ashland, but now I don't think he was."

"Yes," Elizabeth added, "I told him that he had to stay close-by for a few years so that when I get married, he can come to my wedding." He said, 'I don't think I can do that, Darlin. I'm so tired, and I'm ready to go home.'"

Family Table

The following Sunday, Peggy and I gathered with Nathan, Betsy, and baby Charlotte at Lindsay and Joel's house to share dinner together—introducing newborn Juliette Grace to the family table. It took no time for us to begin joyfully remembering special times with Coolidge Sims.

Lindsay had missed Papaw's funeral because Juliette had just been born. But she recalled a Papaw story that had stuck with her since she was a little girl: At Dad's house in Ashland, the walls of almost every room were lined with thick pine paneling, typical of ranch-style houses of the 1950's. Not cheap, veneered paneling, but natural pine paneling complete with knotholes, and sealed with varnish. Papaw would point out the dark knotholes in the paneling and say,

"See those holes and spots on the wall, Lindsay? Those are bullet holes from back in the day when Indians roamed the woods in this area." (pronounced, *AYE-ree-ah*.) "We had to battle those Indians, just to get them out of the house, so we could live here." Of course, Lindsay believed every word, amazed at how fierce the battle had raged throughout the whole house since every wall was covered with "bullet holes."

"Anytime I went to stay overnight with Papaw," Betsy recalled, "The first thing he'd do was open his refrigerator and say, 'Look what I got for you, Besty— grapefruit— your favorite!' And each morning he'd wake me up around 7 o'clock. 'Betsy, You gonna sleep all day?' He'd have each individual section of my grapefruit cut so that all I'd have to do is scoop it out. Even when I was a college student he'd do that!"

"There is a picture of Papaw and me when we went fishing in Ashland," Lindsay remembered. "I was about seven or eight years old and had caught a couple of little fish. What I remember was that a fish fin cut Papaw's hand and caused it to bleed. I was so afraid he was going to die of the wound, and I felt badly that it was my fish that caused it!"

Betsy cracked us up when she revealed this: "He'd let me drive the cart on the golf course, He said I drove like Donna, managing to hit every ditch in the fairway. At one point he stood up after a big bump and said *'You sure do give a guy with hemorrhoids a tough time.'*"

I felt the need to get in on the action as well, recounting a story from Dad's days as a deacon at the church.

"One Sunday a pulpit committee came from another church to listen to our pastor preach, and determine if they wanted to invite him to become pastor of their church. It was when Bob Curlee, one of Dad's favorites, was our pastor. Dad greeted the six strangers sitting on the back row of the church. *'It's good to have you here today. I suppose you're a pulpit committee wanting to steal our pastor from us. Well, I'll have to admit to you that when Bob Curlee is sober, he's really a great preacher.'"* The table erupted in laughter again.

Betsy said, "When I think of Papaw, I think of three words: My Pink Pig!"

She was referring to being at the mall with Papaw and Meemaw, waiting in line to ride the big carousel at Christmastime. Papaw asked Betsy which animal character she wanted to ride. Betsy responded, *"The Pink Pig."* Another little girl in line just behind Papaw heard Betsy and began begging her daddy to let *her* ride the pink pig. As soon as the gate opened, Papaw grabbed Betsy and ran like a man leaving a burning house to claim the pink pig for Betsy. Forget the whiny little kid, that pink pig belonged to Betsy!"

The stories and laughter kept coming. Already our great sense of loss was being healed by the richness of wonderful memories. Dad's seat at the table was now empty, but two new ones had just been added. He would be proud of that.

Room 138 Once More

Driving to The Oaks a few days later I noticed how refreshing the cool-air felt against my face, now flowing freely from the truck's air conditioner. Shane, my trusted mechanic, had finally discovered the problem and repaired it. It was a welcomed relief from the blistering August heat on the outside. I parked the truck in The Oaks parking lot for the last time. Peggy, following the whole way, parked her car right next to me. She clutched my hand as we walked together under the awning and into the building, saying nothing, but particularly aware that we were closing yet another chapter in the life of Coolidge Sims. Nevertheless, there was still work to be done in room 138.

Packing up his things from his brief stay at The Oaks was a heart-wrenching exercise for Donna and Allen, and Peggy and me. After blazing a trail to this location most every day for the past five months, it seemed strange to me to leave it so suddenly.

At the end, I stood alone for a few moments in the room and remembered how the conversations that transpired around this place had changed so many of my perceptions. God had given me five months to search and discover the deepest parts of my father's heart and come to a solid resolution. I will carry that wonderful resolution with me all my remaining days.

Calvin Coolidge Sims was not a perfect man, but he was an honest and principled man, finally redeemed from the burden of his time in history. He was among the greatest of the Greatest Generation—a tower of strength, and a well of joy. His story will be shared with his children's children and beyond. His legacy will live in the footsteps he left behind.

When he left this world and entered Heaven, he left nothing undone. His purpose on this earth was fully realized. He left nothing unsaid and left no one unloved. He finished his course. He kept the Faith

"God is patient. Sometimes it takes us a lifetime to get it right."
Calvin Coolidge Sims

Epilogue

1. Eulogy for Calvin Coolidge Sims

(Read by Ben Rosser at the Ashland First Baptist Church, August 26, 2012.)

 Tom Brokaw wrote a book called <u>The Greatest Generation</u>. In it he describes the men and women who were raised in the guts of The Great Depression and then saved the world from tyranny in World War II as "The Greatest Generation" of Americans that ever lived. It's true. They were modest, hardworking, unselfish, patriotic, and courageous. Our father, Calvin Coolidge Sims was a member of that "Greatest Generation." But to us, his three children, Mike, Mark, and Donna—he was so much more. He was the poster child of that great generation of Americans. He was, in our eyes the greatest of the greatest generation. Our Dad taught us lessons about life, all the way up to his passing a couple of days ago. He taught us how to live, and he taught us how to die.

 All of our growing-up years we heard his stories—mostly humorous stories of being raised during the tough times of the Depression. But they were not sad stories. They were warm, powerful stories of a relatively poor family that loved one another deeply, and nurtured that love throughout their lives. From our father, we learned about the value of family. We have laughed a million times about Coolidge and his brother Bremon trying to corner and capture a mad dog from under the house, and of the ways that he tricked Gwynnelle into doing his share of churning. We've heard him tell about riding his bicycle from Ashland to Delta when he was 10 years old, just to spend time with his grandparents. Nothing pleased him more in recent days than to recount those memories and look forward to a reunion with his father, mother, sisters, and brother. He was the last remaining of the Sims children—and he missed them very much—until last Thursday.

We especially enjoyed Dad recounting his amazing relationship with our mother, Marylyn. They were sweethearts from the second grade on, where Dad won her heart with his wit and charm. The teacher asked her students on the first day of school in 1930, "Each of you tell me what you had this morning for breakfast." Coolidge replied, "Syrup and biscuits, wanna see?" The class giggled as he opened wide his mouth and stuck out his tongue to let the teacher see. He's kept all of us laughing ever since. With Dad around, it was almost impossible to be sad. We loved riding in the car and coaxing him to sing his songs: Paper Doll, I Took a Leg from Some Old Table, and The Wreck of the Old '97.

Dad taught us how to love our spouse—for a lifetime. He adored our mother and served her unselfishly until her death thirteen years ago after a lengthy illness. They were married almost 53 years. Three nights before her passing in 1999, our Dad said to her, "Marylyn, it's ok. You can go. But I want you to know, you're the only woman I've ever been with, and the only one I've ever loved." She whispered back, "And you're my one and only too." What an example of faithfulness! What an example of marital love! We, three children, vowed that we would each live in a way that we will someday be able to say the same to our spouse with our last breath. He always said that Marylyn was more than a wife—she was his best friend. Their reunion this past Thursday was especially sweet.

Our father was a tireless worker, providing more than we deserved, and did it not out of duty, but love. He worked hard as a child, a teen, an adult, and even in retirement. We were amazed to find out that he was a school bus driver at age 17! He, of course, ran a family business in Ashland since 1953—the Ashland Pharmacy. And every worker he ever hired will tell you, it was more family to him than business, because every employee he considered a part of his family. He treated the public <u>and</u> his employees fairly because he truly cared. Over the years the Sims family has had to endure many a Christmas when Dad had to leave the house to get someone's medicine on Christmas Day. We sometimes didn't understand it then, but now we do. Good businesses are not built on slick business plans, but on treating your customers with kindness and respect—a quality in which we never saw him fail. This is the truth. No one, black or white, was ever turned away from the pharmacy if they could not afford the medicine they needed. His generosity was unheralded but constant.

Our father taught us about Christian character, not with lectures, but by watching the way he lived his life every day. Just a few years ago we learned about something that only strengthened our opinion of his honest character. It was not a story that we heard from him, for he would never have considered making anything of it. Here is the story: John Adams, the owner of Adams Drug Company, was Dad's only competitor in Ashland. (What are the chances that the two drug stores in town were owned by Calvin Coolidge and John Adams!) While Mr. Adams was out of the country for an extended time, he had hired someone to run the drugstore for him. The replacement left unexpectedly, so it seemed that Adams Drugs would just have to close down until John returned. Dad knew that such a move could threaten any business's viability, so he volunteered to fill prescriptions at Adams Drugs for John until he returned— and he did not allow any customers to switch their prescriptions to Ashland Pharmacy during that time. When we recently asked Dad why he did it he said, "Because it was the right thing to do. John and I were friends, and it was a way I could help him save his business. It was no big deal." He never told that story, so we wanted to tell it today.

 Coolidge Sims was patriotic. He loved his country. In recent times, he has expressed his worry that his country is declining. At age 21 he landed on Utah Beach in Normandy. His field hospital unit was attached to General Patton's Third Army. When the war ended, his unit was halfway between Frankfurt and Berlin. He never thought his military service was extraordinary, but he was a proud veteran. He saw it as his duty to a country he loved. He told both of his sons, "I did it hoping that you would never have to." Because he was in a hospital unit, he jokingly called himself a "bedpan commando," but in our eyes, he was a true American hero.

 Just a couple of months ago, Coolidge and his lifelong black friend, Banny Heard, sat in their wheelchairs talking about their World War II experiences. A relative had brought Banny to see Dad in the assisted living center. Both were experiencing failing health and got together for what they sensed would be the last time. Their friendship went back to the late 1930's when they worked together at a service station on the square. They laughed and talked for over an hour, but then their conversation turned serious. Banny said, "Coolidge, remember when we went up to Anniston together to pick up that load of tires?" Dad replied, "Banny, that was about 70 years ago, what are you talking about?" "I remember it like it was yesterday," Banny said. "We picked up the tires, and then went to a little café to get a sandwich. That white man came out and told me to get out, that I wasn't welcome. But you took up for me, Coolidge, and I ain't never forgot that to this day. You're about the best friend I ever had." Their conversation ended with both of them pledging to soon see each other in "glory."

 We know that Coolidge Sims' faith was authentic. It was real. We, his children, actually heard him pray. Many times we heard him give testimony to being saved. He was not ashamed of Jesus Christ. We knew that he wanted us to always follow the Will of God in our lives. How did we know that? Because he actually told us that. Nothing pleased him more than to know that we followed the example that he and Mom had set before us.

He was not just a church man, although he loved his church—and proved it through many years of service to it. He was first and foremost a Christian man of integrity. He gave us many gifts, but the greatest one of all was the gift of "stability." We never had to wonder if he was going to keep loving our Mom. His love for her was unconditional, as was his love for us. We never doubted it. We never had to worry about him not coming home, or how we were going to get our next meal. We never had to fear that he could come in drunk, or that he was the same man in private that he was in public, and that his world was a good as gold.

When he left this world and entered Heaven, he left nothing undone. His purpose on this earth was fully realized. He left nothing unsaid, and he left no-one unloved. He finished his course. He kept the faith.

We just discovered that he left his "loved ones" a hand written notebook, in which he summarized the important facts and events in his life. Let us share with you his closing words, as an inspiration and a witness to all of you. He wrote:

"I want to thank all of you again for sharing and being a part of my life. I apologize for my shortcomings, and the times I've disappointed you.
Now, I would encourage all of you to continue in the Lord so that one day we will all have a great reunion.

*With my deepest love, Husband and Father,
Coolidge."*

An important message to you from the Sims family:

You remember that our father once said,
> "God is patient. Sometimes it takes us a lifetime to get it right."

God gives us one lifetime to make life's most important personal decision—"What shall I do with Jesus?"

If you have not yet chosen Jesus Christ as your Savior and Lord, please use this opportunity to invite Him into your life. His death on the cross and resurrection from the dead provided all you need to gain eternal life—on this Earth and ultimately in Heaven.

God loves you and above all things, wants a personal relationship with you. In your own words, talk with Him.

God is closer than you think.

2. Q and A with the Author

- ***Did you have to change any names in the book?***
  Yes, there were a few that were necessary to change, but most of them are accurate. All changes were incidental and did not alter the narrative in any way.

- ***Not much is mentioned about Coolidge's younger sister. What's her story?***
  Gail was eleven years younger than Coolidge, fourteen years younger than Gwynnelle, and seventeen years younger than Bremon. Still, they were all very close to one another in adulthood. Coolidge actually came up with Gail's name—Audrey Gail. He had seen a western movie with a cowgirl named Audrey and insisted that his little sister be named after her. His parents agreed and added Audrey to their chosen name for the new baby, Gail. Gail Sims Carpenter was the first of the Sims siblings to die—dying from cancer in 2002.

- ***Whatever happened to Sadie Thompson?***
  Sadie helped me gather first hand information from contacts with her contemporaries who were still alive at the time of writing, as well as from her own recollections. She allowed me to read to her large portions of the manuscript while I was writing it, and was an excellent resource for accuracy. Sadie was thrilled about my writing this book, and could hardly wait until it was finished.

Unfortunately, Sadie passed away peacefully in early 2017, just a few months before I completed the manuscript. <u>Is That You, Coolidge?</u> is dedicated to her memory.

- **Did Coolidge stay in touch with Johnny Wise, Tommy Grantham, and Dunwoody—his army buddies?**

    Dunwoody's address was in Coolidge's little black book, but they did not remain in contact more than a couple of years after the war. There was an interesting story that I did not include in the narrative involving Johnny Wise and Marylyn. Johnny was injured in early 1945 and was shipped to his home in Chicago for treatment. Coolidge gave Johnny money and asked him to wire roses to Marylyn once he got to the states.

    Coolidge never heard anything from Marylyn about receiving the roses so he assumed that Johnny had forgotten to send them or had lost Marylyn's address. Not long after they married in 1946, Coolidge asked Marylyn if she had ever received them. She told him that she had received some beautiful roses from a man named "Peetey" in Chicago, but had no idea who he was!

- **Is your information about the 180th General Hospital and the Normandy invasion factual?**

    I based my information on Coolidge's first hand recollections as well as my own historical research on the movements of the 180th General Hospital from its creation in the summer of 1944 to its inactivation on the 31st of January, 1946. The *USS Nevada* and the *USS Bayfield* were in the waters of the English Channel during the Normandy landings.

- **How far did Coolidge follow General Patton into Germany? Where was Coolidge when the war ended?**

    Coolidge's unit followed the invasion force from Utah Beach on the Normandy coast of France through St. Mary's Eligse, Carentan, St. Lo, Dreux, Versailles, and Paris. They crossed the Rhine River at Frankfurt am Main and progressed as far as Fulda Gap before the German surrender in May of 1945. Coolidge was in Fulda Gap when the war ended.

    Fulda was halfway between Frankfurt and Berlin, and later became the focal point of the defending West Germany from the Soviets during the Cold War.

- **Was the song "Wreck of the Old '97" ever recorded professionally? (from Chapter 9)**

    The original ballad, released in 1924 by Vernon Dalhart, was based on the real story of a tragic 1903 train wreck that caught the attention of the nation. It became a country music hit and was possibly the first million-seller on the country music charts. Later it was recorded dozens of times by singers like Woody Guthrie, the Statler Brothers, Johnny Cash, Boxcar Willy—and if only I had had a tape recorder, *Coolidge Sims*.

- **Are any family members named after Coolidge?**

    Coolidge and Marylyn's first son, Mike, was named for his father, "Michael Coolidge Sims." Mike's first grandson was named "Asa Coolidge Sims" by his parents Michael and Misty Sims. My daughter, Betsy and her husband Nathan Smith, named their second child "Dalton Sims Smith" in 2014.

- *What about your wife and children?*

    My wife Peggy Skinner Sims was born in Paraguay (South America) into an amazing family of missionaries. She is my sunshine, and we work together daily in training young men and women in the Master's Commission at Kingwood Church.

    Our oldest daughter Lindsay and her husband Joel are Family Ministry pastors at Kingwood and have three amazing children—Sophia, Grant, and Juliette.

    Our youngest daughter Betsy and her husband Nathan have blessed us with two more wonderful grandchildren—Charlotte and Dalton.

    We are fortunate that our children and their families live close-by and we all attend Kingwood Church together.

- *What about your brother and sister?*

    My brother Mike and his wife Kathy live in Columbus, Georgia where Mike is a family practice physician. Their oldest son Michael, also a physician, and his wife Misty have two lovely children—Asa and Vivian. They presently reside in Greenville, South Carolina. Mike and Kathy's remarkable daughter Hope is a teacher and children's minister in Columbus, and their youngest son Keith and his wife Anna live in Macon, Georgia, where Keith is in medical training.

    My sister Donna and her husband Allen Taylor live in Hoover, Alabama. Their two beautiful daughters Elizabeth and Meredith both attend Auburn University.

- *Have you written and published any other books?*

    Yes. I wrote Call It Incredible in 2007. It is the powerful story of Ron and Susanne Cox, available on Amazon and at **marksimsblog.com**.

    I also publish a weekly blog called *Paradigm* that can be found online at **marksimsblog.com**. I invite subscribers to my free blog—focusing on Spiritual Growth and Biblical Truth, History, Humor, and growing up in small town America.

3. Glossary of Coolidge-isms

"Check your britches." *[Did someone just soil (poop) his pants?]* In the book: "'Thanks to you, Johnny, I've got to go back now and **check my britches**. And I probably won't be able to fall asleep for days.' I made my way back to my tent and stayed awake the rest of the night." (p. 113)

"… my hind leg!" *[A sign of great irritation in a parent toward their child, and serious disbelief in what was stated.]* In the book: **"A wreck, my hind leg!** That was your Christmas present! Toys cost money! What were you thinking, Son?" (p. 89)

"Got a wild hair." *[Followed through with a bad or dangerous decision; a really bad idea.]* In the book: 'Bremon, how deep is it?' He suddenly **got a wild hair** and said, 'Coolidge, why don't you let me put you in this bucket and I'll lower you down in there so you can find out?' (p. 59)

"Rode hard and put up wet." *[Looked used, like a worn out mule.]* In the book: "I don't remember her name, but she looks like she'd been **rode hard and put up wet."** (p. 34)

"Stinks like c'airn." *[C'airn (pronounced "k'yarn") is something that stinks so badly dogs won't eat it; it has a very disagreeable odor]* In the book: "A few drops into a hollow

tree would bring a rabbit or possum out instantly, **and it stinks like c'airn."** (p. 38)

"Stove-up." *[suffering discomfort from soreness, tiredness, or aching muscles]* In the book: "You must be ready for your workout!" "I sure am," he responded. **"I felt all stove-up** when I got out of the bed this morning. (p.161)

"Coons age." *[a very long time; it is an Americanization of the old British expression "crows age" with the same meaning; first known usage in 1843]* In the book: "It's full of old pictures that I got from Mama before she died. I actually haven't seen most of these pictures **in a coon's age,**…" (p.49)

"Madder than a mule chewing on bumblebees." *[truly mad; spittin' mad]* In the book: 'Well now you've done it!' she exclaimed, **madder than a mule chewing on bumblebees!** (p.158)

"...spit, wind my watch, or go blind." *[totally clueless as to what to do]* In the book: "Mark, I couldn't believe she said it was cancer. **I didn't know whether to spit, wind my watch, or go blind."** (p. 101)

Acknowledgements

My special thanks go out to my wonderful wife, Peggy, for her daily insight, support, and encouragement, and to our daughters Lindsay and Betsy for their sincere impressions, memories, and creative know-how.

I especially thank Mike and Kathy Sims, and Donna and Allen Taylor for input and participation. Without them this book could not have been written.

Thank you Charlotte and Elton Denson you're your irreplaceable input.

Thank you Michael, Hope, and Keith Sims; and Elizabeth and Meredith Taylor for your recollections of Papaw.

In addition to all the Sims family members who helped in gathering, editing, and describing information used in this book, I also wish to express my appreciation to these friends for your contributions:

- June Creel, *for your excellent insight during the editing process;*
- Bill Woodard, *for your detailed proofreading of my grammar, and for your expertise in all things military;*
- Wilma Stewart, *for your insight into relevant history and culture;*
- Hannah Rettig, *for your creative artwork, cover designs and ideas-- you're a genius;*
- Donna Wallace, *for your direction and inspiration in honing my writing skills;*
- Stanley Smith, *for helping me remember the important things;*
- The warm, wonderful people of Ashland, Alabama;
- Sadie Thompson, *for your treasure chest of memories. We miss you very much.*

"I thank my God for every remembrance of you…"
Paul the Apostle, Philippians 1:3